Linda

*Avamere –
Santy
Save your
wisdom.
Linda*

WISDOM
Under the Bridge

THE PROPHETS FROM SKID ROW

ACCLAIM FOR:

WISDOM UNDER THE BRIDGE: the Prophets from Skid Row

We may not expect to hear wise stories from those living under a bridge, but Swanson takes our hand ever so gently, sits us down, and deftly shares such stories with us in ways that entice us to listen. Without glorifying or judging the life of indigents who experience addiction or mental illness or otherwise damaged lives, she finds the stories of grace among them and lets us in on both the grittiness and the hope they contain. She helps us see the longings, the courage, and the grief in the hearts of those who beg on the street corner. She reminds us whom Jesus hung out with, and she makes us want to join him there. This is inviting writing that gives new eyes to the reader for seeing both inwardly and outwardly with more compassion and less arrogance.

—Pat Samples, author of *Daily Comforts for Caregivers* and *The Secret Wisdom of a Woman's Body.*

Rather than breaking readers' hearts with the tragic and the terrible, **Wisdom Under the Bridge: the Prophets from Skid**

Row is a book about overcoming adversity, finding hope, and welcoming peace. With keen insight and spiritual acumen, Swanson opens readers' eyes to the disenfranchised grief that recovering alcoholics and addicts on the streets endure. Swanson makes clear that God imbues all of us with wisdom and insight on our long journey toward wholeness. *Wisdom Under the Bridge* convinces readers that the rich tapestry of humanity is comprised of everyone's story, without exclusion.

—Sr. Helen Prejean, author *Deadman Walking, The Death of Innocents: An Eyewitness Account of Wrongful Executions*

Wisdom Under the Bridge: the Prophets from Skid Row is a powerful book. Beyond the stories, it is a reminder to those recovering from addiction as well as to those that seek to assist, the inherent losses and consequent grief that one has to encounter as one strives toward sobriety.

—Kenneth J. Doka, PhD,
professor of gerontology at the Graduate School of
New Rochelle, author, *Disenfranchised Grief: New
Directions, Challenges, and Strategies for Practice*

Wisdom Under the Bridge: the Prophets from Skid Row, showcases the bravery of souls striving to live normal lives despite battling mental illness,and/or addictions daily. Like,

NAMI's (National Alliance on Mental Illness) *In Our Own Voice Program*, this book raises the self-esteem of its narrators byrecognizing the wisdom and worth revealed through sharing stories of recovery. *Wisdom Under the Bridge*, showcases the soul-baring of the disenfranchised, helping to correct the false images of mental illness, addiction, and homelessness held by the general public.

> —Judy Redler Winter, Educator, and,
> In *Our Own Voice* Coordinator
> National Alliance on Mental Illness (NAMI)
> - Clackamas County

⚘

Reading *Wisdom Under the Bridge: the Prophets from Skid Row* was a spiritual experience reminding me of how extreme trauma and adversity can create huge openings into the Divine.

> —John Callahan, nationally recognized
> cartoonist & author, *Don't Worry He Can't
> Get Far on Foot* (1951-2010)

⚘

Wisdom Under the Bridge: the Prophets from Skid Row is an interesting and challenging book. If you want to know what goes on in the heads and hearts of many of our homeless poor and those who live, work and minister among them, then this book is a good place to start.

—Gary Smith, S.J., author *Street Journal, Radical Compassion, They Come Back Singing*

Wisdom Under the Bridge: the Prophets from Skid Row takes the reader on a journey of heartbreak and hope. In reading the life stories of the "prophets on the streets" the reader finds the wisdom gained through the grief of poverty and addiction and the realization that we are all a part of one another.

—Jan Elfers, Director of Congregational Outreach and Peace Programs, Ecumenical Ministries of Oregon (EMO)

Dedicated to Glasker Rankin
1954–2005

TABLE OF CONTENTS

ACRONYM LIST
12-STEPS OF
ALCOHOLICS ANONYMOUS

AA—Alcoholics Anonymous

ADHD—Attention Deficit Hyperactivity Disorder

ARC—Adult Rehabilitation Center

ACT—Assertive Community Treatment

CADC—Certified Alcohol and Drug Counselor

CAG—Civic Action Group

CEP—Community Empowerment Program

CIT—Crisis Intervention Training

CPE   Clinical Pastoral Education

CSD—Children's Services Division

CSC—Congregation of Holy Cross (priests)

DUI—Driving Under the Influence

GED—General Education Degree

HP—Higher Power

IADL—In a Different Light

ICU—Intensive Care Unit

IOOV—In Our Own Voice

NA—Narcotics Anonymous

NAMI—National Alliance on Mental Illness

NAMI-CC—National Alliance on Mental Health Clackamas County

NIV—New International Version (Bible)

OHSU—Oregon Health Science University

PAHC—Portland Alternative Health Care

PCRP—Project for Community Recovery

PO—Parole Officer

PTSD—Post Traumatic Stress Disorder

RAP—Recovery Association Project

RCIA—Rite of Christian Initiation for Adults (in Roman Catholicism)

SNJM—Sisters of the Holy Names of Jesus and Mary

SRO—Single Room Occupancy Hotel

UA—Urine Analysis

WFI—Working for Independence

VOA—Volunteers of America

YWCA—Young Women's Christian Association

12-STEPS OF ALCOHOLICS ANONYMOUS

These are the original Twelve Steps as published by Alcoholics Anonymous:

1. We admitted we were <u>powerless</u> over alcohol—that our lives had become unmanageable.

2. Came to believe that a <u>Power</u> greater than ourselves could restore us to sanity.

3. Made a decision to turn our will and our lives over to the care of <u>God</u> *as we understood Him*.

4. Made a searching and fearless moral inventory of ourselves.

5. Admitted to God, to ourselves, and to another human being the exact nature of our wrongs.

6. We're entirely ready to have God remove all these defects of <u>character</u>.

7. Humbly asked Him to remove our shortcomings.

8. Made a list of all persons we had harmed, and became willing to make <u>amends</u> to them all.

9. Made direct amends to such people wherever possible, except when to do so would injure them or others.

10. Continued to take personal inventory and when we were wrong promptly admitted it.

11. Sought through <u>prayer</u> and <u>meditation</u> to improve our conscious contact with God *as we understood Him*, praying only for knowledge of His will for us and the power to carry that out.

12. Having had a spiritual awakening as the result of these steps, we tried to carry this message to alcoholics, and to practice these principles in all our affairs.

In some cases, where other twelve-step groups have adapted the AA steps as guiding principles, they have been altered to emphasize principles important to those particular fellowships, and to remove gender-biased language

INTRODUCTION

On January 4, 2007, a chilly morning in Portland, Oregon, R. J. Anheier, an elderly gentleman, dressed for the season. His ensemble included a red-and-blue checkered wool shirt under a nearly new red-and-black ski jacket, a pair of ragged blue jeans, and some well-worn camel-colored suede gloves. On his head he wore his favorite navy-blue Chicago Bulls baseball cap, which made his white hair fan out in all directions. His full, bushy, white eyebrows seemed to challenge his long, fuzzy, white beard.

R. J. picked up his stack of *Street Roots* newspapers (an advocacy publication) from the newspaper's office. He then set about his morning trying to sell the paper for whatever change people coughed up. R. J. was cheerful that morning, greeting folks who walked by. "Morning, sir, would you like a paper? How about a little reading this a.m., miss?" He hoped someone would stop soon and press a fiver into his hand, which was more than enough to buy an Egg McMuffin and coffee at the nearby McDonald's.

Commuters urged their way forward through the sluggish traffic on West Burnside Street. R. J. felt slightly nauseated. *Must be the exhaust*, he thought. As he stood anchored in place by his sturdy, new-to-him, Downtown Chapel–issue boots, he started feeling worse, light-headed, dizzy even. Thinking automobile fumes were the cause, R. J. tossed a quick prayer to the Big Guy Upstairs and ventured to a nearby bench. As soon as he'd planted himself, a strange heaviness crept into his chest, and then it dived deeper and deeper into his body, at last compressing most of the air from his lungs. He placed a hand over his heart, and as he did, the newspapers slipped from his lap, the wind flipping the winged pages throughout the park. R. J. slumped over, his body slowly leaking its life away. R. J. would soon find his way home to God.

Within a short time, a police officer discovered R. J. on the bench. At first, he thought the man merely drunk, passed out in the park, but within seconds, he realized he had encountered a critically ill person. He called for an ambulance.

The preceding narrative is my fictional account of what happened the day R. J. Anheier collapsed on a downtown Portland street and subsequently died. No one actually knows what was going on around him or what was on his mind at the time, so I've taken the liberty of creating the scenario.

I share his story and the others in this book because I consider all of the people within these pages part of my tribe. My mother was mentally ill, and I was her caretaker from age 12 until she died at 83. Two of my brothers were alcoholics and lived on and off the streets for years. I am also an alcoholic, with 25 years in recovery. My oldest brother, Gary, died at age 59 from alcoholism and cancer. About 10 years ago, my younger brother found his way into recovery. Until recently, he lived in one of the clean and sober hotels—the Mark O. Hatfield, located right across the street from the Downtown Chapel.[1] I cannot tell you how many prayers I said and masses I offered up for him. I was so afraid I'd have to go to the morgue one day and identify his body. Apparently, all that praying influenced Mike's decision to get clean and sober. He's now back in the family fold. Praise be to God.

It is true that when R. J. reached a nearby hospital, he was officially pronounced dead—the cause, heart failure. Because of his disheveled appearance, it was assumed that R. J. was homeless, despite keys and identification in his pocket.

On January 5, 2007, officials contacted a man named Jeff Anheier, thinking he might be R. J.'s next of kin. He wasn't. No other attempts were made to locate family or friends. Officials didn't realize that R. J. was merely four blocks from his apartment when discovered. But, since he was assumed homeless, his body was automatically declared "unclaimed." No one took the time to empty R. J.'s pockets, which revealed the location of his apartment, where, on his nightstand, he kept an address book with contact information for his sister and best friend.

When R. J. didn't show up at his apartment and no one saw him at one of his favorite hangouts—Sisters of the Road Café—for a few days, his friends went looking for him. Fearing the worst, one of them called the medical examiner's office. That was when they all learned that R. J. had died from natural

---

1 The parish is currently in the process of changing its name to St. Andrè Bessette, CSC.

causes and that his body was taken to the Oregon Health Science University Hospital.

According to Oregon Statute 97.170, any "unclaimed" indigent body must be offered as a cadaver to OHSU. The awful truth is that R. J.'s body was given to the university hospital for a paltry $37.50 and was awaiting dissection and study by medical students, while his family and friends looked for him. Sisters of the Road Café and *Street Roots* newspaper advocated for this law to be changed, and it has since been rewritten.

R. J. was loved by friends and family and highly regarded by advocates for the poor in the area. The staff and clientele of Sisters of the Road Café considered him a dear friend and former coworker and mourned his death.

The Oregonian published an article written by reporter Michelle Roberts titled "Death on a Portland Street Turns into Sorry Tale of Disrespect," which was published on March 27, 2007. On May 15, 2007, *The Portland Independent Media Center* published a similar article, "Perception Leads to Heartache and Grief," written by Matt Barrett.

On any given day, in cities across the country, people die on the streets, in parks, and along waterfronts. The treatment R. J. received wasn't intended as malicious or disrespectful. It came from city officials who were undoubtedly numbed by daily heartbreaking experiences.

I share R. J.'s story to exemplify how society treats people who are homeless, or in R. J.'s case, *assumed* homeless.

Judgments slide off people's lips, blaming individuals for huge systemic problems, which our society refuses to admit and/or address. We criminalize, ignore, and ridicule people for being homeless and poor. If only we could all decide to give eye contact and friendly acknowledgment to those less fortune when we pass them on the street; these gestures are crucial to all people, as it validates our humanity.

This book attests that wisdom doesn't discriminate. *Wisdom Under the Bridge* captures insights not only from the formerly homeless, the mentally ill, and the recovering addicted but also advocates who work in the many helping agencies in Portland, Oregon. Their mandate follows the Corporal Works of Mercy, which includes the following:

1. Feed the hungry.
2. Give drink to the thirsty.
3. Clothe the naked.
4. Shelter the homeless.
5. Comfort the imprisoned.
6. Visit the sick.
7. Bury the dead.

I've dedicated this book to Glasker Rankin, a true street prophet, who helped me appreciate the Burnside Street community here in Portland. Glasker taught me that the deepest, most enduring epiphanies result from adversity, not from a sheltered life. Glasker, along with his brothers and sisters in recovery, grace these pages. Their stories are compiled in a letter format, forming a Wisdom Will®, which is a legacy letter based on the Jewish tradition of an ethical will. Wisdom Wills document what people have learned in life thus far, what got them through the tough times, their experiences with the divine, blessings and prayers for the future, family stories, and anything else the person wants to share, including how they want to be remembered.

Formerly, legacy documents were bequeathed to loved ones and the community, along with legal wills after a person's death, but these days, legacy letters are often given to commemorate special occasions such as a graduation, a marriage, or other significant event. Dr. Barry K. Baines wrote the book *Ethical Wills*, which was published in 2006. An ethical will is a mitzvah, or commandment, in the Jewish tradition—one of hundreds. It seems that after the events of September 11, 2001, when the World Trade Center and the Pentagon were attacked by terrorists, Baines noticed there was an interest in writing them again. How comforted loved ones and their communities would have been had those who perished in the September 11 tragedy left behind Wisdom Wills. Certainly, some of the anguish people went through would have been assuaged by such a letter, as it can serve as a comforting talisman for grievers, a message from beyond that keeps memories alive for generations.

John Kunz, a geriatric psychotherapist, educator, and author, reminds us of the following:

> Remembering and sharing painful life experiences promotes greater emotional healing and acceptance of life's unfortunate circumstances. Remembering the way we faced difficult times in the past helps us better face difficult times today. Reminiscing helps us maintain an awareness of who we are, where we've been and what roles we've played in our lifetime. (website.http://members.aol.com/johnkunz/hand1.htm).

We all carry memorable stories through which we can offer our wisdom, understanding, and compassion. In Barry Lopez's book *Crow and Weasel*,[2] there is the following quote which I love because it strikes at the very purpose for documenting our wisdom and collecting stories. There's no point in learning, having insights and epiphanies if they are going to be buried with us when we die.

> Badger says to Weasel: I would ask you to remember only this one thing [...] the stories people tell have a way of taking care of them. If stories come to you, care for them. And learn to give them away where they are needed. Sometimes a person needs a story more than food to stay alive. That is why we put these stories in each other's memory. This is how people care for themselves. (60)

If it weren't for stories, Bill W. and Dr. Bob S. wouldn't have founded Alcoholics Anonymous. Their victory was based on believing in someone else's success story and following their example. It gave them hope. They then shared the stories of their own journey and that of many others in the *Big Book of Alcoholics Anonymous*. And just like Badger said, "Sometimes a person needs a story more than food to stay alive."

---

2 Lopez, Barry, *Crow and Weasel*. North Point Press, Sunburst edition, 1998.

Statues All Over America

*Let there be statues of migrants
And soup-kitchen workers,
Steam-vent homeless families
Vagabonds riding the rails,
Runaway teens in the Tenderloin,
Kids at orphanage windows,
Wheel-chaired elderly in
Rest home hallways,
Train porters and fry cooks,
The blind with canes or dogs,
Sweatshop seamstresses,
Waitresses at truck stops,
Salvation Army kettle collectors—
Statues for all the taken-for-granted,
Avoided, abandoned, or forgotten—
Unique, historical.*

© BAKER, CLAIRE J., 2005, REPRINTED FROM *Street Spirit,* (AFSC).

PART i

CHAPTER I

Harvesting Grief On Our Journey To God

There is nothing—no thing, no person, no experience, no thought, no joy or pain—that cannot be harvested and used for nourishment on our journey to God.

—MACRINA WIEDERKEHR, *A Tree Full of Angels*

I left the Roman Catholic Church for nearly 20 years but returned in 1997. I conducted a search for a parish most reflective of my personal beliefs, one that supported social justice, the poor, the mentally ill, the addicted, and the homeless. I felt blessed upon entering the doors of the Downtown Chapel on 6th and West Burnside Streets. The congregation is all-inclusive. There are people from the street, benefactors, those using and recovering from alcohol and drugs, and young and old families, as well as people visiting the city. The chapel actively feeds, clothes, and gives comfort to the poor. Programs are developed based on the needs of the skid row/Old Town neighborhood. Included are depression retreats, anointing of the sick, support groups, blood pressure checks, art classes, bus passes, and even "Undie-Sunday" on the first Sunday of the month. On this day, the congregation donates new underwear and socks for those without.

At the time, I was in a marvelous period of discernment and open to the mysteries of the Holy Spirit. My faith meant wrapping my arms around the body of the church, which, for me, is all the people of God, not just those belonging to Roman Catholicism, but *all* people, whether believers or nonbelievers. I attended the Rite of Christian Initiation (classes) for Adults (RCIA) under the guise of helping Father Ron Raab, CSC, the associate pastor. The truth is I wanted and needed the instruction as much as any new convert. It was there I first met Bryan E., one of three formerly homeless people recovering from heroin addiction who attended the Downtown Chapel. In the pages ahead, you'll meet Mary, Bryan E., and Jason E., my friends and teachers.

For a time, all three attended the same 10:00 a.m. Sunday Mass that I did. Nowadays, I usually just see Mary there, as Jason E. is a new father, and his baby, Clementine, naps at that time of the morning. And Bryan E., newly married, goes to Mass these days at St. Mary's Cathedral. I rarely see any of them beaten down by life. They've all learned to lean on each other, the program of Narcotics Anonymous, and their NA sponsors. They do their best to attend church each Sunday. All three have a close relationship with Father Ron, and he is an important part of their recovery and their spiritual lives.

In Mary's Wisdom Will below, you'll see that besides attending Mass at the chapel, Mary gives back to the community by volunteering every Thursday in the hospitality center, located in the Chapel's basement, which offers emergency aid to the neighborhood. Mary is on disability because of mental illness.

She attests that living on the streets is a precursor to great losses. Yet, it may be surprising for people to learn what she endured psychologically after she moved into her single room occupancy (SRO) apartment. Though she was grateful for a roof over her head, there were other challenges she hadn't anticipated, and I, too, hadn't considered prior to meeting Mary.

As a woman living on the streets, Mary was particularly vulnerable. Hypervigilance became her middle name. She developed 360-degree vision, for no one was trustworthy. Most sleeping occurred in the daytime because evil serpentined the streets, the alleys, and the cubby holes at night. Fear was her companion. Finally, Mary entered the world of recovery, saving herself from herself. Housing was found for her as well as all required emergency aids—healthcare, medications, clothing, and food.

When Mary closed the door of her apartment, she found everything quiet. Still. There was nothing outwardly to fear, and hunger no longer nagged. Mary lay outstretched on her bed, and it truly was *her* bed. Almost giddy, she thanked God for these blessings. Then night came, and with it, the haunting! She was no longer in an excitable state worrying about her physical safety, but something else disturbed her peace of mind. Memories marched through the doorway and into her being. Grief and remorse filled every nook and cranny of the room. Flashbacks of tragedy, danger and horror illuminated the walls.

When on the streets, Mary didn't have time to think of anything other than her next fix, food, and a place to sleep. Now everything was taken care of, and she no longer needed or wanted a fix. The appalling drama that had been her life began to rewrite itself page by page. Where was Mary's new script?

Her character only knew how to play out the tragic and the terrible, only knew how to fear. In this new way of being, Mary was forced to act in fresh scenes a moment at a time, an hour at a time, and a day at a time. It was different than before, but the intensity of fear remained. Mary held tight to her friendships with Bryan, Jason, and others like them who were also recovering heroin addicts. She clasped hands with her Narcotics Anonymous sponsor and attended NA meetings. If she didn't, she might use again.

Today, there are times Mary wanders into the confessional at the Downtown Chapel, more to talk to Father Ron than simply unload her wrongdoings. He manages to affirm her every time she visits, and that makes her feel better. Still, she struggles daily with mental illness, thoughts of using to get relief, and the tremendous unresolved grief in her life. Lately, her longing for her deceased mother has intensified.

What I found remarkable about Mary is how well she manages day-to-day living with such an ominous background. She shares her story, which includes a history of mental illness, heroin addiction, prostitution, and homelessness, with unbelievable candor, faith, and peace. I am honored to count her among my friends.

Wisdom Will Of Mary

Dear Friends and Family,

For those who don't already know my story, I lived by the Ross Island Bridge until I moved into an abandoned van by a golf course. I started using drugs at 15. I didn't get into recovery until I was 35. The day I found myself homeless was the worst day of my life. I had nowhere to go, no money, and no one to trust me inside their house. I had nothing, and this was the most horrible feeling. I sat down by the river and said to myself, "I'm going to live here by the Ross Island Bridge, near the cement factory on Holgate Boulevard." For a year, I slept there with one of those emergency blankets. That was a time of total despair. Now, I thrive and enjoy being alive, but back then, I didn't.

My partner, who I lived with for seven years, was a drug dealer. We ended up losing our apartment. I had a dog and he had a cat, so we struggled to find people who would accept us and our animals. We came up with the money, but once the landlord found out we were using, he changed the locks and called the police. I was strung out on heroin every day. During the last eight years of my drug addiction, I was prostituting and stealing books to sell at Powell's Bookstore to support my habit. My partner had a job at a thrift store, so he'd lift books from there, or I would come in and steal them.

I started using heroin when I was a teenager and went into treatment when I was 20 years old. I've been diagnosed with bipolar disease. Once, when I was desperate, I looked up a therapist in the phone book. She asked me what drugs I used. I told her heroin. She said she couldn't help me until I got off of it.

So I went through treatment and stayed clean for about a year. Then I relapsed for another eight years.

The turning point was my 35th birthday when I had a stroke from doing speed. I blacked out, and when I woke up, my left side was paralyzed. At the time, I was living in a tent. It was pouring rain. I had to lie on my back with my right foot holding up the roof of the tent so the rain wouldn't drench me. Besides being strung out, there was a warrant out for my arrest from a six-year-old DUI. I was afraid of going to a hospital. My controlling partner didn't want me to leave. He wouldn't call an ambulance or anything. I just lay there while he went out every day and got our dope. It took me a week before I could walk or speak without slurring my words. After the stroke, I realized that I'd had enough. I bought some methadone from a friend of mine who was dying of AIDS, used it for a few days, and then I went to Hooper Detox Center.

I went through a program called the Mentor Program. My mentor's name is Jill, who has 17 or 18 years clean. The first thing she did was get me some food and clothing because I had nothing but my purse when I checked in. She took me to 12-step meetings, found me housing, helped me enroll in treatment. I checked in with her on a daily basis, and she encouraged me to get a sponsor and start working the 12 steps in the Narcotics Anonymous program. Thanks to the Hooper Detox Center, Portland Alternative Health Clinic, and the Mentor Program, I got back on my feet.

I overdosed on heroin seven months ago and almost died. I am really afraid of it now. I'm back on the wagon. I had three and a half years clean, and then I relapsed. The set of circumstances was just like in the movie *A Perfect Storm*.

I attend the spiritually based Narcotics Anonymous meetings developed around a relationship with God or a higher power. I consider God and the Holy Trinity as my higher powers. I work the steps and reconcile the past by writing out resentments, including my part in the situation. Then each of us in NA shares our results with God and another human being.

I volunteer with the homeless at the Downtown Chapel. I don't share my story very often, but last week, a young man came in and just started telling me his story. He'd been on methadone for the past seven years and was doing heroin as well. He was homeless and stole things to support his habit. When I told him I was clean, he couldn't believe it. My story gave him hope.

I grew up Roman Catholic and went to church until my mother was murdered. After that, I experimented with other religions. Mom always said that someday I'd appreciate her raising me a Catholic. I started recovery five years ago, with the whole premise of developing a close relationship with God. That's when I returned to Mass and discovered she was right.

My friend Bryan is also recovering from heroin. I met him when he was attending the Downtown Chapel and taking classes to become a Catholic. Three of us recovering heroin addicts—Bryan, me, and our friend Jason—go to Mass together. Jason was baptized into the Church last year. I like bringing people from NA to Mass with me. I like the simple atmosphere of the church. Since its location is on the corner of Sixth and West Burnside, in a very poor district of Portland, it's open and available to all kinds of people—the homeless, the addicted, and the mentally ill. I feel accepted there, even with my tattoos. I can be myself there, and it's okay. Bryan, Jason, and I support one another in our recovery, especially now that we are all Catholics.

When I first started going to Mass at the Downtown Chapel, I wasn't receiving Communion. Finally, I made an appointment with Father Ron and told him my entire life story. It took me an hour and a half to confess everything, like the fourth step in NA. After Father Ron gave me absolution, I felt reinstated into the Church, into God. I felt so good I cried.

My most recent relapse came after surgery. I was on pain-killers for one thing. Then I swiped someone else's muscle re-laxant prescription. Even though they were non-narcotic, my sponsor made me change my clean date [when a person stops using]. She ended up on my resentment list for a while. A short time later, I did heroin again. It wasn't fun anymore, though. The whole process of being strung out, going through with-drawal, and hustling to get another fix scared me to death.

What I've learned from all my struggles and pain is how to be compassionate. As long as people are not hurting me, I feel compassion for them because I've been where they've been. Over the past five years, really listening has changed my life from self-centeredness to openness to other people's stories.

It took me a long time to get around to reading the Bible. I finally sat down and read the whole New Testament. It took six or seven months, a little bit every day. Now, when I go to Mass and hear scripture, I'm familiar with it. When I read it, I don't try to interpret anything. I just absorb it.

A lot of my friends don't believe in Jesus; even my sponsor doesn't believe in Jesus. When I realized that I was a believer, I felt so overwhelmed that God and Jesus actually loved me! That's what inspired me to read the New Testament and start going to Mass.

Today, I believe that Jesus is the son of God. I used to think, *How could we be so vain to think that God sent His son, a part of Himself, into the world to communicate with us?* I said this to someone one night, and she said to me, "Well, what do you think He'd send—a turtle?" Now that I believe in Jesus, I feel comforted to know a living presence continues to teach me ways to live and understand. I no longer feel alone.

One of the challenges of living in my apartment building is my former dealer lives there, too. He bums cigarettes off me. It's kind of enticing to run into him. So I use a lot of prayer to stay clean. I get down on my knees and pray. Every day I say the "Third Step Prayer" in the *Big Book of Alcoholic Anonymous*. It goes like this:

> *God, I offer myself to Thee*
> *To build with me and*
> *To do with me as you will.*
> *Relieve me of the bondage of self*
> *That I may better do your will,*
> *Take away my difficulties, that*
> *Victory over them may bear witness*
> *To those I would help, of [sic] Thy power*
> *Thy love, and Thy way of life.*
> *May I do Thy will always. Amen.*

—Big Book of Alcoholics Anonymous (63)

I have a routine, a program that I do every day. I pray in the morning. I do some step work. I'm really diligent about working the 12 steps, so I do a little writing. I regularly attend 12-step meetings, maybe four or five times a week. I make sure to talk to my sponsor every day. I bounce my plans off her and let her know where I am. At night, I review my day. I'm attracted to the 12 steps because they offer structure and support through the fellowship. Besides developing my relationship with God, Narcotics Anonymous provides a constructive distraction for me to focus on—something besides getting loaded.

All the time, I walk around saying, "I love this," and "I love that." I feel like the queen of the world because I have my own apartment. I enjoy eating and being with my cat. I have cable television, and I'm going to get an air conditioner. I find a lot of peace in my life right now. Since I'm finally on the right medication, I haven't had a manic episode for about a year. My life is full of serenity now, so I don't have racing thoughts. One of the aspects of my mental illness is audio hallucinations. I can get extremely paranoid, agitated, and stressed out. Also, I suffer from depression, so I can really feel down and hopeless. It's really hard during those times. Because I have structure and consistency in my life now, and I'm on the right antipsychotics and antidepressants, I feel pretty safe. I'm grateful that I don't have to constantly struggle to survive like I did before.

My advice to people is to live in the moment and appreciate what they have. They should love God and express love for Him through their actions toward others. My wish for my friends and family, and all people who don't believe in Jesus, is to at least consider Jesus is God, and that Jesus loves them, and there's a place for them in God's heart. I'd like them to know that God knows our hearts and our thoughts. Having a relationship with God on such a level is very comforting. I want others to have what I have.

One of the things I pray for is more women's homeless shelters. There's no place for homeless couples, either. I pray that people develop deeper compassion for the homeless. In terms of the addicted, one of the biggest stumbling blocks for getting into recovery is the inability to form a relationship with God. My prayer for people who are using drugs and alcohol is that they surrender and form a relationship with God or their higher power.

When I run into folks who are homeless, I say, "Find faith in your community. Trust in yourself and your intuition. Trust the community of homeless people because they can give you support." When I was out there, I developed a close-knit family, and we all looked after each other. "Build community with the people around you." People don't realize all the opportunities and resources available to them if they're willing to get clean. I had to change everything in order to recognize those opportunities in my life. Even if you're homeless, there is still hope within your community if you build relationships with your street family.

I have a lot of guilt about my past. I wasn't involved in church or anything. I remember being admitted to a psych ward once because I was suicidal. I passed up a lot of opportunities when I was using, too. My friend's mother asked me to go to the rain forest with her to track macaws. She collected eclectic parrots and macaws and was doing a research project at the time. I couldn't go because I was strung out. The truth is I couldn't go anywhere because I had to have drugs. That was the most important thing in my life back then.

My process of self-forgiveness has been a long one. I hurt most of my old friends, and I was estranged from my family. I'm reconnected with them now. When my dad got cancer, I was strung out and couldn't go see him. After I'd been clean for a year, I wrote him a letter and apologized, begging his forgiveness for not being there when he was sick. Even though I'd been clean for a year, he refused to see me. It really hurt my feelings that he didn't trust me enough to let me in his house. A couple of years went by before he allowed me to visit. When I got absolution at the Downtown Chapel from Father Ron and started going back to Mass, I eased into forgiving myself. Receiving the Sacraments continues to help me. It was a real relief to get absolution for all those years that I'd been doing wrong. I love the Church; I like the entire ritual of it. Today, I work on forgiving myself and others. I concentrate on making amends by staying clean and doing the next right thing.

My mother was a functioning alcoholic and was addicted to Valium. One of my brothers got run over by a truck when he was 13 and died. At the time, I was 11. Then another brother came home from the service diagnosed with schizophrenia. The hospital wouldn't keep him, and he wouldn't take his meds. He would just get crazy. After Jimmy (the brother run over by a truck) died, my mother fell apart and started drinking and taking Valium again. When I was 17, both her and my oldest brother where murdered by someone with a shotgun. I was the one who found them. I think that's what spun me into my drug addiction and why I suffer from PTSD (post-traumatic stress disorder). I get flashbacks about that, and about the time I spent prostituting and being homeless. I have nightmares and lots of anxiety. Once, I tried to commit suicide by climbing into the bathtub and slitting one of my wrists. When the blood started pouring out into the tub, I panicked. I thought it was too horrific for my roommate to find me like that. So I cleaned everything up and wrapped my wrist real tight with gauze. Luckily, I'd missed the artery.

My mom was only 42 when she died. She kept the house immaculate and made sure the five of us went to church and good schools and wore nice clothes. One of her hobbies was gardening. She was also an artist and drew life portraits. She also wrote three science fiction novels. I miss her all the time. After she died, I went into therapy, but I started doing drugs and acting like a crazy teenager, so I didn't get much out of it. Drugs kept me from dealing with my grief. Mom was my go-to person for everything. I have questions now that I want to ask her, and it's sad that she's not here for me in person. Still, I have a good relationship with her. I talk to her like she is still here and have photos of her all over the apartment. I pray for her.

I have a good relationship with my sister. We talk on the phone at least once a week. We're really close. My other brother lives in Costa Mesa and is a really hard worker. He's married to a kindergarten teacher. He doesn't call, but he sends me cards and I know he loves me. We aren't that close, but we still keep in touch. He was the most forgiving of everyone about my drug addiction and my past behavior. He's proud of me.

I have a good support system these days to keep me on track. There are people I call every day as part of my recovery program, and I've been in therapy for the past three years. With PTSD, my mental illness, and wanting to do drugs, I never know quite what's going to happen each day. I've learned to live one day at a time and to do the best I can every day to stay clean and sober.

When I die, I'd like to be remembered as a crazy, punk rock street urchin and as a compassionate, caring person who served as God's eyes and ears in the world. I'd like people to say that I was a servant of God who tried to do God's work every day.

Love, Mary

I believe that everyone needs help. Everyone needs God. Everyone needs people. Everyone needs community. Everyone needs to learn to love themselves so that they can love other people. Someone once said, "I'll go wherever God drags me!" That very well could be a motto for all of us in recovery—at least until we learn to embrace God's omnipotent forgiveness and grace.

Mary is currently in therapy, takes medication for her bipolar disease, and is actively involved in NA. Without outside help, the onslaught of memories, post-traumatic stress, mourning, and victimization will remain a threat to her sobriety. Mary embraces a strong spiritual program, which includes her volunteer work. She is an example of what's on the other side of recovery; her presence is a symbol of hope for others. Mary has a deep abiding faith in God. She believes God lifts our burdens and transforms our lives, if only we allow it. Every day, Mary inches forward to a life filled with peace, grace, and joy.

On November 8, 2011, I met with Mary to celebrate her fifth recovery birthday. She has a new love in her life and is looking forward to enrolling in college.

CHAPTER 2

What Would Katherine Hepburn Do?

We are taught you must blame your father, your sisters, your brothers, the school, the teachers—but never blame yourself. It's never your fault. But it's always your fault, because if you wanted to change you're the one who has got to change.

—KATHERINE HEPBURN

Mary's mentor in recovery is Jill K., who walks beside her modeling life after addiction. A female role model is crucial to Mary's healing because her mother died so young, and in the past she'd alienated herself from everyone else.

Regarding her own heroin addiction, Jill talks about being alone in the world without a single person to turn to. It's ironic that she became that which she was deprived of—a person to support and encourage another when all seems lost and insuperable. Jill believes that all addicts are salvageable—herself a prime example. This urges her forward with strength, compassion, and love. Jill, who is not easily manipulated, embodies the old maxim, "You can't bullshit a bullshitter." Jill's story defies the naysayers who label all addicts as hopeless.

WISDOM WILL OF JILL K.

Dear Loved Ones and Friends,

As you all know, I'm a recovering heroin addict. By the time I got clean, I had two children and had left my husband, John, because he wasn't interested in recovering with me. During my addiction, I ended up in some really, really horrible places, including an abandoned house, with huge rats scurrying around. That was when I was still with my husband and my two-year-old son. The woman I was back then had no sense of worth. I believe the core of all addictions manifests itself in low self-esteem. When addicts don't feel good about who they are, they rely on drugs to forget.

In my elaborate system of denial and bullshit, I was convinced that people with jobs were losers. If they had the guts to hustle, they wouldn't be tied down to stupid jobs. I actually thought it was pretty cool living in that abandoned house with my husband and kid with no more worry about paying rent or utility bills; in fact, there weren't any utilities like electricity or water. Looking back, it was really awful.

When I was very young, my mother convinced me that sex before marriage would ruin me, and no man would ever want me. At age 15, I lost my virginity, and within a year, the guy dumped me. There I was—ruined! I can't say I became promiscuous, but in my search for human affection, I had a number of partners. I convinced myself that I liked only bad boys—criminals, rebels, and guys on the fringe of society. I fancied finding someone and scooping him up, taking him home, and caring for him. Then he'd see I loved him, and la, la, la, I'd be in *Cinderellaland*.

My first wedding to John was a debacle. We had to postpone the ceremony so he could go cop for some people. I was so drunk it was a wonder I didn't just roll down the aisle. Half of our gifts were drugs. We'd been living together for two years, so I knew it was a safe bet to inform him, "You need to marry me or move out." And he said, "Okay, whatever." He'd been married three times before. It wasn't any big deal to him. He didn't have any other place to live, anyway. How romantic was that? I still had it together enough to carry a Meier and Frank credit card, with which I bought my own engagement ring. Within six months, it was in the hands of our drug connection.

When I finally left John, I thought he'd see my seriousness about getting clean, he'd want the same, and everything would turn out like in the movies. I suffered from incredible codependency, which nearly crippled me with the thought, *If I leave, what will happen to him?* Finally, I began thinking, *If I don't leave, what will happen to me?* What a shock to learn John got clean before I did!

I nearly had my children taken away. In fact, I almost called Children's Services on myself because I knew I wasn't a good mother! If I had lost them, I wouldn't be here today. My children kept me from robbing banks and, ultimately, serving jail time. Robbing banks was preferable to getting a job; however, robbing banks wasn't an option for me, since there was not one person in the world who I could call and say, "I need some help. I'm in jail. Can you watch the kids?"

Through the years, I searched for some kind of spiritual connection. But a person under the influence cannot establish a spiritual connection. When I decided to quit using, I weighed 85 pounds and was desperate. I prayed to whatever was out there. I was smart enough to know that if I asked for help, I'd have to hold up my end of the bargain. For starters, I had to leave my husband, which I did. My second challenge was to stop stealing. *Shampoo and toothpaste—who pays for that stuff? Only those stupid people who have jobs!*

While living in my car with the kids, I survived a series of fiascos. My daughter was about a year old and my son was five. Throughout my pregnancy, I used scores of drugs even though my thoughts screamed, *What's wrong with you? Look at what you're doing! How could you do this?*

I fell to my knees because I couldn't listen to those assaulting thoughts anymore. In my heart, I knew my behavior was killing me. *Killing* me! But I couldn't stop. I didn't know what to do. In the summer of 1988, I was on methadone, which disqualified me from entering detox. Plus, even if I wasn't on methadone, I couldn't go because I had the kids. What would I do with them? There wasn't anyone to watch them.

Leaving my husband meant leaving the drug house; our house *was* the drug house. For about a year and a half, I'd tried to clean up there, but of course, it didn't work. Every month, I'd tell myself that as soon as my welfare check came, I'd leave. The check would arrive, and the next thing I knew, the money was gone. Then, I'd beat myself up, saying, *You've done it again! You've done it again!* This went on month after month. By leaving John, I was able to get clean on my own. To me, that meant not sticking needles in my arms. This was huge! Gigantic! To be just on methadone and alcohol was an incredible first step.

I don't know how I found the courage to leave my husband. We had been together nine years. He was the father of my children and the only person in my life besides the kids. Somehow, one month, I ended up with $200 left over! This was the first of many miracles. With my kids and a few items that fit in the car, I left. I didn't care what happened to what I left behind. Months down the road, the kids and I were living in a little studio apartment. I was detoxing from methadone because I wanted off of it.

Methadone never worked for me, anyway, because I never wanted to just feel normal, which is the whole rationale for that drug: "Here, we'll put you on methadone so that you don't have to commit crimes and stick needles in your arms. You'll be able to get a job and lead a productive life." I didn't want that kind of normalcy. I'm an addict. I wanted my brain turned off, whether that's up, down, or sidewise. When I was on methadone, I also did cocaine and drank alcohol. Now, I wanted off of everything, including Methadone. My life revolved around the clinic and whoever supplied the pills. As soon as I'd hit the clinic, people in the waiting room would say, "Jill, Jill, Jill! Guess what John's doing?" I didn't want to know. "Don't do this to me," I begged. "It's too hard. I know what he's doing."

Then I started hearing my husband was in treatment! The only way this could have happened was if he had been picked up on a parole violation. And, sure enough, while he was talking to his parole officer, he came out of the fog enough to remember that he was a veteran. At the time, he had no place to live because all the welfare money left with me. He had to come up with something. So it struck him, *I'm a veteran.* He knew he could go to treatment at the VA drug recovery facility in Vancouver, Washington, instead of going to jail, so John told his PO that he had a big drug problem and needed treatment. Ever since then, he's been clean. I left him to get clean, and he ended up with six more months of clean time than me! How paradoxical!

After I was convinced that John was serious about staying clean, I met with him a few times in a park. At first, I didn't want him to know where I lived. Eventually, the change in his behavior convinced me to let him visit me at the apartment.

We weren't thinking about reconciling. It was more about being familiar with each other and raising two kids together.

I still felt yucky, and before long, I thought about using. Voices in my head screamed again: *You left your husband. You went through months of excruciating symptoms. Finally, you have a little apartment. Your husband's clean and doing his thing. You're on the right road, and you're thinking about using? What's wrong with you?*

One day, when my husband came to visit, we went to the movies. I'd been drinking in secret, which I'd never done before. I knew that I shouldn't be drinking in front of him. So I ran to the Plaid Pantry for "milk," where I chugged some wine coolers and chewed gum to hide the smell, thinking he wouldn't notice. At the movie, John was very cool. About halfway through it, he leaned over and said, "If you're going to drink, I can't come see you anymore." That was all he said. It wasn't mean or anything, just a statement of fact. A couple of tears ran down my face, and I said, "I don't know what to do, and I'm scared that I can't stop." He said, "You know, Jill, you might want to check out these meetings. They're full of people just like us, but they're clean." He handed me a 12-step meeting schedule and that is all he said about it. He didn't preach; he knew it wasn't his business.

John was so involved in his own recovery that he didn't have time to worry about mine. Thank God! He was doing some codependency and post-traumatic stress work as well as working the steps. I wasn't doing any of that yet. No new information was coming to me. I wanted the old me gone, but I wasn't sure who I wanted to be. I had no good examples to follow. Katherine Hepburn was the only person I could think of wanting to model after. She wore pants before other women did. And she wasn't a weakling. In the movies, she didn't take crap off of anyone. Katherine was bright and spunky. That's who I wanted to be like. In fragile moments, when I didn't know what direction to turn, I'd think, *What would Katherine Hepburn do?*

I also made a deal with God or whatever IT was: If the 12 steps and going to their meetings helped, I promised to do the right thing. It took a while for me to clean up some of my bad behaviors, but all in all, I did pretty well. Nowadays, people comment on my ridiculous honesty. But, to me, if something is not the truth, it's a lie. I'm real clear on that. So that's how I found 12-step programs and recovery—through my husband and Katherine Hepburn.

I started going to meetings, which I hated. I thought Alcoholics Anonymous, Narcotics Anonymous, the readings, and the *Keep Coming Back* slogans—all of it—was stupid, cheesy, and corny. I also thought that the people in the meetings weren't really clean at all. I believed they were using in their cars before they came in the door. They were only attending meetings on judge's orders to get their little slips of paper signed. These were my evil twin's thoughts. At my third meeting, I entered the room and saw an old girlfriend sitting there. The last time I had seen her was the previous Thanksgiving, when my husband, son, and I lived in a house paid for by a benefactor. We told our three-year-old son he had to give up his bedroom so that friends could have it. They had drugs, and drugs always took priority. We made a list of the food we'd need to have for a real Thanksgiving Day meal. Someone had already given us a turkey; if we wanted a regular Thanksgiving dinner like normal people, all we had to do was steal the rest of the groceries.

Suddenly, this friend began miscarrying! She wasn't going to leave for the hospital, though, because, first, the meal wasn't ready, and second, there were still drugs left to do. She knew if she left, we'd use up her share. She didn't go to the hospital until both the food and drugs were gone. It was a miracle that she didn't bleed to death.

Two years later, I walked into a meeting, and there she was sitting in a chair. She had two years clean! She might as well have said a hundred. I couldn't even manage having a day or a week clean. If such a thing were possible, she'd been a worse user than me. Now, her hair was clean! She had a light in her eyes, and her blouse was buttoned! She looked like somebody was home. I thought, *Okay, first, here's my husband who originally didn't want to get clean, and he's clean. Now, this woman who was worse off than me has two years clean!* I still thought the 12-step programs were corny and stupid because I didn't know how they worked. But, I decided to go for it. A friend hooked me up with my first sponsor, who showed up every Saturday morning to take me to a meeting. Sure, I believed in the program, but I still didn't like it. I'd see her car pull up, and I'd think, *Oh God! It's that woman again to take me to that damn meeting.* I tried every excuse I could think of. *The kids aren't ready. I don't want to make you late. You go ahead without me.* She'd have none of it. Eventually, I quit making excuses and was ready when she arrived. Now, I have more than 19 years clean and sober. I still attend that same Saturday meeting. It's my home group. If my sponsor hadn't been persistent, I wouldn't have connected with this group.

When I first met someone who'd relapsed, I thought, *Wait a darn minute!* I thought somehow we'd made it, that we were safe. We'd have to do some things like go to meetings, but we didn't go back. This man in my home group had been attending meetings all the time. After his relapse, I'd see him once in a while at meetings trying to make it back. Each time, he looked worse than the time before. The last few times I saw him, he was walking with a cane! The guy was in his thirties! What did he need a cane for? One day, he sat next to me at a meeting, with his head in his hands, and cried. "Jill, I can't get it back again!" Ultimately, he threw himself out of a window! He killed himself rather than stay stuck in the disease. It broke my heart.

As I move forward, I have my little apartment, I've found my home group, I attend regular meetings, and I'm continuing to detox. My head kept telling me that 20 milligrams of methadone wasn't holding me, so what was the point of going every day and dealing with the darn stuff? So I made a plan about getting clean, and this time, I did it. I got down to five milligrams of methadone, then three milligrams. I had to fight to get off drugs because the prescribing doctor made a written recommendation that I stay on methadone for the rest of my life and said that I should just accept the fact that I'd never be clean. Thank God I didn't listen!

When the kids and I moved into the apartment, we didn't have any possessions, not a towel, or a plate, or a pan—nothing. Plus, I didn't know of any resources where I could get these things. As a result, I'd push a shopping cart, with my daughter sitting in the little seat and my son walking alongside me (or he'd get in if he were tired), and we'd hit the apartment dumpsters. People throw away perfectly good, useable items. I'd dig through and see what I could bring home. It was an adventure. I have fond memories of those days. We'd find magazines and then cut out the pictures of food and play restaurant. We'd serve one another the food or play grocery store. Once, I found a coloring book and some crayons. We colored and then cut out the pictures and glued them onto Popsicle sticks to make puppet shows. It was such a relief not to be in chaos anymore. It didn't matter that we didn't have much. We had each other.

My husband and I didn't move back in together right away because we both had a lot of work to do, but we hoped to recreate our marriage into an entirely different relationship. We did just that, and we've been together 27 years now.

The first five years of our recovery, we were just poor, poor. The first five years clean were like that. We had a lot of financial wreckage. We both worked minimum-wage jobs. Half of my check went to the babysitter for the two kids. John couldn't drive for the first three years because his driver's license had been revoked. One day, he called me and said he needed me to give him a ride. I asked, "Where to?" and he said, "Well, never mind where; I just need the ride." I picked him up from work, and he took me to a hawk shop. I wondered what we were doing there. Somehow, he'd managed to save a hundred dollars, which was huge for us. He said, "You need to have a wedding ring." With the hundred dollars, he bought me a wedding set.

When I was two years clean, we held a potluck at our house, and a friend of mine handed me a clipping from the classified ads. She said, "You need to apply for this job." It was working at a treatment center for woman with children. Ironically, it opened up the month after I got clean—May 1989. I told her that I'd never been in treatment and didn't know a thing about it. But she insisted, "Just go apply!" I went and got the job at Letty Owens Treatment Center, which is now part of Central City Concern. At the time, Ecumenical Ministries ran it. I worked there for four years. In the end, I dreaded going to work, so I gave my notice. My brain immediately started haranguing me. *What are you doing? You don't have another job to go to! You can't just quit!* But I knew if I didn't quit, I'd stay stuck there. I hated it because so many of the women coming through were only participating to regain custody of their kids. The Department of Human Services (DHS) demands that people go to treatment to get them back. So the women agreed. I knew they weren't going to stay clean. I watched these already-damaged kids being reunited with their moms. I still had my own issues. I'd felt guilty about what I'd put my own kids through. But these moms weren't serious about cleaning up. They only went through the motions, doing what they had to do to be compliant. I could see their lack of conviction. It was a vicious cycle—mothers getting loaded again, followed by the kids being removed again. I worried about the children placed back in foster care. It was too difficult for me to witness anymore. I left and vowed I'd never work in the treatment field again.

A friend of mine who cleaned houses said I could work with her until I found a job. So when people asked what I was going to do after I resigned, I'd tell them. Pretty soon, someone would say, "My neighbor just lost her housekeeper," or "I just lost my cleaning lady." The next thing I knew, I'd established my own clientele. That was my business for four years. It worked out well. By that point in my life, I'd established a good, strong spiritual connection with whatever's out there. I knew that IT had my back as long as I kept doing the right things. Did that mean I was ever going to have a lot of money or things? No. But it was okay. I knew that I was never going to be homeless again because now I had friends with couches. I'd always have a place to sleep, and they'd feed me, too. I wouldn't go hungry. It was okay. I liked me now. I understood that, no matter what happened, loving myself wasn't something that could be taken away. Today, I have self-esteem. I'm proud of myself. I'm a good mom. And none of it hinges on my job.

When I got clean, my son was only five years old. He'd grown up in the most incredible mess. There were syringes all over the house. Violence and crime were common visitors, as were the police. Our babysitters were bank robbers who got busted by the FBI! And that's only part of the story. Inevitably, when my son grew up, he had problems. I went to the school right away and said, "I need help because I don't know how much of my son's behavior is normal little boy behavior or how much is because of how he was raised. Or maybe there's a chemical imbalance." I just didn't know. But the school labeled my son a product of drug-addicted parents. Through the years, they passed him on from one grade to the next. Teachers told him that he was bad, lazy, and stupid! They said they liked it better when he didn't come to school! Gee, do you think he wanted to go to school and give it his all after that? Hardly. Come to find out, he was off-the-charts ADHD (attention deficit hyperactivity disorder)! The only reason it was diagnosed was because I took matters into my own hands when he was in eighth grade. Up until that time, I kept thinking, *Well, they're the experts. They know what they're doing*. But they didn't. I was at the school all the time, saying, "He's not bad. I know he's a handful. Believe me, I know that! But he isn't bad, and he isn't lazy, nor is he stupid, by any means. He's very bright. Something is going on with this kid, and we're just not finding out what it is." I was so frustrated. I felt like I was standing on a table jumping up and down and screaming at them that the building was on fire, and nobody was hearing me, let alone listening to me. I decided I was done waiting and took it upon myself to find out how to help my child.

My house-cleaning business was perfect because I could leave whenever I wanted to. I had a flexible schedule, which was my priority at the time. If I needed to go to my son's school, I could go. I was my own boss. My husband works for Central City Concern. He came home one night and said that he had heard about a new program for heroin addicts that they were implementing. It was 1999, and that year, there was a crisis in heroin overdose deaths. The county was desperate to do something to stop the epidemic. The Recovery Association Project (RAP) had been around about a year at that point. Fortunately, they had developed relationships with some city commissioners and other people in the county. Because of their connections, the county knew that RAP was filled with recovering people and that they might have an answer. How insightful of them!

A coworker of mine dreamed up the idea for a mentor program because people were going into detox but weren't making it from there to treatment programs without relapsing. A person gets to the exit doors of detox and says to themselves, "I've been a heroin addict for years. My life is a mess. I've been in detox for eight days now. I'm standing at the door ready to leave. I have the same dirty clothes on that I came in with. I have this piece of paper telling me where I can go sign up for treatment, but I haven't seen my parole officer since God knows when. I can't go back to where I was living because everybody there uses."

After detox, it is still overwhelming for people. They don't feel that great. So, naturally, they think, "I'll just do a little something until I can figure things out." And then they're right back out there. The people at RAP said that if they'd had someone come into Hooper Detox Center saying, "I know what you're going through because I've been there. I want to help you make it on the outside," then physically took them from detox to clean and sober housing, it would have been really helpful. In the beginning, the Mentor Program didn't have a vehicle, so the mentors went over to Hooper Detox and got on the bus with the people leaving detox. They bussed across the bridge and took them to get food boxes, utensils, clothing, and whatever else they needed to meet basic needs. They'd only have to worry about their treatment and get involved in the 12 steps. When treatment comes to an end, what are they going to do without the support of a 12-step recovery program? The mentor pushes to get them involved in 12-step recovery. There are meetings all over town, so people have lots of choices. When they find a home group and a sponsor, then they can begin seriously working the steps. They need to get to know folks with some time in the program so that they have a support system in place. That's how the idea of the Mentor Program developed. I applied for and got the job in August 1999.

The gentleman that thought it up and one other woman and myself were the three original mentors. They gave us an office down in the basement of a building that doesn't even exist anymore. It had originally been a storeroom. The man and I didn't know the first thing about having an office, but luckily, the other woman was well trained. She knew how to do spreadsheets and other forms on the computer. I thought, *Well, we'll need some pens, some paper, and a file of some sort*. The thing we all had in common was what had worked for us in recovery. The challenge was how to put that into an office, into a program. We had the advantage and opportunity to create the Mentor Program from the bottom up. Thank God Central City Concern let us to do it the way we saw fit.

Until then, I didn't know there were agencies around that handed out food, so initially, part of our job was locating all the programs that might help us out. We introduced ourselves around town and told people about the Mentor Program. We learned the best places to get free groceries, clothing, and pots and pans. We also learned who offered hygiene services. I was, and still am, so excited when I meet a new client. The beauty of our program is that we get to pick who's going to be our client.

No one mandates anyone to us. Clients aren't determined by their ability to pay. Initially, everyone came right out of Hooper Detox. Nowadays, we get them from Hooper, Inverness Prison, Coffee Creek Women's Facility, Columbia River Correctional Institution and the Oregon State Penitentiary. I think the only place we aren't cleared for is Sheridan, which is a federal prison. We hold face-to-face interviews with referees. If it's a woman, I go. If it's a guy, then a guy goes. The institutions know what we are looking for in our clients. Ideally, it's someone that everyone's lost confidence in and don't believe can or ever will get clean. We want people who've done a number of treatment programs and now really want to get clean. We offer them hope: "You know what? It doesn't matter that you've been in treatment thirteen times. It doesn't matter that you spent the last twenty years of your life in prison. It's okay. You can still make it."

I work with a woman I'll call Tina. She's probably the most memorable client I've ever worked with or sponsored in a 12-step program. She endured the most horrific childhood I've ever heard about. I don't know how a person's psyche can survive her heinous background. Tina does have mental health issues because of it and is on a number of medications. This woman spent five years in Damasch State Mental Hospital [now closed] located in Wilsonville, Oregon. She received messages from everyone there that she was a waste of human flesh and that there was no redeeming value to her at all!

Meeting Tina ended up being one of those God shots! I was supposed to interview her at Inverness Prison. It was Christmastime, and I was really busy. I kept meaning to get out there, and finally, I knew I had to go because they'd be releasing her the next day. When I arrived, she'd already been let go. I felt terrible, but I knew if it were meant to be, it would happen. I've learned that I'm not responsible for everything and everybody in the world. This is a *big* truth of life, which took me a long time to understand. In the past, I felt like a failure because I could never do enough for everybody, so I was bad. Today, I let everybody have their own God. And their God can take care of them. It isn't my job.

After a week or two, the phone rang in my office, and it was Tina. What's so bizarre is that she can't see anything without her glasses, and that day she didn't have them. When she left the jail, someone had written my phone number on a tiny little slip of yellow paper, which had been tossed in a plastic bag with her clothing and a mishmash of other things. She was sitting on the bed in a disgustingly filthy house. Tina is a woman suffering from obsessive-compulsive disorder; she has to have everything clean. So there she was on the bed in this gross house—a similar place where I'd found myself when I hit my knees begging for divine intervention. Tina didn't want to *do this* anymore! She looked down and saw that yellow scrap of paper and miraculously was able to read the phone number and called me! I didn't give her my usual spiel about what my expectations are of people when they work with me. If I had, she never would have met with me. That was five years ago. Tina put a number of years together before she relapsed. Her addictions were heroin, alcohol, pills, and whatever else that came her way. Most of her life was filled with abusive relationships, incarcerations, and institutionalization. She had very little time on the streets. When she did find herself there, she survived abusive relationships. Tina was so damaged, so broken! In fact, when she first came to us, she was animalistic. I feared she'd stab somebody in the elevator because she was so backed up. Even when people didn't have ill intentions, she was overly defensive: "Don't you look at me! Don't you touch me! I'm not going to be abused anymore! Back off!"

After her relapse, Tina made it back to sobriety. Since I've known her, she's had three relapses, the longest of which was six months. But she keeps coming back. She has almost a year clean now. She's involved with an agency that I won't name, but they specialize in dual-diagnosed people. The message Tina gets in their group setting is, "You have mental health issues. No one expects you to ever stay clean because it's harder for you. So if you have a slip, you don't need to change your clean date." She let's them have it! She'll holler, "What are you talking about? I relapsed; of course, I'm going to change my clean date! I may have mental health problems, but I know that I can get clean and stay clean." She's a pistol and an amazing woman. Tina attends the meetings at this agency only because it's required for her to maintain housing. I tell her it's okay to have an opinion and to voice it. Sometimes, she confronts people in the group, like one woman who comes week after week and says she'd used. This incenses Tina. And she'll say something to the woman like, "How is it that you have a 'slip'? I've never seen you in recovery. How can you have a recovery date?" It just makes her angry. I tell her, "Maybe this isn't about them. Maybe this is about you being there so they can hear what you have to say. Tell them, 'Here I am, the most miserable person in the bunch, and I get it. I'm doing it, and you're not!'" Even with all of her challenges, Tina has held down a job for years.

Tina reminds me that where there is breath, there is hope, and that no one is beyond redemption. No matter how damaged someone might have been, there is hope for finding inner peace. Tina is still tormented and has very little inner peace, but she does have some. I hear my clients complain about the stupidest things. But that's what we do as addicts. We complain to take the focus off of ourselves. I think of Tina and all the obstacles she's had to face with no help from society at all; in fact, it has only hindered her every step of the way. She is evidence that the resiliency of the human spirit is beyond belief. That's what she reminds me of every day. Tina wants to believe in something greater than herself, but in light of her agonizing background, she reasons that if there is anything greater, then why did it allow those dreadful things to happen? She continues seeking though and hasn't given up on finding IT.

One day, I told Tina, "You need to find a sponsor, because I can't be there for you all the time." (She can be very draining.) After giving a friend of mine a heads-up, I gave Tina her phone number. This particular person is the most tolerant, compassionate woman ever. If anyone would be willing to work with Tina, she was the one. So Tina called her and said, "I don't know why Jill wanted me to call you. I guess she thinks I need to find a sponsor. But I'm not going to attach to you. I'm not going to become your friend. I'm not going to care about you. I'm not working any steps with you. Blah, blah, blah…Now, do you want to be my sponsor?" And my friend said, "Okay."

For years, Tina told me, "I don't really have a connection with my sponsor." Then I'd bring up a few points: "Didn't you call her when this or that happened? Didn't you call her and tell her when such and such was going on? That's pretty personal stuff to divulge to someone you don't really trust." My friend is not only Tina's sponsor; she's my sponsor, too. Yesterday, the three of us had lunch together. And all of us thought, *Isn't it amazing that we have this connection with each other and that we're all clean?* Then Tina said, "You know, I really do have a bond with you [her sponsor], and I really do trust you." My friend holds Tina's money for her because Tina's daughter, who is also an addict, is back in her life. She is constantly using the guilt ticket: "You were never there for me; give me four hundred dollars for this"; "You were never there for me; pay my cell phone bill this month, which, by the way, is three-fifty"; or "I need rent." She guilts Tina into giving her money because she knows her mother can't say no. Now, Tina can honestly say to her daughter, "I don't have any money." Every cent she gets her hands on she gives to her sponsor, and her sponsor won't let her finance her daughter's pseudo-emergencies.

When I go through a difficult time in my recovery, I draw upon the same faith I had when I quit my job before the Mentor Program came along. One of my first God shots came when I started on methadone. I fostered hope that there really was something divine out there to believe in. Through the course of my day, things came to mind like, *I wish I had some little tights for my daughter with some ruffles on the butt. Or I wish I could buy my son some Converse high-top tennis shoes. Red ones would be cool. And he needs some underwear.* At the time, my son was into army guys and ninja toys. So all these thoughts of what I couldn't give my kids flooded my mind. One day, I went to the methadone clinic, and the lady responsible for childcare said, "Somebody just left me this whole bag of donations. I am not set up for this. Will you just take it home, and whatever you can't use, get rid of for me?" So I took the bag home and dumped it out. Everything in the bag was something we could use! Everything was the right size and the right colors! There were even toy army guys! I thought, *I get it!* It was loud and clear in my mind. Boom! A conk on the head! To anyone else, it wouldn't have been such a big deal. But, for me, it was a message that something *was* out there, something that knows my thoughts and what's in my heart. Since then, I've never doubted ITS existence. The fact that I was able to get off methadone and not use was enough divine proof for me that as long as I do my part, whatever IT is will support me.

During the first couple years of my sobriety, my sponsoring style was rigid: "You have to do it this way. This is what I did and it works. And now I want you to do it exactly the same way so it can work for you!" Through the years, I've loosened up a bit. I realize all roads lead to Rome. People can tailor their program somewhat to make it their own. It doesn't have to follow my experience to the letter.

My son is now one of us (a recovering person). He grew up predisposed, and then with the ADHD stuff added, any self-esteem he might have developed was wiped away. According to the school system, he was convinced he was a *loser*, *stupid*, and *bad*! Early on, he started to self-medicate. I was so close to it, but buried in my denial, I chose not to see his addictions. By the time he was 19, he'd been taken to the sobering station five times![3] He'd been shot and stabbed! I told him, "You've been arrested more times than I ever was. In all the years I used, I was never taken, not once, to the sobering station!" Every time he was arrested, I'd think, *Thank You. Thank You.* Then they'd lose his paperwork, or the witness wouldn't show up. Finally, they kept him for 10 days at the Justice Center Jail. He was in there long enough to get a little clarity. There were some really violent episodes there, just like in his life. I always feared a phone call in the middle of the night announcing that he'd killed someone! My son was physically small for a very long time. Then, all of a sudden, he grew into this really big guy. He sauntered around, giving the impression, "Don't mess with

3 The sobering station is located at the Hooper Detox Center. If someone is drunk on the street, really intoxicated, they take them to the sobering station instead of taking them to jail. They keep a person from four to six hours until they sober up, and then they let them go. Sobering stations used to be called "drunk tanks." They were located in the county jails. The police used to be the ones who picked up the people crashing on the street. Nowadays, nobody wants to pay for this service, and as such, they are in danger of going away.

me!" Even though he hadn't started the trouble, he'd go into a rage if someone picked on him while he was drinking. He'd have *rage blackouts*. When he came to, he'd realize that the person wasn't even moving anymore.

So, after ten days in jail, he called and asked us to bail him out. This was a first. In the past, no matter the situation he'd found himself in, he'd never call because he knew full well we wouldn't come to the rescue. Also, he didn't want us to know what he was doing. After all, he'd been on his own since he was 17. But, this time, we said, "Okay, we'll bail you out if you go to treatment. Then you can stay with us as long as you stay clean." It's been five years, and he's been clean ever since. That was a very difficult time for us. I'd pray a lot. I didn't know where he was or what he was doing, but I begged whatever IT was for his protection. I believe that the dead are still with us and that angels are real. I'd rally the troops and ask them to surround and support him. And please just give him a nudge to call me—especially at times when I hadn't heard from him in days. I was always fearful that he was dead somewhere or hurt. I'd light candles and soak in a hot bath. I'd put on relaxing music, and then I'd ask for the angels and other heavenly beings to protect him. It's always worked. I gave up years ago trying to figure out what IT is. It doesn't matter. It's a mystery. I do think, though, that love is the crux of all religions and spiritual programs. Now, my son is not only clean, he works two jobs.

Fortunately, my daughter never had addiction problems. The biggest difference, I believe, is that she grew up with self-esteem. She's 20 now and has a very good head on her shoulders. She's an old soul. The decisions she makes are amazing.

Today, I understand the connection between the faulty choices I've made in my life and the misery it's caused me. Sadly, there are many folks who aren't making that connection and don't know how to be accountable. I've learned that we can live through and survive grief. We can grieve the loss of our loved ones. We can even grieve all the little deaths that accumulate along life's path. And, because we can grieve our losses, we can reach back and help someone else through that awful maze. If we don't do that, if we remain self-centered, we'll never experience the rewards, and worst of all, we won't stay clean. If we do manage to stay clean, we aren't going to be happy. We'll be bitter because we'll never get enough, never make enough money at our jobs, never get those promotions, never acquire houses larger than our neighbors, or whatever it is we're trying to fill from the outside. The truth is the hole is inside of us. I visualize it as a disgusting abscess. We have to lance it. We have to allow it to drain. If we just put ointment and a Band-Aid on it, it's not going to heal. We must cut it open, endure the pain, and clean it out. We have to fill it with faith in something greater than ourselves. Then we have to leave it alone so that it can slowly heal.

Some of the women I work with still want to steal, which I understand. It's a fix. They don't have any material possessions, and they want that cute pair of earrings or cute pair of underwear. It makes them feel better for a minute. The fix might be the guy down the hall who thinks the woman is cute: "I'll go have sex with him, and I'll feel better for a minute." Or the insatiable sweet tooth: "I'll eat this whole bowl of ice cream." They are all fixes. "In the long run," I tell them, "you're going to feel worse about yourself because you did that. And the urges will keep perpetuating themselves." We can't let that hole in our hearts continue to fester. It's important to feel the full impact of it, or we will never even want to develop a spiritual connection.

I want to be remembered as someone who cared for others, someone who didn't take herself too seriously, and someone who gave back. When I was using, I took, and took, and took, and took. Sometimes, it feels like I am almost at the balancing point, that I'm almost there.

Integrity has been one of the most important values that I adopted from the time I got clean. I wanted, and want, my word to mean something because I've been such a liar. No one could believe anything that came out of my mouth in the old days. People (who know me now) know that if I tell them something, it's true. I don't lie. I don't cheat on my taxes. All those years I ran my housecleaning business, people would say, "You don't have to claim this income. Nobody knows that I paid you." But I'd say, "I know you paid me." I claimed every penny of it. If someone gives me too much change, I tell them. You can't have too much integrity. It's important for me to be remembered for holding that value high.

When I die, I want people to have a big potluck and line the walls with goofy photographs of me. I love to travel, so I'd like some of the photos to be of me in different places—pictures of me with my family and pictures of me laughing and having fun. I want everyone to get up and tell funny stories about me, like, "Oh God, I remember the time Jill…" I want them to recall how much I enjoyed life and that I was fun to be around. I want them to acknowledge me as a spiritual person, with lots of integrity and a kind heart.

One of our wedding gifts the second time around was an old-fashioned, weathered-looking sign that says, "Fairytales Do Come True." I have really lived a fairytale life. I am so blessed.

With Love, Jill

One of the doctrines of Catholicism that I hold dear is our belief in the communion of saints. For me, that means we are truly not alone, that there are ethereal beings with whom we can call upon for guidance, direction, and protection. Included are the prophets, saints, martyrs, and avatars throughout time, as well as our own dearly departed. Not replacing the divine, this community is enfolded into it and at the ready to receive our supplications and oblations. For me, this makes the Godhead more approachable, tangible, and personal than the infinite *I Am.*

In recovery, I found great consolation in praying to the Blessed Mother Mary. And today, I often enter discussions with my parents, big brother, and two girlfriends who are now on the other side. I don't believe that love dies with death, but that it merely changes form. Love on either side of the celestial realm provides our lives with meaning and purpose. How shocked and pleased Katherine Hepburn must be to learn that she was an *intervention* tool for Jill's heroin addiction. For Jill, Katherine, angels, and other heavenly beings have been integral to her healing and peace of mind.

Self-love and self-pride are often denounced as *false pride*, *narcissistic*, and *sinful*; however, they are primary to our staying clean and sober. I can still hear my tormented mother preaching, "Self-pride stinks!" I believed her. The word *pride* makes many people squirm. Glasker (Chapter 9) and his parents viewed it as a fault that was steering his life toward grief, pain, and death. Yet, how can we love ourselves without some measure of self-pride? Honest self-pride emerges from self-love. It says, "I'm okay, and I think you are, too." The pride I'm talking about here is not *false* pride, which is what I think Glasker (a later story) dealt with, but that which makes us proud to be alive, providing us with contentment. It doesn't assert superiority; it merely affirms our belonging, our humanness, warts and all. Jill has climbed this mountain.

I agree with her that every addicted person reaches out to substances or things in compulsive and addictive ways to numb their self-loathing and assuage their lack of self-esteem. Healing from any addiction literally means recovering our *self*. Once we learn to love and respect ourselves and our bodies, it's hard to return to self-murdering behaviors. I believe everyone, not just recovering addicts, needs the love and support of people in the past, present, and future to help them learn self-love, to survive, and to thrive.

CHAPTER 3

I'm Going To Love You Until You Learn To Love Yourself

Life is filigree work. What is written clearly is not worth much, it's the transparency that counts.

—Louis Ferdinand Celine

*P*eople living on the streets are in survival mode, so there's no noticeable psychological or spiritual growth. But as they begin to recover, every single unexpressed loss gallops in. Peace only quiets one's soul when a strong measure of darkness is dispelled. It's challenging to wrap one's arms around the negatives in the past and embrace them as implements for growth. It is, however, necessary in order to accept God's forgiveness and, ultimately, find the strength to forgive ourselves. Within community, we offer one another absolution, and by integrating the imperfection in our lives with the light of divine love, we discover our wholeness.

As a recovering person, I know that when most of us hit bottom, we beg for God or our higher power's (HP) help. In that moment, we are as transparent as it gets. We have nothing left to lose except our physical lives. If we want to survive, we face our demons and do whatever it takes to unearth our wholeness. Continuing our old ways is more painful, more terrifying, than grabbing hold of our HP's ankles and diving into the *Big Book of Alcoholics or Narcotics Anonymous*. I believe that it takes the *fall* for us to become *real*.

Witness the transparency and the grace of Bekah as she moves in the direction of a healthy recovery, making choices that bring her more fully into life than ever before. I am amazed by the attitude she's developed regarding losing her children to the state. She hasn't given up on them or herself and sees reconciliation in her future. I don't doubt for a second that Bekah and all of her children will one day sit down together and share a family meal. I believe we all need her kind of hope.

Bekah works at Sisters of the Road Café as an employee and as a volunteer. She willingly took hold of the microphone I offered her at Backspace Internet Café, located a couple of blocks away from Sisters. It is a place to rent Internet time and enjoy light food and coffee. The walls are covered with rotating art. There are tables to play chess and checkers, and best of all, there are three-pronged wall sockets where I can plug in my tape recorder. Bekah was eager to share her story.

WISDOM WILL OF BEKAH W.

Dear Family, Friends, and Community,

Many of you know my story, but I'd like to retell it now. I grew up in the rural area of Boring, Oregon. My parents, who also had biological children, adopted me with my brother, who was eighteen months old. Basically, my brother and I were adopted to be their slaves. We did all the housework. By the time I was seven, my dad started abusing me in every sense of the word—physically, mentally, and sexually. I stayed until I was 13, and then I ran.

When I was 14, he touched me for the last time. It was Christmas. He told me that (his touching me) was my Christmas present. I finally said something to somebody. I couldn't hold it in anymore. I was going to school and attending the church I grew up in. My parents were paying for everything, although I was living with foster families in the area. One day, in youth group, I broke down and told my volleyball coach what I was experiencing because the abuse had been going on too long.

They brought in CSD (Children's Services Department), and I stayed in the state's custody until I was 18 years old. After I turned 16, I became suicidal. This went on for about two and a half years. I carved anarchy and peace signs into myself with safety pins. Once, I carved *I love Lance* because he was my boyfriend. I was just confused. I remained a cutter for a while because, for some reason, the physical pain provided me release from the emotional pain. Also, it gave me a rush. I asked my foster mom to put me in a mental ward; however, she was determined to experience a breakthrough with me. She finally did. I didn't understand why she hadn't given up on me like everyone else. "You've called 911, had the mental ward on hold for two and a half years, and you didn't give up on me. No one's ever done that [been that committed] for me—ever." She answered, "It's because I love you." While growing up, I'd never heard those words, so the tears came. I hugged her and started following her around everywhere she went.

By 15, I'd already completed algebra, trigonometry, and calculus. I was working with MS DOS. When I was entering Canby High School, my math and English scores were at college level; however, they put me in freshman math and English. I rebelled. I said to myself, *I don't care if I fail these classes. This is not where I'm supposed to be.* I thought I was headed for failure because I just didn't care, so I quit after my junior year with 18.25 credits, when I should have graduated with extra credits. Instead, my life went downhill from there. I intend to start the process of getting my GED again. I don't want my children growing up thinking their mom is a dropout. Eventually, I'm going to tell them my life story—and how it was then and how it is now.

When I was younger, I told myself that I was never going to drink or do drugs, smoke, or even have kids. By the time I was 17 I'd done everything. I got into the methamphetamine habit and went on to have three kids. My son was born in 1994, just as I was turning 18. In my twenties, I had a daughter. My youngest was born in 2002. She recently turned five years old. I haven't seen them since they were little. The state took them from me because they said I was mentally unstable. They didn't give me a chance to take parenting classes or any of that stuff that's available. In fact, they told me that any kid I had from then on they were going to take away! That was so hard. It pushed me into more criminal activity.

When I was 17, I'd broken into a house in Canby, Oregon, and caused over $20,000 in damage. One of my friends was house-sitting for another friend's family. We broke the glass backboard on the basketball hoop in their driveway. We were going to take the Corvette in the garage, but the house alarm system coordinated with the car alarm. We figured out the system beforehand, so it didn't go off. We threw a party that went on for two or three days. On the last day, my foster sister and I were sitting up in the attic. She called 911 because, by then, the Canby Police had surrounded the house. We didn't know what else to do. The dispatcher told her that they couldn't send anybody to help us because the entire police force was already there. A neighbor had spotted us going into the house and, knowing we didn't belong there, called the cops. The dispatcher told my foster sister that we should appear at the door with our hands up and turn ourselves in. So we did. We were both really drunk.

When I was two months shy of my 18th birthday, Child Services just let me go. I got really depressed. I'd been in one foster home or another most of my life. And they just dropped me from the system.

Until two years ago, I was living on the streets, running amok. I was doing the drug scene off and on. I was out there running drug deals. I never did tricks, but I might as well have because I was sleeping with my dealer. That's how I got my drugs at the time. Finally, I just gave up on men. When I was 21 or 22, it hit me that I was tired of men, but I wasn't done with the drugs or criminal activity.

My first daughter was taken away from me when she was 20 months old. It was really sad. I had her with me for almost two years, but because the house was messy during the social worker's visit, they took her from me. I'd even quit using for a couple of years prior to that house visit, but CSD refused to let me keep her. That's when I gave up again. I had my own apartment out in North Portland in Columbia Villa [a sub-sidized housing development] before they took my daughter. But afterward, I didn't have anything to live for. I told myself that I didn't care what I did or where I went. I got high, drank, and smoked pot.

Then my roommates (a guy older than me and a younger girl) introduced me to signing checks on closed accounts. We'd make the checks on the computer and put a legitimate account number on them, even though the accounts were closed. We wrote lots of checks to Domino's Pizza—like every day for two weeks. We just kept ordering pizza. Then Domino's caught on. Then we went to Fisherman's Sporting Goods and bought guns. We were trading the guns for drugs, but it didn't take long for them to notice what was going on. Forging those checks was really fun at the time, but obviously, I wasn't thinking clearly. The first time I went in with a check, I told myself, *If this checks clears, I'll come back and get the gun later.* Well, I got a call that the check was good and I could purchase my gun. I spent $489.99 [in forged funds] on a Glock 9mm and took it home. What a rush that was! I was like, *Wow!* The reason we got caught was that the youngest of the three of us went into Fisherman's to buy another gun, and her check was refused. The police arrested us. They asked me a bunch of questions. I tried lying my way out of it. I said so and so came over and offered me this and I did that. Finally, I just broke down and said, "You know what? I'm guilty. I am counterfeiting the checks and signing them inside my house, and these are the people I'm doing it with." I was beginning to fear my roommates, anyway. I didn't feel safe with them. The reason I got hooked on check forging in the first place was because it got me high.

We went back to the apartment with the police. They found five of the seven guns we'd bought. Mine is still out there somewhere. This scares me because the district attorney told me, "If your gun gets used for any criminal activity whatsoever, it's going to come back on you." I thought, *Oh crap!* I have to cross my fingers, even now, that the gun doesn't end up on the nightly news. I'm hoping they have found it already. I'm hoping because it's already been six years.

The first night after they picked me up, I went to jail for 24 hours. The younger girl and I got out. Then we went to court. We got arrested three more times before they actually charged us. The oldest of us, the guy, ended up going to the Sheridan Jail because they didn't want to put him with us. He stayed there for a year.

The only thing that kept me out of prison was the psychological evaluation I'd done with my attorney and the investigator. The judge looked at me and said, "I feel sorry for you." I said, "Why?" He said, "Because you act on impulse!" I just did stuff. If I got overstressed or depressed, or whatever, I'd just do something criminal. I didn't care. All together, I spent 41 days in the county jail. When I got out, I landed five years of probation. That's where I ended up and where I'm at now. My conviction was on February 15, 2003. They were going to charge me with unlawful use of a firearm and fraud for writing bad checks, but because of my psychological evaluation, the judge did what they call a *downward departure* and took off the top two charges and charged me with only check fraud. So that's how I got the five years probation. I felt bad because my codefendants got more than that. They had to sit in prison and basically rot their lives away until they got convicted. I implicated them to save myself. They have no nice words to say about me right now. But I don't care.

After that, I started getting high again on methamphetamines. I found out about the needle before I got convicted.

I'd get high just to pass the time, I guess. It gave me lots of energy. I'd go bike riding, go out in the middle of the night to buy cigarettes, or just sit in the apartment working crossword puzzles. Finally, I got fed up. I'd been in and out of recovery. I didn't care anymore about the probation. I didn't care about anything, really. So I went into treatment. Eventually, I was put in a halfway house at the YWCA (Young Women's Christian Association) by the Safeway Store on Tenth and Jefferson Streets (in Downtown Portland, Oregon). I stayed there for three and a half months. Right before they were going to let me out, I took off. I thought I didn't belong there any longer.

I got involved with a female. She'd called me up when she was drunk, so I "rescued" her, so to speak. I yelled at her. Let her puke. Let her do that and other things. I poured her bottle out. I was clean then, with almost a year behind me. I looked at her and said, "You know what? This is not the life." But, even though I knew that, I wasn't done. I started abusing myself with alcohol. I went back to the YWCA program twice. So I'd actually been there three times. Then my old PO (parole officer) put me in jail. I sat there for two weeks, got out, and he said, "Okay, Bekah, you can live on the streets as long as you check in with your PO once a week and do UAs [urine analysis] as often as he asks you to." That went on for a month.

I lived in and out of shelters, like Harbor Lights, or stayed with friends. Or, when I didn't have another place, I'd sleep out-of-doors. I wasn't particularly afraid to be out on the streets because I have a reputation for being tough. When I was dealing drugs, this chick came into the park where I was dealing and tried to step on my toes, so to speak. Tried to take all my customers away. So I put her in the hospital for two weeks. I developed a reputation really fast. Now, I try to show people that I really do have a softer side. But, so far, it's not working. They say, "We know about you."

When I got involved romantically with this new girl, I'd relapse with her. If she relapsed, I'd follow her. I went everywhere she went. She had this control thing with my mind. We had dated for almost two years when I started getting physical with her—like hitting her and stuff. I became the abuser, and ultimately, I left her to go out with men. I was doing my thing, sleeping around all over the place. I was depressed,. Eating a lot, and gaining weight. I'd walk everywhere, but I wouldn't exercise. Occasionally, I'd go back to her and then cheat on her with someone else. I got involved with her best friend at the time, who then became my best friend. It was this big triangle.

My turning point came when I was introduced to Sisters of the Road Café. I met a girl who had a reputation like me. I'd met her before when I was on the streets, but I started going to the café just to see her. I started to get to know the staff. I realized that I couldn't keep doing the things I was doing anymore. I connected with PAHC (Portland Alternative Health Care) in 2006 and cleaned up. The girl and I got married last year. We changed each other. She has almost 12 years. Even though she doesn't go to meetings, she's a good influence on me. She pushes me to go to AA meetings because she knows it suits my background.

When I started working at Sisters in October, I decided that I was too tired and too old to abuse myself anymore. I just turned 31 in May. Before Sisters, I was living in this fantasyland. The first time I set foot inside Sisters, I felt a sense of peace. When I walked in, everyone welcomed me. They told me their names, and I introduced myself. Immediately, I felt at home. I could be open about my sexuality. I can't cuss in there, but I can talk about whatever I need to talk about with anyone in there. It's hard not to cuss. But Sisters' philosophy is one of nonviolence, and that includes words. Nobody cusses in there. You pretty much leave all the drama at the door. We've had more than one customer say to us, "You know what? Everything that was wrong for the day I just left at the door. It's gone." That makes the staff and me feel good. We get goosebumps over it. Sisters is a loving, warm place. We practice our philosophy of nonviolence every day.

When I started working there, I was cleaning the bathrooms and, once in a while, bussing tables and sweeping the café. I lived in an SRO on Second and Couch and was in drug rehab through PACT. I moved from the shelter to the Estate Building. After eight and a half months, I went to the SRO. I've been there for over two years now. I got a job at Sisters that paid $8 an hour, and I'm lucky if I get 20 hours a week. There aren't any benefits, but there's a chance to get full-time work down the road. I just got a raise on the first of July. I'm still a temp worker, doing mostly cashiering. I help with the floor managing if they need me. When I look around and see how clean the restaurant is and what I've accomplished during the day, I feel good about myself.

Lots of the customers know me now. If they're in a bad mood, I try to crack a joke. It makes me feel good because I came from the same place. I'm learning who I am and that I don't have to abuse or be abused anymore. I can sit here and tell my life story to a total stranger. At first, I wouldn't have been open to an interview, but today, I don't mind.

These days, when I want to drink or get loaded, it's because I get stressed at work. I call my wife on the phone, and she'll let me vent. I'll spill it out, just throw up on her. She'll be like, "Okay, so what do you want to do?" And, I say, "I really want to come home, but I have to work." So she's like,

"Do you want me to come see you tomorrow?" And I say, "That'd be nice." She lives at our apartment in Gresham, and right now, I'm staying at the SRO because I need to work on myself by going back into recovery and doing my thing. So I stay in town most of the time. My PO finally came out and met my wife. When she knocked at the door, I thought, *No, it can't be her.* But then I remembered that she did ask for the address, the zip code, and my partner's full name. She came all the way to Gresham for a home visit. And that's when I told her I'd gotten married back in August. She said, "Don't be afraid to tell me anything. I'm going to respect you no matter what decision you make." She's very happy for me and tells me that whatever day I decide to make our Gresham apartment my primary address to let her know. When the time comes, she said she'd arrange with the Shelter-Plus care people to move in all my stuff. She's really become a friend. I just have seven more months, and then I'm off probation. I'm going to order a virgin daiquiri to celebrate!

I have a great support system at Sisters, and my wife is an amazing person. She's 46 years old, so there's a gap in our ages. She has two boys who, one day, are going to start calling me Mom, too. I think that's fine. Right now, one lives in Medford, and the other one lives in Santa Fe. We have a brand-new grandbaby that's eight months old now. She's a joy to look at on the photo CD. We both feel a sense of belonging, of family, to watch her walking and stuff. I'm going to ask my PO if I can go to Tennessee to visit her for Christmas. It will be two months before I get off paper. I've been paying off my fines and doing my UAs. I finally got off the color system. That's when you have to call your PO every day, and if your color comes up, you have to go out to a facility at Eightieth and North Columbia Street for a UA. I've been doing my treatment and going to my Thursday-night class. I'm now a responsible person, but it's hard at times. Last week, when it was really hot, I thought, *This would be a good day to have a wine cooler.* But I picked up a cigarette instead and drank some coffee. I drink a lot of iced tea, too. It doesn't make me jittery like coffee.

I don't want my kids to grow up without a mom. My oldest is going to be 14 this year. There's only four years to go before he's 18 and can come find me. (I'm in the adoption registry.) I'm going to make a copy of this Wisdom Will and save it for my kids.

I'm not really religious, but I am very spiritual. I believe in a higher power and a god out there. There has to be because I've experienced miracle after miracle. When I thought the end was coming for me, Sisters came into my life. These days, I believe that everything happens for a reason. We are all here for a purpose—and mine is to help others. My dream has always been to find ways to help the homeless people.

I'm involved in the Five-Year Planning Committee at Sisters of the Road. We're going to create a proposal to end homelessness in Portland. Monica, the director, is in charge of the committee. I became her co-chair last night. I'm pretty proud about that. I went to the meeting last night, the first one they've had, and at the end, they asked if anyone wanted to be the co-chair. I looked around, and no one raised their hand. So I said, "I'll do it." This gives me a chance to open up more and learn more about the philosophy of Sisters. Then I can make a difference in people's lives. If I can change for the better, then anyone else can, too. I want to stand for hope and encouragement.

I believe that the people who live on the streets are there for a reason. They're experiencing what they need to. Most of them have a chance to go out and work or whatever. That's when they discover Sisters. They get experience volunteering, which they can list on their resume. That's how I started—as a volunteer. Look at me now. I'm 31 years old, with an awesome job, awesome support system, and I'm getting involved. This confirms my number one belief that I'm here for a reason.

I'm grateful for my higher power, of course. My higher power comes first, but I'm grateful for the whole recovery system—the education, the programs, the facilities—because if it wasn't in place, I wouldn't be here. I'm grateful for my PO, because without her, I'd be running amok somewhere. I'm grateful for Sisters of the Road, my life, my partner, my friends, even the customers at Sisters who I hardly know. I'm grateful that I have a chance to give back that which was freely given to me.

I don't like to future step, but in five years, I'd like to be living in a home I can call my own, with my partner and our kids. I see myself reaching my goal, which is to raise and train dogs and horses and match them with the personalities of humans—like animal therapy. When I grew up, I had a lot of companion pets—dogs, cats, chickens, and goats—and I know how important they are. You can sit there and talk to a dog, and as long as you're talking in a friendly voice, it will just sit there and listen to you. You can hug it afterward or take it for a walk. Being around animals has always provided depression therapy for me. Right now, my wife and I have fish and plants. If we can keep those going for a while, then we'll move on to getting a German shepherd and, eventually, a horse. That's what I see for myself. I don't see myself working at Sisters in five years. I'll be starting a whole new career. I see myself growing up and loving life. That's really important. Sometimes people forget that life is what you make it. I choose to make it a happy place for myself and others.

I'd like my kids to know that I struggled with life and I'm a fighter. I managed to go through what I went through to get to where I am today. I also want them to know that I didn't give up on them because I didn't give up on myself. I want them to know that they are loved, no matter what. If they turn out gay or hating me, I'm still going to love them because they're mine. They may be with other families, but they're still mine, a part of me. On every one of their birthdays and every holiday, I say a prayer for them. I feel blessed because I married into a make-shift family, and it serves as an extended family to me.

I need to make amends to a lot of people, and a lot of people need to make amends to me, but I don't hold grudges. I'm not someone who says, "I'm going to hate you until you say you're sorry." If somebody has a problem with me, I expect them to come and tell me, instead of learning this indirectly from some-one else. I'd do the same for them.

My life motto is *I'm going to learn to love you until you learn to love yourself.* I truly believe in that, and I like spreading it around. I came into Sisters not liking anybody, but they accepted me for who I was, no matter what I'd done. The main thing I want people to remember me for is that I spent my life giving back that which was given to me, not just during my recovery, but at Sisters. *I'm going to love you until you learn to love yourself.*

I also want to be remembered by people the same way I want my kids to remember me. I want them to know that I'm a fighter, somebody who never gave up on life. I took a turn for the worse before I got better. I took my dive, hit rock bottom, and then brought myself to the top of the mountain. I want them to remember that I was a person who loved everyone, because that's what I expect from myself.

Love, Lois Rebekah W.

Many of us from dysfunctional family systems adopt other people who we call our family. We don't get the chance to choose biological parents, but we can choose others who satisfy our familial needs. I tell people that sometimes it's necessary to love our biological parents/family from a distance and find surrogate parents and siblings. The chosen family for most folks on the streets is the one that nurtures and encourages them. People in Old Town consider the staff and customers of Sisters of the Road Café their family, and after spending some time in the area, it is clear that there is a thriving community, or neighborhood, of disenfranchised folks. They love and support one another. My friend, Mary Sue, who is the former spiritual director of the Macdonald Residence in Old Town, once told me about a disabled person who was offered a room at an assisted-living facility. He turned it down because he didn't want to be separated from his friends. Every day, when he was ready to go upstairs to his rundown hotel room, he'd find one of his disabled friends sitting at the top of the stairs to make sure he was able to scoot his way up. True friends watch over one another, no matter what the circumstances. These are the people we call family. Bekah found such a family, which, I believe, doubles her chances for a sustained sobriety.

When I presented Bekah with 12 copies of her finished Wisdom Will, she was so grateful. She later told me that she knew her story backwards and forwards, but there was something about having it documented on paper and rereading it that made her appreciate how much she'd grown. She was thrilled to be able to give her Wisdom Will to her friends and loved ones, including, some-day, her children. Today she engenders self-esteem and is a remark-able example of recovery, courage, peace, and ever-present hope.

CHAPTER 4

My Creator Takes All My Pain Away

Under heaven all can see beauty as beauty only because there is ugliness. All can know good as good only because there is evil.

—LAO TSU, *Tao Te Ching (Number Two)*

I met Shorty just before the grand opening of Sisters of the Road Café's Personalist Center. The center physically connects the café to an indoor waiting area. Prior to this addition, lines of hungry people waited outside and down the block, foul weather or not. The Sisters' newsletter, *Sisters' Voice*, September 2007, mentions that the area allows space for people to receive their mail, hygiene products, and hospitality phone service. It is also a place for them to receive vital information and enjoy Sisters' ever-expanding barter program. The center also addresses Sisters' systemic change work by creating easy access for customers to get involved in the issues that affect their daily lives.

I could barely see Shorty over the tallest counter, a testament to her nickname. She sported a blue Mohawk haircut and, by the look on her face, seemed full of spunk and fun. But, like the other poor and homeless who live in Old Town, Shorty hasn't had it easy, as we witness in her Wisdom Will.

WISDOM WILL OF SHORTY D.

Dear Friends and Family,

As many of you know, I was born in Sacramento, California, on August 25, 1976. From the time I was five years old, my mother physically and emotionally abused me when no one was around to see it. Most kids get timeouts for punishment. I got hit with belts, shoved to the ground, and then kicked in the head and sides. Going to school was difficult because I had to hide the bruises and come up with excuses to explain injuries. My mother told me that I was a mistake and that she wished I'd never been born. The abuse didn't stop until I was 25.

I always felt that my brother was more loved. Mom bought his clothes at Nordstrom or other nice stores, while she took me to Goodwill and Valu-Village for used, crappy clothes. I never met my real dad, but I remember my stepdads. Unlike my mother, none of them ever laid a hand on me.

I was born with hydrocephalus (water on the brain), and the doctors put in a shunt for drainage. One day in 2006, when I was with Bekah, (Chapter 3), she noticed me rubbing my chest and looking sick. Something was sticking out, and I thought maybe it was a pulled muscle. I hurt for two or three days straight. Finally, I went to the emergency room, where my shunt was replaced. It goes from the top of my skull down into my stomach. My hospital stay lasted two weeks. At first, the doctor thought he just needed to adjust the top part of the shunt. But because I was so sick and unable to keep anything down, he went back in and replaced the whole thing. I think the original damage occurred during all the abuse I experienced as a kid. My shunt's working better now, although I occasionally get migraines from it.

As a child, I moved to Billings, Montana, for about three years and then to Portland, Oregon. Our house was in the outskirts of Portland, in Clackamas. I attended Clackamas High School, graduating in 1995. My freshman year, I felt safe because my brother was a senior. He was six foot two and weighed over 200 pounds. He told me to tell anyone that messed with me that they would have to answer to him. However, my brother rarely took my side at home; he'd just watch as my mother beat me.

During high school, I worked at Fred Meyers, McDonald's, and Jack-in-the-Box. One night, at Fred Meyers, my manager took me into the office. I was afraid I was going to get fired. He sat me down and said, "What's going on? I've noticed you come to work every day with bruises. They go away and then come back." I broke down and told him I was being abused at home. Once in grade school, when I broke down, the cops came and talked to me there. I told them my mother was abusing me. They wanted to know if I'd turn her in. I said no because I was afraid of what would happen to me and where I'd go. I thought that if my mother went to jail, then my brother would hurt me.

My only way out of the pain and frustration was by drinking. I'd stay out late so she'd be asleep when I came in. A couple of times, I ran away from home. I lived in Salem for six months at a shelter for women. One time, when I was driving around in Salem, my mom found me and told me, "You'd better get your ass home, or I'll beat you!" I said, "I can't go home. I can't do this anymore." But I came home, anyway. So my aunt stayed with my mother for a couple of weeks, and things were okay. Once my aunt left, the beatings started again.

The only time I ever felt close to my mom was during the September 11 attacks on New York's World Trade Center buildings and the Pentagon. I was getting ready for work, and my mom said, "You're not going to work today." So I stayed home. We both shared the sorrow of all the families that had lost loved ones in the attack. Things were okay at home for a while.

In January 2002, I came home from work thinking, *Okay, Mom's in a good mood. Maybe she won't abuse me today.* But she did a 360-degree turn by beating me and then kicking me out of the house. With a bloody nose and black eyes, I went to a neighbor's house crying. I told them that I had to get away to be safe. They asked me what happened, but I didn't tell them my mother had attacked me. I just said I needed to leave. The man took me to his friend's house in Tigard. I stayed there for a year and a half. Then they kicked me out because I wasn't helping to pay the rent. I also drank and partied with friends. The mom there didn't like me, so this gave her a reason to kick me out. These days, the sound of people arguing triggers me. I completely shut down and experience flashbacks because I suffer from PTSD (post-traumatic stress disorder).

In 2003, I moved to downtown Portland because I didn't want to go home, especially since I knew Mom was looking for me. At that time, I was living on the street. A couple of my street friends would tell me that my picture was posted around town, showing me as a missing person. I met some cool people downtown—at least I thought they were cool at the time. We'd party every night. We did what we had to do to get drugs and alcohol. Finally, I got tired of hanging out with those friends, sleeping on the street, and not feeling safe. I went to Harbor Lights, part of the Salvation Army. I felt safe there because nobody could come in asking for me. That's how I found Sisters of the Road Café. I was hungry and without money or food stamps. One of the women in the shelter said, "Come with me.

I'll take you someplace where you can work for your food. And it's hot food."

When I first walked through the door at Sisters, I felt safe because the staff and customers were so caring. They have a policy of not identifying people in the café if someone comes around asking for them. I lived on the streets until October 15, 2006; I was into drinking heavily and using drugs. I got clean for about nine months, but I went back out until I realized it wasn't fun anymore. I'd gone partying and got kicked out of the housing project I was in. When I went back out on the streets for the second time, I knew I was done. I found SRO housing at the Estate Building through Central City Concern. Then I moved to another SRO, the Sally McCracken. I've been there for almost five years now. While I was at the Estate Building, I entered an outpatient drug and alcohol treatment program through PACT. I participated in groups and classes. I went to Sisters regularly for hot meals and started volunteering when they needed it. I'm coming up on two years clean and sober. I would have had four years, but I went out and drank again. This time I know I'm done. I like living the clean and sober life.

In 2003, I met my best friend, Bekah. Everyone at the café knows her. I feel safe and comfortable with her. We have our ups and downs, but what friendships don't? I'm really happy to have her in my life. Last October, I was inside Sisters volunteering and one of the employees said, "How would you like to work here?" I thought she was kidding. I said, "I'm already working here." She said, "How would you like to get paid to work here?" I asked her, "What made you ask me?" She said, "We notice how much you volunteer and what good atmosphere you bring with you." So I've been working there almost a year. In April of this year, I got a permanent position, so I'm a full-time employee. I work part time in the café and part time in the development office. I like working here because it's a safe place. I get along with and like all of the staff. This is the first time ever that I've gotten along with everyone I work with. I don't have to hide anything from them. They care about me, no matter what. The one staff person I feel closest to is Kate, the associate director.

When they did the new remodel, Kate asked me to help her smudge out the new space. That meant a lot to me. No one's ever asked me to help with something like that. My family is from the Rosebud Tribe, which is in South Dakota. I'm half Rosebud Sioux. There are times I miss my family. My brother's wife had a baby, who's almost a year old. I've only seen my niece twice. I miss my grandmother, but if I try to contact either my brother or her, they will tell my mom where I am. I'm afraid she'll come after me. I've seen my mom a couple of times in the area and I ran. One time, we even ended up on the same bus! She just stared at me, as if saying, *If you weren't on this bus, I'd attack you!* I have a restraining order against her. A couple of times, I came to work scared, and my coworkers noticed something was wrong. I'd share about it during our check-in time. This is another thing I like about Sisters—every morning, we have check-in where the employees and customers of the café get together and let each other know how they are doing. Sometimes, I've arrived crying. They'll ask what's going on. I like everyone, but there are a few of the staff I feel closest to. When I'd open up to one of them and tell them what happened, I'd get a hug and know I was heard. They treat the customers with as much respect and love as they do the staff.

What gives me strength is sitting in my room talking to my higher power, which I choose to call My Creator. I sit there and just talk rather than calling friends. Either sitting on my bed or kneeling, I pray and cry. I know that My Creator can take all my pain away. Nowadays, I go to AA meetings. There, I feel safe and comfortable, too. Sometimes, I go with staff members to the Backspace Internet Café or out for Mexican food with Kate. She says, "You can open up to me now. There's no one around to hurt you."

I'm trying to get my life back together. I want to go back to college. I have an awesome partner. I've been waiting for her all my life. We've liked one another for two years and have been together as a couple for three months. Her name's Alysha. She's incarcerated right now for a parole violation. She'll be out in November. Alysha and I don't argue; we get along great. No fighting or arguing. She's coming up on a year of recovery, and it's sad that she'll still be incarcerated for her birthday. I visit her twice a week and write her letters. She's at Inverness Prison. It's a bus ride and a walk for me, but it's worth it.

Alysha is my guiding light. Our goal is to get married on Christmas Day and then get our own place. She wants to get a pug puppy, and I want a pit bull. For now, we'll probably just get her a dog. I want to go back to college. In the past, I went because my mother wanted me to. I'd meet up with my friends and smoke pot or whatever, just going to classes here and there. Now, I'm ready. I want to get a degree in social work. I want to give something back. My other goal is to get in touch with some family members, not my mom or my brother, but maybe my grandmother. She hasn't been doing well lately. I miss my family, but I consider my friends and staff at Sisters my real family. In December, Orion G., one of the employees, asked to do my story for their newsletter. It goes out to thousands of people. I was so honored. Everyone who received that newsletter knows about my past and how far I've come. At first, I was afraid to talk about my past.

Once, a lady came into a staff meeting from Cascade Aids Project. As soon as she walked in, I knew who she was. I used to work with her when I worked with my mom at the NW Indian Health Board. When I saw her, I ran into the back room. My boss followed me and asked what was wrong. I told her that if this woman saw me, she'd tell my mother. She'd done this in the past, so I didn't trust her. Fortunately, the lady didn't see me.

I get strength from my higher power, my recovery program, Alysha, Bekah, and Kate. I enjoy my job, working with people who are at a place where I used to be. I'm called "Shorty, the lady who gives hugs," or "Shorty, best known for her hugs." I'm happy about putting my Wisdom Will together. At first, I thought, *I don't have any family members to bequeath it to.* Then I realized that my friends and the staff at Sisters are my family; plus, I have Bekah and Alysha to give it to.

My meaning for life is to be happy. When I was a kid, clear up to age 25, I didn't think I should be here. A few times in my past, I wanted to die. I felt unloved and uncared for. Finally, I'm learning to love myself, so I no longer feel that way. If I have a problem, I know people who give me space and listen to me, like some of the people in my AA meeting. Right now, I'm not able to forgive my mom because she never loved me as a daughter. I don't feel love for her since she didn't give me any opportunity to love her. Right now, there are a couple of females in my life that I call *Mom.* They both represent the mother I never had.

I believe in God, but I don't go to church. My spiritual program is AA. This past month has been hard on me because Alysha got locked up three weeks ago. Life isn't the same without her. I'm used to her being by my side, except at work. I spend my paycheck on her. I met her through one of her ex-girlfriends. She scared me about a month ago. We were in my bedroom, and she had a grand mal seizure. I've been around other friends who've had seizures, and I've had petit mal ones. I had one last year. When Alysha didn't respond, I called Bekah's wife, Taz, and asked her what to do. She told me to, first, calm down before I set myself up for a seizure, too, then to call 911. At first, Alysha's mom didn't like me because she doesn't approve of two women being together. She wanted her daughter to be with a man and have a family. But after the night of the seizure, she and I've been close. I think, in the long run, she'll approve of our marriage.

I watch people judge the homeless when they walk past them. They act like everyone living on the street wants money or digs around in garbage cans for food. How do they know if the person isn't just looking for a pop can for its deposit? Most people don't want to live on the street; they are just running away from something. People also assume that someone down on their luck also abuses drugs and alcohol. Many on the streets are mentally ill and have no other place to go. There's only one place for homeless women to go to in Portland—the Salvation Army. But they can only stay for 30 days. I feel sad for judgmental people. That isn't me. I'll be your friend, whether you're homeless or not, colored or not, or whatever. People end up on the streets for many reasons.

Another goal for me is to open a year-round women's shelter. It's dangerous for a woman to find something to do all day long or to find someone to trust. Nighttime is really scary walking around downtown Portland, especially near Sisters. I see women getting beat up, raped, and abused.

I want to make the world a better place. I pray for an end to the war in Iraq. I'm sick of hearing about our soldiers dying. It saddens my heart. I want the world to be one happy place, with everyone getting along. I never want to see anything like the tragedy of September 11. I always take time to pray for the people who died on that day and their families. When it's my time to go, I want to be remembered as the Shorty who was loving and caring, as well as wild and crazy. I want them to remember the smiles, the jokes, and the hugs. By the time I die, I hope I'll also leave a legacy as a good social worker, giving back what was given to me. I want to be remembered for just the good stuff and none of the bad.

I want all my friends in Portland to know that if it weren't for them, I wouldn't be alive today. A big thank-you goes to all the Sisters of the Road's staff, past and present, for all their love. I especially want to thank Kate. On days when she is busy, she still makes time for me. I also want to thank Bekah. I couldn't ask for a better best friend. When I was in the hospital getting the shunt replacement, Bekah visited me every day, and that's what I call a good friend.

With Love, Shorty

When children are psychologically or physically abused, they feel broken and unworthy of love. Shorty felt she was a mistake from birth, and it filled her with shame. Shorty was rendered helpless and hopeless because of a tyrannical mother. I believe we either develop an emotional depth from childhood adversity, exhibiting potential for tremendous compassion, wisdom, and spiritual acuity, or we become cynical, angry, resentful, and abusive ourselves, standing firm in our victimhood. We get to choose which person we will be. In the book *Legacy of the Heart:*

The Spiritual Advantages of a Painful Childhood[1], Wayne Muller notes the following:

> A painful childhood invariably focuses our attention on the inner life. In response to childhood hurt, we learn to cultivate a heightened awareness, and sharpen our capacity to discern how things move and change in our environment. Childhood pain encourages us to watch things more closely, to listen more carefully, to attend to the subtle imbalances that arise within and around us. We develop an exquisite ability to feel the feelings of others, and we become exceptionally mindful of every conflict, every flicker of hope or despair, every piece of information that may hold some teaching for us. Thus, family pain broke us open and set our hearts on a pilgrimage in search of the love and belonging, safety and abundance, joy and peace that we were missing from our childhood story. Seen through this lens, family sorrow is not only a painful wound to be endured, analyzed, and treated. It may in fact become the seed that gives birth to our spiritual healing and awakening. (xii, xiv)

Muller's comments are true for me. At the age of 12, I became my mother's caretaker by default. Since my father worked out of town, coming home only on weekends, and my older sister and brother were married and out of the house, it fell to me to take care of my mentally ill mother and two younger brothers. As such, these tasks and responsibilities were an emotional assault, depriving me of a healthy childhood. I remember my hypervigilant behavior. I spied on my mother's every move and

---

4

mood. I was concerned that she might exhibit more psychotic behavior, hurting herself or one of us. I monitored her obsessive-compulsive tendencies and watched for any frenetic acting out of the manic phase of her bipolar disease. I was ever on the alert to the tension in the house, to her moods, and to the needs and emotions of my siblings. I'd been caught off guard by my mother's first psychotic episode, and I never wanted to be that shocked, that unprepared, again. For survival reasons, I became quite introspective, spending hours and hours in prayer, searching for safety, peace, and reassurance. I developed an intimate relationship with the Blessed Mother. Internally, I traded my biological mother for the mother of Jesus. I felt at ease, comforted, and warm when I talked to her. She gave me respite from my fear and anxiety and continues to do so today. At times, I've been accused of being oblivious to my physical environment, but as Muller alludes, I am ever aware of the energy coming from the people around me.

Shorty recognizes that heredity and childhood trauma launched her into addiction, just as I am certain that my childhood pain contributed to my alcoholism. Alcoholism, as well as any other form of addiction, merely masks our pain, a temporary fix that ends up viciously biting us. It imprisons us in its clutch, choking our emotional maturity and feeding our already sturdy victimhood. But when we finally admit that we are powerless over it and our lives, then, and only then, we are given an opportunity to choose whether we want to remain a victim or use our past to motivate our development as mature, critical-thinking adults with a purpose.

Besides the loss of her childhood, Shorty grieved the loss of the mother she would never have and the unconditional love, safety, and hope that should have been hers from the start. Shorty grieved the lost time that was spent fleeing from her mother's abuse, hiding out, using drugs and alcohol, and look-ing for shelter and other basic needs. Finally, she grieved her old way of being to make room for the new, entering into a recovery lifestyle, where, at last, she's finding love and peace.

Not one person interviewed for this book buried their head in the sand and blamed life for blocking the sun. Everyone stood tall and purpose-driven. They were grateful for divine intervention and anxious to give back, even if their recovery was in its infancy. They realized that, when all was said and done, they needed to forgive their pasts in order to create new hope-filled futures.

CHAPTER 5

"God Enters Through Our Wounds"

—Bryan E.

> Abandon yourself to God as you understand God. Admit your faults to Him and to your fellows. Clear away the wreckage of the past. Give freely of what you find and join us. We shall be with you in the Fellowship of the Spirit, and you will surely meet some of us as you trudge the Road of Happy Destiny.
>
> —Big Book of Alcoholics Anonymous

M ost of us know that the withdrawal from alcohol is hideous in itself, but the sickness from heroin withdrawal (and I understand it is similar with methamphetamines) is something else. In his autobiographical novel, *Shantaram,* Gregory David Roberts describes what it's like to go *cold turkey* off of heroin.

Think about every time in your life that you've been afraid, really afraid. Someone sneaks up behind you when you think you're alone, and shouts to frighten you. The gang of thugs closes in around you. You fall from a great height in a dream, or you stand on the very edge of a steep cliff. Someone holds you under water and you feel the breath gone, and you scramble, fight, and claw your way to the surface. You lose control of the car and see the wall rushing into your soundless shout. Then add them all up, all those chest-tightening terrors, and feel them all at once, all at the same time, hour after hour, and day after day. And think of every pain you've ever known — the burn with hot oil, the sharp sliver of glass, the broken bone, the gravel rash when you fell on the rough road in winter, the headache and the earache and the toothache. Then add them all up, all those groin-squeezing, stomach-tensing shrieks of pain, and feel them all at once, hour after hour day after day. Then think of every anguish you've ever known. Remember the death of a loved one. Remember a lover's rejection. Recall your feelings of failure and shame and unspeakably bitter remorse. And add them all up, all the heart-stabbing griefs and miseries, and feel them all at once, hour after hour, and day after day. That's cold turkey. Cold turkey off heroin is life with the skin torn away. (650)

When we look at dope sickness in the above light, it's no wonder that the success rate for lasting recovery from heroin and meth is so low. Finding sobriety after such addictions is nothing short of a miracle.

Bryan was the first person I've ever met whose drug of choice was heroin. When using, I surrounded myself with other alcoholics and pot smokers. Bryan's unbelievable hardships and desperation were beyond what I'd known as an alcoholic. Heroin devastates faster than alcohol, so his downward spiral far accelerated my own. He first shared his story with me during our days in RCIA at the Downtown Chapel. I look at him as a son because I have children near his age. After hearing his story, I wanted to hold him and tell him how proud I was of his commitment to heal, to do whatever it took to be whole again. I also found his faith in Christ profound. Like Father Ron, I am amazed by the recovering heroin addicts in the congregation at the Downtown Chapel. They continue to teach me the omnipresence of God's love. Bryan, as you'll see, is extremely intelligent, but in the past, his brilliance didn't always serve him. Here's Bryan's Wisdom Will depicting his great fall and his miraculous rise to a new drug-free life.

WISDOM WILL OF BRYAN E.

Dear Friends and Family,

My name is Bryan E., and I'm an addict. I was born in Portland, Oregon, in 1972 into a stable and loving family compared to other people. And, though I didn't appreciate it at the time, it was really a very safe and loving place for me. Ours was a tight-knit family of aunts, uncles, and cousins, with most of the relatives living nearby. Both sides of my family migrated to the Northwest from the South. Because of my mother and father's life example of self-sacrifice, I've always been puzzled why I have the disease of addiction. I've never seen my parents drink, use, or exhibit any other vices.

One of the first things I came to realize was that *real love is usually manifested in some kind of a sacrifice for other people.* The form it took in my family was the sacrifice of time, resources, and personal desires on the part of my parents so that we children enjoyed some of the advantages they lacked. My family is what you'd consider blue collar, or lower class. Because of how my father devoted his time to working, my family emphasized a strong work ethic. At the time, I considered that outlook repressive, sterile, and inhibiting, but my recent experience has informed me that a genuine work ethic is a matter of personal freedom, involving constant discipline. Over these last couple of years, I've come to recognize and fully appreciate something my father showed me from the very beginning. He didn't articulate it as such, but he demonstrated it on a daily basis. Frankly, he hated his job. Why would someone put so much effort into something they hated? Now I see why he made these sacrifices for us, his family. Above all else, I've come to respect this about him. Some of the qualities I value most now are honesty, willingness, and discipline. As I reflect on influential people in my life, my father is the first one who comes to mind.

My father's often been accused of being distant. Sometimes, he lacks the ability to articulate his feelings or talk about emotional topics. Although my mother and father share many of the same values, they express them differently. My mother is a very physical, expressive person. There was always a lot of physical expression of love in my house because of her. We always held and hugged each other. My physical intimacy with other people has always been healthy and strong because there was no history of abuse in our home. I can express my love for other people in physical, demonstrative ways, and that gift comes from my mother.

My mother doesn't have a sophisticated theological upbringing. What she does have is a way to demonstrate religious truth through action. That has made me realize people usually aren't listening to what I say; they are watching what I do. One of the values I've learned from her is that real honesty and real truth, and living for the truth, can best be expressed by perfectly lining up what you say with what you do. Her actions never indicate anything different from her beliefs. Only recently am I developing the kind of integrity she exemplifies.

After my formative years, I went to college. My strong streak of rebellion was due to my struggle for personal identity, my resentment of authority, and my self-centeredness. At the time, I wasn't using hard drugs, but some of the symptoms of the disease of addiction appeared at a very young age. I'm a deep believer in the concept of addiction as a disease. Drugs and alcohol have been out of the equation for me for a year and a half now. But the disease is still alive. Operating on complete self-will and self-centeredness caused me to turn away from my family and from any resources they offered me. When I look back, my rebellion didn't hurt anyone but myself! This rebellion was evidenced at all levels of my existence—against any spiritual understanding and against my parents or any authority figure.

I enrolled in college in 1990, the same year I graduated from high school. There, I sought out people, ideas, and ideology that fed my self-centeredness. I was seeking ways to reinforce what was already wrong with me. I didn't enjoy myself a lot; however, I did learn a lot. I realize that I'm jumping from my childhood all the way up to my early twenties, because the in-between years were a fallow period. Throughout college, I pursued whatever I wanted, none of it of any practical value. All of my behavior was geared to reinforce my own self-will.

At the time, I benefited from the values I received from my parents through my absorption of their work ethic and self-discipline. However, I wasn't able to acknowledge where I'd received these values. Back then, I lacked any sense of religious understanding. Most of my energy went toward literature as a creative outlet. I didn't do much creatively, but I was obsessed with literary art. I was influenced in ways that I still do not completely understand. During this time, I discovered many people who could influence me through the medium of art, and eventually, I graduated with a degree in literature. Celebrated writers had no effect on me. I find the works of many popular writers in the Western literature canon meaningless. Then there are those whose words changed my very life.

I discovered people like Shakespeare, Tolstoy, Franz Kafka, and above all, Dostoyevsky. When I read *Crime and Punishment*, I recognized myself. To reinforce its identity, part of a self-centered nature wants to see the self all around it. I discovered a character in one of Dostoyevsky's novels who I completely identified with. The character starts out living in his intellectual vanity, pride, and superiority to other people. He spends a lot of time in solitude reading and thinking. The novel develops this hypothesis: There is a moral standard and a moral law, but it only applies to about 90 percent of the population. There's another 10 percent that it doesn't apply to, and this 10 percent are the elite. The intellectual elite are beyond good and evil. They are beyond the constraints that apply to the masses. Of course, along with accepting this hypothesis is the belief that the reader is one of the people in the 10 percent. Operating on this theory, the character commits a murder for murder's sake—to prove that he was one of the 10 percent. He believes it takes an act outside oneself to solidify one's theory and to make it real. So the murder has no motive as far as gain, or revenge, or any of the other human motives we ascribe to the act of murder. The motive is only relative to proving that he can do it without getting caught or feeling guilt. Guilt is for those people living under the moral law from which he exempts himself. Anyone familiar with the book knows what happens. He successfully commits this murder, but he is not successful in freeing himself from the guilt. As the book continues, his mental state deteriorates, and he comes to a spiritual awakening. He realizes that he is, after all, subject to the moral law, like everyone else. His notions of superiority and intellectual pride are destructive, and even untrue. They don't have any place in a world where there is a real God.

As the novel continues, the character breaks down. I see this Christian motif of the spiritual awakening descending upon him only when he's in a period of complete destruction, one of complete brokenness. Only then can this awakening occur. It's like *God can only enter through a wound.* In the end, he turns himself in and accepts the punishment for the crime and accepts God's punishment. Only after this does he find a kind of contentment, or peace, or happiness.

I read *Crime and Punishment* once, and then I read it again. I had a very strong reaction to it. Even so, I didn't really apply the book or its character to me. I said to myself, *Why do I identify so strongly with this character?* I was afraid to admit that *I was this person.* I hadn't accepted the fact that the moral law applied to me. I didn't realize that my lack of humility was actually hurting me. I was resistant to what my family, or to what others, had to say because I felt they had nothing to offer. I was pursuing literature so I could find the answers from the greats like Shakespeare and Dante. I surely wasn't going to find them from my parents or peers. My opinion at the time was that those people weren't intellectual or creative enough to learn from. When I read about Raskolnikov, the character in Dostoyevsky's book, I didn't understand that I *was him.* On a subconscious level, however, I understood the spiritual or moral things that happened to me before my graduation from college. If someone were to ask me about the most important thing that happened to me during the last 10 years of my life, when I was going to school, I'd have to say that it was discovering Dostoyevsky. There were others, but his books, especially *Crime and Punishment*, made a profound impact on me.

I want to spend the balance of my time with this letter talking about what happened afterward, because that's where most of the change and recognition in my life has happened.

On the day I was supposed to graduate from college, the day my parents invited my family to come to town, I chose not to show up for the ceremony. This is *the Big Disappointment* in my family. I didn't want to be around my family members, and I especially never wanted to be the center of attention. Feeling the way I did, I had no choice but to leave. Everyone got tickets to the graduation. But I didn't show up. I thought it was funny. But they didn't. It's still a big scandal in the family. Instead of going through the ceremony, I was using IV heroin for the first time. I thought using heroin was romantic and glamorous. I was obsessed with the Beat Generation writers and their ethics, so I thought heroin was cool. My interests were in art and literature. I thought that a person with those leanings needed to get as much experience in the world as possible. So I shot heroin for the first time on the day I should have been graduating from college. I was certain that I wasn't an addict or a junkie. I was certain that I was a person who could do these things and not suffer any ill effects. Why I was certain about it, I don't know. But I was certain. I think that it has to do with addicts feeling exempt from absolutes, and from natural laws, and from the spiritual realities that everyone else lives under. Like the character in Dostoyevsky's book, the rules didn't apply to me. My behavior was basic denial, born of self-centeredness. However, I wasn't someone who had a slow digression into addiction. I was an everyday user from day one. The ironic thing was that I didn't wake up to the reality that I was the same as every other addict!

For the next four years, from 1999 to 2003, I was an everyday heroin user. I was sick. I was dope-sick. I stole to support my habit. I exploited other people. I lived on the streets. I estranged myself systematically from everyone I'd ever known. I was the person society doesn't want to have around! Until the very last day of my using, I never thought of myself as having a serious problem. I never thought of myself as falling under the same dangers as other addicts. Now, I'm a member of Narcotics Anonymous, where we emphasize that this disease always leads to three eventualities: jails, institutions, and death. I never, ever, thought I qualified. I just assumed, "Not me, that won't happen to me."

Once my disease became completely active because of daily drug use, it gained total mastery over my life. Today, I am a person with a healthy respect and fear of this disease. Back then, my disease generated denial; a veil descended upon my mind, clouding my judgment. I wasn't going to die. I wasn't going to go to jail, or catch any diseases, or suffer violence at other people's hands. And, for sure, I wasn't going to overdose. Then these things began to happen to me.

I had problems with the police. Next, I had nowhere to live except under a bridge. I started having physical problems because I was mutilating myself with the constant IV drug use. The wall of denial that I'd built could not keep out the rising tide of reality. A "normey" can do something harmful, suffer the consequences, and decide that they shouldn't do it again because they didn't like the results. A normal person can put their hand to a hot stove, see and feel that it's burning them, and not do it again. Yet, a person with the disease of addiction doesn't have that ability. The fear of death, the fear of going to jail, or the fear of hurting others never stopped me from using. My disease projected a pretty elaborate fantasy world for me to live in. I felt like I was doing fine. I had the courage of a margin walker. I had more strength, more stamina, than other people, or else I couldn't have sustained the lifestyle. Other people were afraid to do what I was doing. My denial kept me going for a long time. I mention all of this because when I talk later about some of the values I hold now, you'll understand how I needed to embrace these new values in order to heal. Looking for solutions in the light of spiritual truths has definitely been the answer for me.

During the years that I was using IV drugs, I suffered what everyone else out there suffers. I didn't agree with the concept that drug addiction was a disease. I thought I just had a drug problem. If I left the drugs out of the equation, I could go on and have a normal life, like I intended to have when I graduated college. But I took a detour. If I could just get away from the drugs, I'd be fine. Operating on this lie led me to try various solutions. I'd been to detox five or six times during those four years. I'd always go to detox. Even though it was uncomfortable, I would kick the drugs. I'd leave feeling physically okay, but I couldn't get the obsession out of my mind. I always went back to using within a few hours or a few days. I always had a plan when I was in detox—to go back and solve my own problems and think my way out of my difficulties. As a result, I stayed addicted, actively using with only the briefest of interruptions in this cycle.

This cycle culminated on August 7, 2003. I woke up that day, and I was completely paralyzed! I couldn't move at all. This was the result of using IV drugs and getting an infection from dirty needles. I was picked up by ambulance and spent seven days in the hospital. I had to have surgery for an abscess. This was the first serious brush with my own mortality. There were others. The most critical event in my life was after an overdose. A doctor came into my hospital room and told me, "Your arm is probably going to be cut off, and you may not live." This broke through the denial, the lies, and the assertions that had kept me going for the four years of drug abuse. Reality finally chiseled through my defenses. When I look back, that was the turning point in my life.

That event meant I needed to enter reality immediately. It convinced me to start living in the truth. I finally woke up to the fact that this disease was real. Drugs weren't my only problem. I knew there was something wrong inside me. My problem was self-obsession and choosing to live based on who I thought I was and wanted to be rather than who I really was. At that point, I surrendered. I admitted complete defeat. At 30 years old, I finally said, "I don't know what I'm doing. I don't have any answers, and I can't think myself out of this problem." It was the first time I ever asked for help. I felt differently at that point. I was honestly facing my own mortality.

In my twenties, I was convinced that I wasn't going to die. Death didn't apply to me. There's a line in the NA basic text that says, "Through our inability to accept personal responsibility, we are actually creating our own problems." I finally realized that every problem was completely self-created. I had to take responsibility for that. It took me four years to use up all my excuses, but I had reached the end.

One of the key relationships in my life started on the day the doctor told me I was going to lose my arm and probably die. The doctor was convinced I wasn't going to make it. I had a 105-degree temperature for three days in a row from the infection. He kept asking what my religious beliefs were. I thought he was just interested on a personal level. Later, I found he wanted a spiritual adviser to speak with me so I could receive some kind of last rites or spiritual counseling before I actually died. He was concerned about my soul. I had no answer for him. Because of his concern for my imminent death, he decided to grab anyone he could find in the hospital. A Franciscan nun happened to be nearby. She was brought to my room. I was not coherent through all of our conversation, so I don't remember a lot of it. But I have flashes of lucidity about what happened. Things I remember are her singing to me and her asking me if she could read to me from the Bible. I remember her praying for me and touching my face. It's impossible for me to articulate what her appearing meant to me. I ascribe the time of my complete surrender to Divine Providence. It's not possible for me to accept another explanation.

The hospital sent me to Hooper Detox again. I'd been a client there four or five times already, so they knew me really well. Hooper almost didn't take me because of the surgery on my arm. I made one phone call in the seven days I was there. It was to Sister Therese, the Franciscan nun from the hospital. I didn't call to seek anything; I called to express gratitude. That's a miracle in itself because I had not expressed gratitude most of my adult life. Self-centered people can't be grateful for anything but themselves. This was one of the first times that I'd expressed sincere gratitude to anyone. I'd been a very manipulative person during my addiction. I told people what they wanted to hear in order to get something from them. This was the first time I had no motivation other than gratitude. The feeling demanded to be expressed, so I called her and told her. Every time I went to detox they offered to send me to treatment or to an agency that would help me stay clean. Previously, I always refused because I didn't recognize the problem. This one time, I accepted their offer and did enter treatment at the end of August 2003. I was in a pretty flexible treatment program that allowed me time to spend the way I wanted. Some places are on lockdown and severely regimented. Since I was not in one of those, I was able to go visit the sister. I developed a capacity for honesty because I realized no one could help me until I knew what was wrong. Earlier, I didn't have the capacity to receive help, so I couldn't very well express what I needed.

I discovered that honesty wasn't just for other people; it was for me, too. The great breakthrough occurred when I realized I was like everybody else. This was a very difficult transition for me because of my self-absorption and pride. Accepting this truth, and choosing not to avoid the reality anymore, was really uncomfortable. However, I was able to acquire new resources and hope—hope for the first time in my life.

At last, I was opened-minded enough to talk to the sister. She never pushed Catholicism; what she did do was give me an honest example of her faith. She explained its doctrines. She taught me how to use new criteria for assessing my spiritual understanding. Prior to that, my criteria were what is popular, what is acceptable, what makes me feel good, what keeps me from feeling bad. Sister Therese suggested that my new criteria should be what is true and what is false. So much of my problems resulted from not living in reality, not living in the truth. We talked a lot about honesty involving a dedication to the truth. Either the truths that orthodox Christianity teaches are true or they are not. It makes no difference whether the concept of hell makes me feel uncomfortable or not. The only question is whether hell is real. Either there is an eternal punishment or there is not. I was reluctant to accept Catholicism because much of what it taught didn't make me feel very good. For example, sexuality is only healthy and acceptable in God's sight if it's done within the marriage covenant. That was so alien to my lifestyle that this precept alone was enough to make me reject religion. My discomfort wasn't a reason anymore to reject it. Whether it's true or not is the only criteria. I learned that from Sister Therese. I realized that if I was going to recover from my disease, if I was going to have any kind of meaningful, purposeful existence, or if I was going to experience any kind of deep internal change, I had to embrace the "true or false" criteria absolutely. When I surrendered, I surrendered my opinions, my own ideas, and my prejudices; I surrendered everything unrelated to the facts. I embraced her faith because I decided it was true. As a convert to Catholicism, I fully participate in the Church, and I consider myself devout. If anyone asks me why I'm a Catholic when I wasn't raised as one, my answer is, "Because the Church is true." That's the only answer I can give. I learned that from Sister Therese. I learned a lot about comparative religions, philosophy, love for the truth, and many other things from her; however, the most valuable gift was that of *living in the reality* that I am powerless over my addiction. I have a disease that is larger than me. The reality is that God is real, and I'm completely dependent upon him. All the truths of my present life have been built upon those two foundations. Because of seeing Sister Therese on a regular basis, speaking with her, and being honest with her, my life is a lot different today.

I received Sacraments of Baptism, First Eucharist, and Confirmation as an adult. Sister Therese was my Godmother and served as a sponsor through this process. Now, she is my spiritual adviser and counselor. Sister Therese has a lifelong commitment to teach me about the faith. As a convert I have a lot to learn. My relationship with her has been valuable for me. She is the first example in my life of someone who's almost sacrificed themselves for the truth of God. Sister Therese has reinforced much of what I learned from my mother—that real love is about sacrifice. When we love something, we are willing to sacrifice a part of ourselves for it. If we're not, then it's not real love. I met someone who loved God more than they loved themselves. I didn't think that was ever possible until I met her.

Now, I know what a saint is. A saint is someone who loves God more than they love themselves. I wasn't told this; I was shown this. Here is someone living the truth and not just talking about it. Sister Therese has also reinforced some of the values I learned from my father. She came to embody my parents' virtues and values, allowing me to recognize their origins. I learned about obedience, discipline, and I hesitate to use the word, orthodoxy. Even though these are not popular concepts in our culture, I consider them essential.

Sister Therese insisted on discipline, and she taught me that many of the freedoms we enjoy result from discipline. She taught me that much of my difficulty was due to my avoidance of pain. I would rather avoid a conversation if it caused pain. She also taught me about vigilance and obedience. For the first time, I studied the Bible. Sister Therese invited me to model my life after Christ's. I always wanted to be an original thinker. I wanted to be creative. When I started examining myself, I found out that I was neither. That was hard to accept. Now I accept the fact that I look to other people to teach me. Now, I'm humble enough to be teachable. A selfless person will tell you that God is the true origin of these ideas. That's what the sister told me consistently.

My first temptation was to hold her up and put her on a pedestal, saying, "You know you are a spiritual giant, or you are this and you are that." She discouraged me from the first day. She said, "Everything I've learned, I've learned from Christ. And you, too, can learn directly from him." That had a real impact on me. When I look at someone like her, the first thing I think of is, *If I possessed her spiritual accomplishments, I'd want to be congratulated. I would want to be considered an authority.* Sister did not want these accolades. I've always been drawn to people with assets I lack. I was drawn to her because she appeared an egoless person, with no desire for praise. That was mysterious to my way of thinking. I could talk all day about her and what she's given me. Without her, I wouldn't still be clean today. I know I wouldn't be a Catholic.

Sister Therese introduced me to my religion, the truth about God, and the truth of spiritual discipline. These are the most important values in my life because of my introduction to the program of Narcotics Anonymous. When I first went into treatment, I was blessed to fall in with a very serious crowd. I've always been drawn to serious people, fanatical people, and passionate people. NA was a requirement for my treatment program. We had to go to 90 meetings in 90 days. I didn't have any feelings about it either way. I simply did what was suggested because I'd reached the end. When you reach such a point, when you have no worthwhile opinions and you feel defeated, finally, finally, you are willing to try something different. I'd reached that point. I wasn't convinced that NA would work for me or that it applied to me necessarily, but I was willing to go. This was a good start. When I first went to meetings, I was introduced to NA's program, philosophy, and methods. I thought that I definitely qualified, but I wasn't sure at what level I wanted to participate. All these things paralleled my developing relationship to Sister Therese.

Rather than listen to other people talk about how to get the program of NA to work for me, I was told to simply let the literature speak for itself. I was already familiar with appealing to the authority of the Bible and religious tradition. The members of NA consider the basic text essential for anyone as far as recovering from the disease of addiction. As a literature major, someone obsessed with texts, I was drawn to this idea. There's something authoritative about the objectivity of a book instead of someone's subjective opinion. That's always made an impact on me. I said, "Okay, I'll let the program speak for itself." As I read the basic text, I found a line on page 96 that troubled me: *Our ongoing recovery is dependent upon our relationship with a loving God.* That alarmed me because I didn't have such a relationship. My success in recovery depended upon my relationship with a god I wasn't even certain existed. At that point, I realized the importance of a spiritual life. Sister Therese became critically important to me because I was using many of the truths she was exposing me to, not in an abstract way, but as a way to stay alive, as a practical necessity. I didn't have the luxury of working on my spiritual life in my spare time as a hobby or as an esoteric interest; my very life was at stake. My life was dependent, as the basic text said, on my relationship with God. I was forced to get serious. As it turns out, Sister Therese's criteria of "true or false" ended up saving my life. I couldn't afford a projection of God. I couldn't afford some kind of a wish-fulfillment God. I could only afford that which was real. I needed to discover God, not to create Him.

Terrible things happened to me in my addiction. I've overdosed four times. I almost died. I've been beaten unconscious. So, I got very serious about living. If the basic text of NA said that my life depended upon my relationship with God, then I took them at their word. That's why Sister Therese was so valuable in my life at this time. I got clean with many people who are not clean today. I got clean with a lot of people who are dead now. I got clean with a lot of people who are now in jail. I can't give any statistics or figures. All I have is my own experience. My own experience is that one out of a hundred addicts stay clean longer than a year and a half to two years, especially when they are addicted to heroin. I had to be that *one*. I had to be *that* person. The fear of not being the one survivor out of the hundred was very strong in me. A lot of the people no longer alive and the ones in jail failed because they couldn't find a god to be in a relationship with. That inability depends on the person. We work the 12 steps in Narcotics Anonymous where the second step says, "We came to believe that a power greater than ourselves could restore us to sanity." Those who failed were never able to embrace that step. They couldn't come to believe in something greater than themselves. I have many opinions why that happened for them, but I don't consider them valuable. I only have my experience. My experience tells me that a self-centered person cannot accept a higher power because then they'd have to accept something more important than themselves. This is where the criteria of true or false come in. Many people created comfortable gods for themselves. I realized that wouldn't work for me. Sister Therese taught me how to discover the reality of God, with true and false as my measure. The result is that I have a *real* God. If you have a real God, then, and only then, can you have a *real* relationship with Him. I use the words *real* and *reality* frequently because they are important concepts for me today. Even after 16 months with no drugs in the equation, I still feel my disease fighting for its existence every day. The drugs are gone, but my disease has gone underground, and it continues to look for new outlets. So I have to stay rooted in the concepts of reality.

Much of my struggle today involves communicating my experience to others, about discovering rather than creating God. I run the risk of sounding judgmental, of being seen as dogmatic, and as acting superior or narrow-minded. These are acceptable risks for me because of my deep and abiding belief in what Sister Therese taught me. The resulting relationship with God that I learned from that encounter has been the only thing that's kept me alive for 16 months. It's the only thing that's kept me from returning to active addiction. This truth is so strong in me that I can't communicate it by relying on the language of NA. I have to carry the message. I have a burning passion to tell other people what happened to me and that what I've found works.

There are a lot of ways to die of this disease besides an overdose; there are automobile accidents, disease, and violence. One can die in a mental institution or in a jail cell. The death certificate may not always mention addiction as the reason for demise, but we know the real cause of death. The way out for me has been selflessness. It goes back to what my parents taught me about self-sacrifice. I have a limited amount of time now.

Part of being in recovery for me is that I've gotten my life back. I have a good job and some security. I have many things competing for my attention. I have to carry this message to others. I have to sacrifice my desires and my spare time to do this because that's how I stay clean.

There is another dimension to my life in NA, and that's the influence of my sponsor. One of the things we are encouraged to do when we come into the program is find a sponsor while working the 12 steps. I didn't choose my sponsor; he found me. After a meeting with me, he told me that he felt God wanted me in his life. Any other time I would have laughed at this notion, but I happened to hear his words at a time when I was very receptive. As a result, I said, "Okay." My choice has to do with the surrender that I practice. I try to rid myself of opinions and judgments. If I look at people and assess them, then I leap to judgment. I may end up distancing myself from them because they won't measure up to my expectations. When you have surrendered, you are willing to accept help from anyone. Then you've finally become teachable enough to learn from anybody.

Every single day I meet somebody who knows something that I don't. I finally realized this through practicing humility, the humility that led me to accept the reality of God, the humility that helped me become teachable, the humility that helped me admit that I am capable of nothing without God. That same humility allowed me to be sponsored.

I've been working with my sponsor for two years now. He's not a Christian. He doesn't even have a concept of God similar to mine because NA allows freedom in choosing the god of your own understanding. That freedom has kept many people alive and clean. If NA offered a dogmatic concept of God, many people would choose to be exempt and, quite possibly, couldn't stay alive.

The program has been organized in such a way that we have that kind of freedom. So my sponsor has a different God concept than me. Even though he's not a Christian, I respect his right to differ from me. Still, the parallels between him and Sister Therese are really eerie sometimes. One of the commonalities is that he didn't tell me how to do the program; he showed me how. A chapter in NA's basic text is called "Living the Program," and he is somebody who lives the program. I knew that was the only thing that was going to work for me. I had all this resentment toward authority figures when I was growing up. So if I had someone just telling me what I needed to do, I doubt if I would have done it. My sponsor's real merit is that he showed me what to do. He lives this program. When working the 12 steps, we are also learning the spiritual principles behind each of them. My sponsor applies these spiritual principles to his life: honesty in all of his affairs, willingness to do whatever it takes, and simplification of our resistances. When I first read the basic NA text and saw what it suggested we do, I doubted it was possible, just as I had my doubts that living the gospel was possible until I met someone who did. For four years, I had only one constant theme in mind—getting and using as well as finding ways and means of getting more. That's what I thought of every waking moment. I didn't believe I could obtain freedom from that obsession. Then I met my sponsor who was doing it. He told me his story, where he came from and his present life. I wanted to know how he did it. When he told me about the program of Narcotics Anonymous, I had hope for the first time that I could recover. My hope also arose from one of the most unlikely places. Referring back to *Crime and Punishment* and my belief systems not in accord with reality, I felt exempt, or superior. Any word you want to use that emphasizes a difference between other people and me, that word described me. I'm better. I'm worse. I'm smarter. I'm more ignorant. I'm more depraved. I'm more dishonest. Anything that created a difference between other people and me, I employed. This was the source of my problems. When my sponsor told me his story, I recognized how similar it was to mine. That is where my hope came from. If someone is just like you, then what they did, you can do. If you do what they did, you can go where they go. You can achieve similar results.

I know many people insist on their individuality. I used to be interested in creativity and uniqueness and how everyone's got their own voice to express. I appreciate that for what it's worth, but I'm one of those people who really insists that, fundamentally, we are all alike. At first, that was difficult for me to accept. In essence, everyone with this disease is just like me. Now I can go to a meeting and listen to people who appear unlike me, from a different place, dependent on a different drug, and talking a different way. If others have this disease, I can learn from them, and they can learn from me. Only when I accepted this did the program begin to work for me. That's where my hope comes from. If this program can work for me, it can work for you. That's the message I carry. I insist on one thing: I am not special. That's why this program will work for you. These things I learned from my sponsor might sound depressing to some people who are still insisting on their individuality, still insisting on their uniqueness. If there is one person who can live the gospel, then it means I can live out the gospel, too. If there is one person who can stay clean from addiction through NA, then so can I.

I believe in diversity, but I'm referring to strength on a deeper spiritual level where we are all in the same boat. I am really on my guard against any kind of a theory or ideology that encourages separating me from other people. My sponsor and

Sister Therese have reinforced what I've learned from my mother and my father. They are the four most influential people in my life. By working the 12 steps, participating in my faith, and receiving the Sacraments, I've made my discoveries and had spiritual awakenings.

I have this deep need to express gratitude to my parents, Sister Therese, and my sponsor, because I wouldn't be alive if it wasn't for them. These people haven't taught me abstract, sentimental virtues; they've taught me how to live, how to stay alive. I've been called militant concerning the Church and about the NA program. I'm willing to accept that label because of the gravity of my situation. These four people came into my life just at the right time. Without them, I probably wouldn't have survived. This has taught me a great deal about the love God has for me. It's impossible for me to doubt this is a manifestation of God's mercy or God's love for me. Without these people in my life, I wouldn't be alive or free or enjoying life on life's terms. As a result of these realizations, I've been able to speak to my mother and father. I have resumed a relationship with my father again, one that I haven't enjoyed since childhood. I've been able to express myself about how I feel toward him. I know that he recognizes my sincerity and is touched by it. When I express my feelings to my mother, she cries, so it's hard. All the seeds, every single one, were given to me by my parents in my childhood. It took Sister Therese and Lawrence, my sponsor, to allow those seeds to come to fruition. It took these two people to express the same realities in a different way for me to come full circle and acknowledge where these truths came from.

I'm at a point in my life today where I can experience gratitude and humility. I see my complete dependence on God, and I can thank God for the people He's brought into my life. One of the most motivating things in my life is the need to express these truths to others. I wouldn't bother if I thought people were different than me. I only do this because I feel my brothers and sisters, especially in the recovery community, are just like me. I search for new ways to express the truths that I've discovered. Not everyone has been as blessed by God as me. Because God has chosen to reveal himself to me, he gave me my parents. He brought Sister Therese to that hospital. He brought me close to death's door, without actually killing me, which woke me up. He brought Lawrence into my life, and he brought me into the Church. I have a need to be God's instrument in the same way these four people have been instruments of God's will in my life. I want God to use me now as a channel to communicate the truths He's revealed to me. Sister Therese, my sponsor, and my parents have all been messengers. I want to resemble them. I want to carry the message of the 12 steps, the message of God's reality—the Gospel message. You can destroy the messenger, but never the message. I want to be a servant now. That's it. My self-obsession and my waking up to its damaging effects have caused me to want to detach from my ego and my pride. I don't want to concern myself with how I appear. Rather, I want to be concerned with the clarity and integrity of the message. That's what drives me now.

Appearances are deceiving. I think it was the Sufi Poet Rumi who said, "Take no notice of my appearance, and just simply take what is in my hand." That phrase means a lot to me today because I'm carrying something valuable now—the experiences I've had and the discoveries I've made. My only job now is to serve and communicate this message to other people. All four of the instrumental people in my life sacrificed themselves for me, out of love for me. Even though it was inconvenient and difficult for them, they all believed in me enough to deliver the message. Now, I need to do the same thing.

I'm glad to be alive. I'm glad that God's revealed himself to me in a very real way. As strange as it sounds, I'm glad that I was a heroin addict for four years. I'm grateful for that because experiencing such pain and brokenness is what finally allowed me to receive some spiritual truth. I lived my life so long with a closed fist and self-obsessed that nothing could get in. Only by being so broken down by my addiction was I finally forced to open my hand and receive something new. It was then I could open my mind and begin to let go of my pride, superiority, and self-obsession. My addiction did that for me. Sometimes, I shudder to think what would have happened if I'd graduated from college, went out, got a job, and lived my life out without going through this spiritual crucible. I don't think I'd have had any spiritual awakening. I would have gone on operating my life on self-will alone, probably without any understanding of my dependence on God. My addiction gave me that gift. If that's the price I had to pay, if all that suffering was necessary to bring me to a point in my life where I could hear God's message, then I'm glad it happened. I would have suffered twice that amount if that was the price it took. I had to be weak and broken down enough to accept help. I had to become humble enough to look at God and God's reality.

I'd like to be remembered as somebody who realized his complete dependence on God's love. As a result of this love, I am a man who has surrendered to the program of Narcotics Anonymous and to the authority of Christ's church. It would make me happiest if those who knew me remembered me as a servant to his brothers and sisters, a devout member of the Catholic Church, and a man who sought and believed in his reunion with God.

Love, Bryan

I interviewed Bryan in 2005, but didn't meet Sister Therese until August 2007. I met her at Our Lady of Peace Retreat House in Beaverton, Oregon, where she lives and works. Sister Therese acknowledged going to Bryan's hospital bedside, rosary in hand. As he fell in and out of consciousness, she held his hand and prayed. Occasionally, he'd awaken. Sister Therese suggested he pray to the Blessed Mother Mary. She told him Jesus's mother understood his pain. During one of his lucid moments, Bryan grabbed her hand and copiously wept. His physical and psychological pain appeared unbearable. Bryan feared the loss of his arm and the very real possibility of dying. By this time, Sister Therese had visited his hospital room many times. So she changed tactics, sternly addressing him:

> Bryan, I don't have any sympathy for you! Stop crying! Stop feeling sorry for yourself! If you don't stop, I'm going to walk right out of here! You're the one that got yourself into this situation.If you want to recover, pray. Ask God for forgiveness. Ask for God's help. You have to make up your mind that, from here on, you're going to stay clean. It's your call. If you want to recover, you have to do this.

This launched the beginning of Bryan's recovery from the wicked grasp of heroin.

These days, Sister Therese continues her prayers for Bryan, but she's turned his recovery over to the Almighty, knowing she's done what she could do. Sister Therese doesn't worry if weeks go by without hearing from him. As Bryan's Godmother, she's made it clear that her commitment to him is for life:

> It's my job to bring you to heaven, or at least show you the way. We're connected at the soul. Even if you should relapse and feel so remorseful that you can't look at me, I'll still love and forgive you. My purpose is not to judge you, but to encourage you to keep trying. You see, Bryan, I understand that every day you don't use is a day of Grace.

Sister Therese is a grateful witness to Bryan's growing humility. "We all need a good measure of humility. Sometimes, God floors us, just to keep us humble," she says.

I know firsthand what Sister Therese means. There's no greater fodder for personal growth than humility. It is when we finally bottom out and give up that we become receptive to divine intervention. Some of us are asked to *enter through the narrow* gate[5], letting go of the baggage we carry, stripping ourselves clean of false self-images; otherwise, we'd never clear the passage or awaken to the New Jerusalem stretching forth just beyond.

---

5 "Enter through the narrow gate. For wide is the gate and broad is the road that leads to destruction, and many enter through it." —Matthew 7:13 (NIV)

CHAPTER 6

Oh My Darling, Clementine

Before I formed you in the womb I knew you, before you
were born I set you apart; I appointed you as a prophet to
the nations.

—JEREMIAH 1:5

J ason E. is part of the triad of heroin addicts I interviewed
from the Downtown Chapel. He prepared his Wisdom
Will primarily for his little girl, Clementine. As Jason spoke,
I reminisced about my own father. Years before he died of heart
failure, my father gave my mother, Pat, an envelope telling her
to "open this after I die." My mother tucked the letter away,
along with a few other treasured items at the bottom of her
underwear drawer. In December 1983, the time came to retrieve
it. My sister Gail and I sat anxiously at the kitchen table with
Mama wondering what our father had to say to us now that he

was gone. I watched as Mama opened the envelope and slipped out a single sheet of paper. After she read the note, she looked perplexed and handed it to us. We were stunned by what was written and especially by what was not! I knew that my father detested writing, and when absolutely necessary, he was terse to say the least. But none of us was prepared for his pronouncement:

Dear Pat and Children,

Children, take care of your mother. And never, never tell anyone the year I was born. I've lied about my age, and I don't want the government to find out.[6]

Love, Dad

That was it! That was the message our father wanted to convey to us from beyond the grave! What kind of legacy was that to leave of one's life? We had expected some words of wisdom, some enlightened direction. We were sad, sitting in stunned silence wondering why he wanted us to keep his age a secret after he died. What difference would it make to the government now? How comforting it would have been to read a synopsis of what life had meant to him, what we'd meant to him, where he'd found meaning, how he got through the tough times, or what he wanted us to remember him for. I would have been happy with a mere list. He wouldn't have needed to wax poetic. Don't get me wrong, I loved my father and have many wonderful memories of him, especially his storytelling. Papa was one of the best storytellers around. Unfortunately, none of us thought to record the Huckleberry Finn–like tales of his boyhood.

---

6 Dad had worked for the Bonneville Power Administration as a supervisor at the convertor station in The Dalles, Oregon.

Knowing how my father's note had let down my mother, myself, and my siblings, I vowed that I'd leave behind a written legacy for those I loved. So I rewrote my life story in a 250-page family memoir, using humor as my guide. You see, I'd inherited some of my father's storytelling abilities, and it worked well for me in writing *Beheading the Hydrangea*. The memoir title was inspired by one of Mama's psychotic episodes when she took a shovel to her beloved garden, destroying all the plants.

After I'd healed from my family of origin issues, I looked back on what once was tragic and discovered humor sprouted in its place. These days, my children laughingly tell me, "Mom, stop writing! We all have more than enough words to remember you by. We're running out of shelf space."

As for Jason's daughter, Clementine, I'd say she is one lucky, loved little girl. As you'll see, her father bequeaths to her his very essence in his Wisdom Will.

WISDOM WILL OF JASON E.

Dear Clementine, Loved Ones, and Friends,

I was born on October 2, 1971, in Jacksonville, Florida, at St. Vincent's Hospital. I created this Wisdom Will for my family, especially Clementine, and my friends to keep me alive in their hearts and memories. If my experiences can assist them in their recovery, my struggles will have been worth it.

The sense of *family* was not held in high esteem during my childhood. Both of my parents were divorced and remarried several times. No one was ever very close. I was moved around constantly. I had many stepfathers and attended many different schools. Growing up, I had no feelings of belonging, no real roots. Now, since I've been in recovery, I enjoy relationships that I consider family. My male friends seem more like brothers than friends. I consider some older men almost like uncles whom I can look up to and emulate.

I wrestled with addiction from my early teens through my early thirties. As a result, I've been homeless and suffered from depression and many drug-induced psychoses. In my darkest times, heroin and cocaine brought me to my knees.

My drug abuse led to homelessness. Without life-management skills, as a substance abuser, all my income went to buy drugs. I was trained as a cook and, for over 18 years, worked wherever they were hiring. I bounced around the country, usually following a woman. These "true loves" were doomed from the beginning because I was an addict/alcoholic. I'm grateful that I didn't marry or make a long-term commitment to anyone—for both our sakes.

For many years, I was able to manage, until I started using heroin and cocaine. Cocaine caused me to use every 20 minutes or so at $10 a hit. I didn't care whether I was homeless or not. Before using heroin or cocaine, my life was still about drugs, but once I found these particular substances, my addiction became a frantic craving unparalleled by anything else I'd ever taken.

I was living with a girl I'd followed from New York to Oregon, but she left me, and afterward, I spiraled downward. I couldn't pay my rent and I was evicted. I put my stuff, including a mattress, in the truck bed and that's where I stayed. Now and then, I could afford a cheap hotel room, or some nights, friends would let me stay in their house. By then, I was a serious addict so I didn't want them to see what I was doing. I preferred to be left alone, burdened with my shame.

Once I began living in my truck, I was in and out of shelters. Neither housing, clean clothing, nor good hygiene mattered. I'd say to myself, *I'll make do under the bridge. I'll make do in the bushes. I'll make do as long as I have my drugs.*

Finally, I sold my truck for a mere $50. While I was at the junkyard, someone else came in to sell a car, which I bought for $20! My truck's brand-new tires were easily worth more than the 50 bucks I got for it. I would've received more money if I'd sold it in pieces. But at least I had a hotel room for the night and my drugs. Nothing could be finer. During the day, I didn't look like a homeless person. If you saw me, you wouldn't believe that in the evening I found shelter under a bridge or in the bushes. In bad weather, I hung out at the library and the public restrooms, although even keeping dry was a low priority.

Finally, I ran completely out of money. In desperation, I tried to rob a couple of Subway shops. Any money I made anywhere went, first, to drugs and, second, to a safe place to do them. On my second robbery attempt, I got caught. The police took me to jail. They interrogated me, assuring me that if I told them what was going on, then they'd try to help me. I believed them and answered all their questions, which led to my entering a program in prison that saved me two years of jail time. I was arrested in Portland, spending four months in the county jail before I was sentenced. I plead guilty to attempted, second-degree, armed robbery—two counts. This plea lessened the charges against me, allowing me to enter the Boot Camp Program. First, I was shipped from Portland to Pendleton. There, I was confined to the Eastern Oregon Correctional Institution in the middle of the desert for 10 months. From there, I entered the Boot Camp Program at Sutter Creek Correctional Institution in North Bend, Oregon, on the coast.

Previously, in detox centers, I'd been introduced to 12-step programs, which hadn't meant a thing to me. Now, in this structured environment, they eased in the tenets of the program. I'm not sure how. First, it was exercise, then change-point classes and cognitive-restructuring, and all of sudden, 12-step meetings. In order to complete the program, there was a test where you had to recite all 12 steps by memory. I not only completed the program without difficulty, but I sailed through it. When I was released, I was on the right track for once. I intended to do *the recovery thing.* Five times a week, I attended meetings, and I found a sponsor. My transitional leave from prison required that I find work, which I did. However, by the time my leave was over, I was using again.

For another year, I used. My isolation and desperation increased. I was living in the Medford Building, an SRO behind the Greyhound bus station. The hotel was drug and alcohol free, but I used anyway. I didn't pay my bills or the rent until I got kicked out and was once again homeless. My sponsor said, "Look at yourself. You had everything going for you, then in three days—in a flash—everything you own is in a plastic bag. You have your coat on your arm, along with your pillow, while wandering around Old Town again! What part of *powerless* don't you understand? What don't you get?"

I tried to stay clean, but I went back and forth, back and forth, for months. I entered Hooper Detox for the second time. Then I returned to school at Portland State University, thinking this might be the solution. I received grants and loans and acquired dorm housing. My sponsor thought I was crazy. "What are you talking about? This is not a decision you should make right now!" I said, "No, no, no, no. It's going to be okay." I had clean time. Clean time. Clean time. The first term at school went well. By the second term, I was using again. My dosages increased substantially until, one day, I packed up all my dirty clothes, went over to Hooper Detox and sat down on the curb waiting for the doors to open, all the while using.

This time while in detox, I began to understand what *powerless over our addictions* meant. I'd heard that phrase over and over again, but what it says in the *Narcotics Anonymous Basic Text* is the following: *What makes us powerless is that we use against our will. We use drugs, even when we don't want to; even when we know it's killing us and causing us to be insane.* I realized that I couldn't stop! At last, it made sense. I *was* powerless. Now, I know that once I introduce something into my body that alters my mind—heroin, cocaine, caffeine, cigarettes, sugar, or whatever—then I'm powerless.

Prior to my using, I lacked self-esteem. At times, I wonder if this is what drove me to the point of using. For many years, I had no idea how to change my life without drugs or alcohol. I was a victim, and I blamed all my problems as an adult on my childhood. I couldn't wrap my head around the idea that the drugs were the source of the problem. Denial is huge when using. Today, I know that my difficulties with drugs were symptoms of much larger problems. People wouldn't like me if I wasn't high; I wouldn't like me if I wasn't high. I'm still working on liking myself, and it's a huge job.

After I had 24 months clean, I became aware of how I was living a day at a time. I'd slowed down. In a 12-step men's group, someone asked, "What is getting in the way of your trusting a higher power in your life?" I wrote down that I no longer try to force an answer or try to solve it right this minute. Now, I seek an answer that can come in a lot of different ways. Maybe I query three, four, or five guys in my support group to see what they think. Or I quiet myself down to pray and meditate on an answer. I experience a daily reprieve because the spiritual principles behind the 12 steps allow me to live in the present. Another insight from that meeting that came up was about what step two meant to me: *My solutions are better sought through an external force, rather than myself.*

My relationship with God, in the person of Jesus Christ, has helped me the most in learning to love myself. In the past, I railed against Christian religious teachings. No way there could be a god with so many problems in the world! But I discovered that, even while going in and out of the program, people still cared abut me; God was appearing in other people. They might be hard on me, or I might not like them, but someone was always there for me. This one guy, Lawrence, made a huge impact on my life. Every time I wanted to get clean, he'd open his door to me, with a few stipulations involved. He would welcome me because he wanted to see me succeed.

I continue to struggle, but I have a life that I like. Sometimes, I even love it. The key to my spiritual awakening is taking responsibility for my life. I became accountable. I no longer blame other people or justify and make excuses for my behavior. Sometimes, it's as simple as I can't do something—like manage my own life. I can't do it alone or without God. I truly believe that God shows up in other people. I've learned to rely on others in the program for their wisdom and experience. Lawrence is not much of a God person; yet, he encourages me when he says, "I believe that you believe."

Right now, I'm going through some difficulties. I have a beautiful, young daughter, Clementine. Her mother, Vanessa, and I didn't live together while she was pregnant. After Clementine was born, I moved in with them. Vanessa and I are both in recovery now, and lately, we've begun to see each other's unpleasant sides. The relationship is just not working, so I have to move out again. A couple of years ago, this would have devastated me. I'd have been in a whirlwind of trauma and drama. My self-esteem would have been blown away. Today, I know there's not anything wrong with me; I'm okay. Sometimes, a relationship just doesn't work, but I want to spend time helping Vanessa raise and enjoy Clementine. We want to agree among ourselves so as not to put our baby girl in the middle. Clementine is such a miracle in my life.

In my addiction, I took risks by being promiscuous. My inhibitions went out the window. I thought I was sterile because of all the substances I'd pumped into my body. One night, when I was in another program on the west side of the Burnside Bridge above the Union Gospel Mission, I woke up with a start. I called Vanessa and said, "I had this lucid dream that you are pregnant." She said, "You know, Jason, I've wanted to talk to you about that." She rushed right out and got a test kit, and sure enough, on May 5—Cinco de Mayo—we found out that she was carrying my baby.

Both of us were terrified. She was a little over a year clean, and I was just six months clean. I was walking away from a very dark, dark side of life. Vanessa had her own struggles with failed pregnancies. She feared she might lose this baby, yet she wasn't sure she wanted to bring a child into the world. I told her, "Look, I don't have any control over what you do. It's your body. I can't physically stop you from doing anything, but I assure you that I will do everything that I can to make this work for us. Some way or another, I'll help to raise our child." People had walked away from me in my family. I wanted to break the abandonment cycle with Clementine. I wanted to be there for her. We decided to have her, even though the pregnancy was hard.

I was committed to working on my program through Central City Concern, so I didn't move in with Vanessa. After I completed the Mentor Program, they suggested I enter the Employment Program, which is connected with the Work Source Center on Northwest Couch and Second Street. Its mission is to give individuals and families tools to launch themselves into self-sufficiency. Self-sufficiency was something I'd never acquired. So I was proud to finish the program. I was hired by a firm that caters events for corporate clients. I don't earn an extravagant amount of money, but it's more than I've ever made. Recently, I was invited to speak at an Employment Program dinner. When they introduced me, they said, "Jason completed the program. He is now living in an apartment, working and enjoying life with his new baby girl."

I first moved in with Vanessa on April Fools' Day. I used to tell her this was a bad omen. I lived with her and Clementine for about a year. Now, we're in the process of breaking up, and my move out date is April 1. I feel all right about it because my perspective has dramatically changed since I've been in recovery. While discussing step three about turning our lives and wills over to God in one of my step study groups, a sentence made me think. I realized that my life was much more than my problems and their related emotions. Life is a gift when I'm with Clementine. I think about that often. She's such a little miracle.

I believe in the Narcotics Anonymous principle of open-mindedness. Things are happening for a reason, even though they may be beyond my understanding. That truth was written into the 12-step philosophy long before I was ever a member. I'm reminded of the Bible verse about God knowing me before I was even born and that he'd numbered the hairs on my head.[7] I've been able to develop a way of being in the world based on the open-minded principle. I don't need to understand everything. I believe there is a God, and it's not me. I just need to let go of control. The only thing I can control is my response to situations. God is going to take care and love me during my breakup with Vanessa. Even in my darkest times, I have known God wasn't done with me. He wants me to get out there in the world and do whatever I'm supposed to do. Instead of telling me what it is, He just reveals it as it comes along.

At my worst, I isolated myself. I rejected help. I rejected change. I was alone. I didn't want to be that way, but I viewed the world as a hostile place. Now, as I'm breaking up with Vanessa, instead of a failure, I'm viewing this as an opportunity. What I'm going through happens to people all of the time. So there's no excuse for me to run back to drugs. Using drugs would compound the situation a hundred times over. I have a gift of *clean time*. I'm not willing to give that up like I have in the past. With my new insight into open-mindedness, I realize that I can learn from other more experienced people in recovery. I can call my support guys and tell them honestly what's going on and how I feel about it. Most of my life, I've covered my

---

7 Matthew 10:30 (NIV).

feelings up with drugs and alcohol. Now, I'm learning that it's totally okay to have feelings.

I want to pass my outlook on to Clementine. I want her to experience the rituals, trials, and pleasures of friendship. I want her to grow up at a normal childhood pace, which I didn't experience. My mother wasn't always around, and my dad left when I was pretty young. After my stepfather left, my mother expected me to be the *man of the house.* I was only 10 years old! That's a huge responsibility for any child. Soon enough, I figured out that she wanted me to take care of her and my sister, who was a couple of years younger. That's how I became a *smoother-overer.*

I'm still learning that my feelings are okay and that stirring things up might not be all bad. I want Clementine to feel what she feels and not suppress things, as I did. I want her to create long, enduring friendships beginning in childhood. Good relationships and supportive friends are so important in life.

Chances are Vanessa and I will never marry, or even associate, as Clementine gets older. But I'm committed to my relationship with my daughter. I won't walk away, no matter what. I don't want Clementine to think she's in any way responsible for the breakup.

I'd love for Clementine to remember me with nostalgia as she tells her friends, "I remember when my dad helped me with this," or "I remember the way my dad held my hand through a hard time, and how, no matter what else was going on, he loved and cared for me. He wanted me to be happy and out of harm's way." I can't say that's how I'll remember my folks, but I want great memories for my daughter.

When I was in prison, I shared with a priest how I'd been baptized a long time ago in the Baptist Church, but I didn't know if this counted. He looked at me and said, "Here's the thing. For you, it may not have counted, but to God, it always counts." That's the kind of love we're dealing with when we speak of God. The Bible mentions how God placed the rainbow in the sky, not to remind the Jews about God, but for God to be reminded of the Jews.[8] God is a loving god. In order to receive that love, we don't have to be perfect. I want Clementine to know that she's going to make many mistakes and fall short in life. But God loves us unconditionally. There is nothing she can do to make that love go away. It took me years to realize this. I was walking through my own dark, dark, dark times, when Pascal's Wager woke me up: "Let us weigh the gain and the loss in wagering that God is. If you gain, you gain all; if you lose, you lose nothing. Wager, then, without hesitation that He is."[9]

Since then, I've been involved at the Downtown Chapel. I go to Mass there, and that's where Clementine was baptized on Easter Vigil of 2007. Bryan E. brought me to the Downtown Chapel for the first time when I was participating in the Salvation Army's ARC (Adult Rehabilitation center) program.

When I was nine, we lived in an apartment where members of Trinity Baptist Church signed us up, even though my mother and her brothers and sisters all grew up Catholic and went to parochial schools. On Sunday, a bus came and collected us for the church service. That's how I came to be baptized in the Baptist Church. Bryan's been a friend for quite a while, both in and out of recovery. In fact, we both have the same NA sponsor. When I told him what they were preaching in the ARC program, he said, "Why don't you check out the Downtown Chapel's program?"

---

8 "Whenever the rainbow appears in the clouds, I will see it and remember the everlasting covenant between God and all living creatures of every kind on the earth." —Genesis 9:16 (NIV)

9 http://plato.stanford.edu/entries/pascal-wager/

I've always been comfortable in the Catholic Church, maybe because my grandmother is a Catholic, and I'd gone to Mass with her on occasion. Right away, I signed up for the RCIA (Rite of Christian Initiation for Adults) program, which offers instructions for people who want to join the church. I didn't do very well in the program because I missed a lot of Sunday morning classes and some important dates at the cathedral, but I was still entered into the Book of Life. I received Confirmation and First Holy Communion at the Saturday-night Easter Vigil of 2005. I've been attending Mass there ever since. I really love the Downtown Chapel. I have a good relationship with Father Ron Raab. He led the RCIA class I was in, and he taught me a great deal about what it means to be Catholic. He taught me about the importance of the Sacraments and the Paschal Mysteries, which is about Christ's dying and rising from the dead for us. Father Ron's gentle, accepting nature teaches me how to be accepting. Every time I go to confession, Father Ron says, "First of all, God loves you, Jason. Did you know that?" How can I feel bad at the end of the day when I hear that?

I want Clementine to know the same sense of community I feel at the Downtown Chapel. Even though I don't know many of the people there, I sit in the same pew every Sunday next to Bryan and Mary. I want to make it a pattern, a habit so she'll learn that this is part of what "we do" on Sundays. I hope she learns as much as I have about God's grace and the mercy of Christ. There are times in our lives when Clementine will need to forgive me and other people. That's one of the biggest lessons I've learned at the Chapel, and I want to instill it in her. We come as we are—with the good, the bad, and the ugly—and we present all of it to God. I believe my life story is already written, with everything in it. I need to accept the bad elements along with the good, for both come my way as gifts.

Right after Clementine was born, Vanessa and I took her to visit my mother, who was in Seattle, Washington, attending a conference. Then, last Christmas, I went back home to Jacksonville, Florida, to continue reconciliation with my mother, and to just spend time with her. My mom loves it when I'm clean because I phone more frequently, and she knows I'm doing what I'm supposed to. She sees the changes in my attitude and behavior. On the other hand, my father is still actively drinking. Although I lived with him once in a while during my teen years when I was trying to escape my mother, or my reality, he and I were never, ever close. My father abandoned me, even though I know it wasn't his fault entirely. I feel angry with him because he didn't give my mother child support. I would have loved it if he had called on my birthdays or if he'd even sent a card. The last time we spoke, I phoned to tell him Vanessa was pregnant. He responded in a loud, boisterous manner. I called one other time since Clementine's birth to talk about her, and he has seen her photos on the Internet. For some reason, my mother wants me to keep in touch with him. Although I have other things to think about right now, I'm concerned he might die before we can heal our relationship.

I'm not too worried about moving to an apartment on my own. I believe that if I continue doing what I've been doing with my recovery everything will turn out okay. I know that God will take care of me, and I hope to grow closer with God as the years go by. I don't always understand God's will for me, but I want to deepen a sense of what that might be. The 12 steps of the NA program states, "I want to continue through prayer and meditation to improve my connection with God as I know God." I pray that I can stay clean each day while continuing to nurture my relationships.

When I die, I want people to remember me as a wise person whose struggles weren't in vain, someone who was optimistic because I experienced God's love for me. I'd like people to say, "He was someone who wasn't overwhelmed by life, with all the problems and emotions connected with being human. Instead, he was a person who recognized something bigger at work in all of our lives." I want to be remembered as someone with great hope, faith, and trust in God, someone who knew everything was going to work out for the best. Those three qualities—hope, faith, and trust—build upon each other. The more we develop these traits, the stronger they'll become.

Love to all, Jason E.

Clementine gives Jason's life so much meaning, as do his friends in recovery and his faith community. Being human requires us to accumulate meaning in our lives. Without it, our spirits die and eventually take our bodies. Sir Laurens van der Post, a famous 20th-century Afrikaner and author of many books, said the following in the 1997 documentary *Hasten Slowly* about the Bushmen:

> The Bushman storytellers talk about two kinds of hunger. They say there is physical hunger, and then what they call the Great Hunger. That is the hunger for meaning. There is only one thing that is truly

insufferable, and that is a life without meaning. There is nothing wrong with the search for happiness. But there is something great—*meaning*—which transfigures all. When you have meaning you are content, you belong.

Jason, and everyone else depicted within these pages, has found *that* something great. They still experience rough patches, but they are primarily content. And I'm sure readers will agree they definitely have a place alongside the rest of us.

CHAPTER 7

Embracing Our Demons

Out of the rubble of my life—so undeserving, insignificant, obscure, and screwed up—Jesus crafts someone who will, in spite of himself, bear fruit for the kingdom and the glory of God. It never ceases to amaze me.

—GARY SMITH, SJ, *Radical Compassion*

Monica at Sisters of the Road Café introduced me to Tim B. He works as a cook in the café. He agreed to my recording his story, but was superstitious about calling his recording a Wisdom Will: "I heard that one of the first people you interviewed died after you recorded his Wisdom Will." I assured Tim that I have no power over life or death, but would, nonetheless, honor his request. The following is hereby Tim's *wisdom narrative*.

WISDOM NARRATIVE OF TIM B.

I am a cook at Sisters of the Road Café, among other things. I ended up on the streets downtown in a kind of domino effect. I was brought up in what is called Felony Flats, spanning from Southeast Fifty-second Street to Southeast Eighty-second Street and Flavel Street in Portland. This span was claimed by a chapter of the Gypsy Jokers, a motorcycle gang. Years ago, before I was born, my mother's brother (now deceased) was a methamphetamine cook for them. Back then, they were called the Brothers Speed. When I was growing up, my uncle said he invented the shit (meth).

My home was really inconsistent—drug addiction, alcoholism, violence, and so forth. I barely had any parenting. From the beginning, my mother was not there, which taught me self-sufficiency. I had to learn very fast at a very young age how to survive. You either work or you do something to eat, or you starve and die. My earliest memory at age 3 was my first foster home. I took my first drink and my first hit of pot when I was seven years old. By the time I was 10 years old, I was drinking and smoking pot regularly.

I was in and out of foster homes all during my childhood. When I was 14, I was pretty much on my own. At 16, I went through ETBS (Employment Training and Business Services), a program for underprivileged teens in Clackamas County. Now, it's a prison program. But, back then, ETBS got me housing and put me through a training program to learn landscaping. At 16, I was emancipated by a judge. I was pretty much an adult by then.

My mother's father was a Baptist minister. He was really strict with my mom and her siblings. They were all fucked up because of it, but my mother's children and her siblings' children actually turned out pretty good. For some reason, they had more stability than the previous generation. My mother gave us a choice regarding religion and so did her siblings with their kids.

I was a landscaper for about 15 years. Then I got into finished carpentry and cabinetry for a while. In the meantime, I was playing bass and guitar, doing vocals, and songwriting. I took a downward spiral in 1998. I had been married for about 12 years and had a son who's now grown. My divorce was devastating. My son lived with relatives in Eugene. I was so drunk and addicted to drugs and depressed and suicidal that nobody in their right mind would stay with a person like me. When my wife divorced me, I ended up downtown. I'd burned bridge after bridge with friends and relatives, so eventually, I ended up at rock bottom on skid row. For over seven years, I moved from place to place, camping under bridges and at Dignity Village (a homeless tent community) for nine months.

I'm not in a recovery program, but I'm not doing drugs anymore. I do drink moderately. I tried Alcoholics Anonymous (AA), but it didn't work because I don't believe in the 12-step program. I do believe in a higher power, as they require, but I have more than one higher power. My higher power has a higher power. It's called the universe. I've studied all sorts of spiritual traditions. I believe in the following saying, although I'm not sure where it comes from. "Religion is for people who are afraid to go to hell. Spirituality is for people who have already been there."[10]

I've had really dark, dark moments, but I don't need medication. I've been studying Practical Magic, Wicca, Kabala, Angelology, and a little bit of Christianity. I think these

---

10 Running Hawk of The Lakota Nation. (http://okiemomconfessions. wordpress.com/2010/07/18/religion/).

traditions share similarities. Like Hinduism, Buddhism, and Christianity, they all have a main focus. I don't know why people are fighting over religion. All they are fighting over is the way you worship, not what you worship or who you worship. It just doesn't make sense. There have been more people killed in the name of Christ than all the world wars. I just don't think He (God) would approve. I believe that wherever He is, in heaven or wherever, He's just shaking his head about what these people are doing in His name.

I embraced my fear, taking all the demons and embracing them. If you embrace your demons, they flee from you. Love your demons. Own your mistakes. That's the key to healing. My mistakes are something that nobody can take away from me. They belong to me. If you look at a mistake as a lesson and learn from it, then it's not a mistake, is it? Realizing this has been a really long, hard road for me.

In 2000, I went to jail on my 30th birthday for a burglary. The funny thing is that it was more of a criminal trespass. I ended up not knowing where I was because I'd blacked out. I had enough alcohol in my system to kill two people, not to mention the meth. The jail psychologists were saying, "How can you be walking around? You're supposed to be dead!" The truth is the cops probably saved my life because I couldn't get up. They were beating me profusely, kicking me, and beating me with a Billy club, while their police dog gnawed on me. After two months in the Justice Center, they switched me back and forth from Inverness Prison to the farm. This went on for 13 or 14 months. The two months in the Justice Center was time served. Then I was on probation for 18 months, which turned into two years because I couldn't comply due to my homeless status. Being homeless is against their conditions.

On three occasions, they *halfway-housed* me out to Salvation Army for 30 days. While there, I met a girl who showed me around, introducing me to Sisters of the Road. I started bartering for food, then volunteering, and finally I was able to enter Sisters' job training program. Working there is what helped me turn my life around and give me stability.

I believe people are out on the street because they don't have anything stable in their life anymore. There are many causes for that. It's a big misconception that everybody who's homeless has drug and alcohol problems. I'd say maybe 65 percent do, but there are also a lot of mentally ill people out there. And don't forget the working class in the USA is only one paycheck away from being homelessness. If you get sick and you lose your job and can't pay your rent, then you're out, out on the street.

Sadly, I lost music, which was something I always wanted to do since I was a young kid. Back then, my goal was to be a rock star and have a good-looking corpse. It didn't happen. I found that God had a different purpose for me. There's this Internet joke that my daughter-in-law sent me that says, "Do you want to know how to make God laugh? Tell him your plans." I finally let go of the desire to be a musician.

My purpose is the same one that all human beings have. I've been shown the meaning of life. It is so simple. We are put here to be the consciousness for the universe, whether it be bad or good. Our God, or the Universal Consciousness, is going to look at us and say, "What were you thinking? This is just flesh." Time on earth is just a blink of an eye compared to the other side. We are spirits with a body, not a body with spirit. That's what I believe. You could say my religion combines Ayurvedic meditation and dream work.

Since I stopped doing pot, I dream a lot more. My dreams tell me what's going to happen in the very near future and stuff like that. Some of it is drivel, or entertainment. I'm also interested in the paranormal. My guides tell me things, and they protect me. I get a lot higher off of stuff like that than when I was using drugs and alcohol. When you are clouded with drugs, you create a veil. It troubles me that I went through so many years in a cloud when my guides were trying to pierce that veil. My mother was psychic, but she was thwarted because of her father's strict religious guidelines. I try to tell her some of the things I practice and believe in, but she doesn't want anything to do with it. She says, "I will try to understand what you're talking about, but I can only do so for a couple of minutes. Then I don't want you to talk about it anymore because it scares me." Her father put her on a real guilt trip.

Do you know what happens when you mix religion and politics? Three hundred years of witch burning! Those years had nothing to do with women as witches; it had to do with greed. It was all about money, control, and power. If someone wanted your land, they'd declare you a witch. Same with the midwives—a lot of them were burned as witches because they were taking business away from doctors. I studied a lot about that period in human history.

I don't trust people, not out of clear maliciousness, but I just don't trust human beings in general, even if I'm one of them. I just don't get some of the tenets of nonviolence because the world was created in violence. Childbirth is violent. Sex is violent. Car engines are violent. Everything is created in violence—in the jungle and in the sea. That's how animals live, in pure, unadulterated violence. When I turn on my stove to cook, that involves violence. I just don't understand how this earthly dimension can function without it. I believe in treating people with respect, regardless of who they are. At Sisters of the Road Café the people treat everyone nonjudgmentally. No matter who you are, you will be served. Even at the café, however, with its philosophy of nonviolence, you will be kicked out if you start causing trouble. It just happened today. One of our main closers here at the café created an incident, and we had to kick him out.

One of the things I'm struggling with right now is acceptance of things I can't change, like in AA, like accepting traumas I've endured from the past. Another struggle is being grateful. I have many, many things to be grateful for, but I always have a duality, or a pragmatism, that I struggle with, especially because I'm a Virgo. Most Virgos are pragmatists, which encourages duality. Every day, I get up and I see so many people in misery and struggling with their own conditions. This reminds me that I do have many things to be thankful for.

I'm learning to accept responsibility for myself, and I've been doing okay with it. But I need to let those close to me do the same and not enable them. There are a lot of guilt trips that come with this way of living.

I want my son to learn just to be. That's what I'm learning to do right now, which is a part of our purpose, our meaning in life. We are to be the consciousness for the universe. Even serial killers are giving the universe information, dark as it may be. That's what God wants from us—information—because each of us can sway the balance. Even the demons in hell will be sucked back into the Godhead and purified one day. Everything goes back into the Godhead. It came out, and it's going to go back in and pass through, no matter what.

I no longer make plans. Plans are what got me into trouble in the first place. Now, I just do whatever the universe puts in front of me. If things get a little bit uncomfortable, then so be it. I'm conditioned for that, and that's okay. Things are uncomfortable now because I'm having serious financial problems. But I don't care about money. I have whatever I need right now. If I need food, I can find food. A person can't go hungry in downtown Portland. People will come up to me on the street or in the café after it's closed and ask about a place to eat. I'm a human referral service/resource. I can tell them where to go for medical attention and what places are serving food right now, or within the next couple of hours.

I always have job leads for people. They come back and say, "Hey, dude, I got the job because of you." And that's what I'm about. That is what Sisters of the Road is about. It's about helping people, serving people. Here at the café, we serve immediate needs for people. But Sisters also handles the more extraneous ones.

I want to be remembered as someone who was just himself, someone who was real. I have flaws, but I try to just be. I've done a lot of things that I'm ashamed of. But I just want to be remembered as I am now, not for how I was in the past when I was out disturbing and hurting the ones I love by hurting myself. Self-destructiveness impacted everyone around me at the time. These days I get to give of myself. Life now is much better!

—Tim. D. B.

A New Good Name

Hanging my head in shame
No denying the weight I've gained
Pain on top of my shoulders pain
I can never show my face here again
It'll never be the same.

Always hanging my head in shame
Thoughts flowing like a river
Sediments selectively deliver
tiny fragments of fate
with whom you may or may not relate
destiny at its all time slowest rate
Herbs and stones flicker of flame
working to give me a new good name
so I won't have to hang my head in shame.

—Tim D. B.

At first, while recording Tim, I struggled somewhat with his philosophy that humanity's purpose is one of gathering information for the universe. Now, I recognize the profundity. I believe Tim views human consciousness as an ongoing growth of order in the universe, or *cosmogenesis*, as Pierre Teilhard de Chardin[11] described it. Tim taunts us to adopt a new paradigm by facing our demons head-on instead of grasping at fear-based control. In her book, *Radical Amazement*, Judy Cannato elucidates the following:

---

11 De Chardin was a Jesuit priest-theologian and a distinguished geologist-paleontologist born in France in 1881. He intermixed theological and evolutionary cosmic concepts with Christian creedal theology. Considered subversive by the Vatican, he was silenced. His works, written from 1924 to 1955, were published after his death in New York City in 1955.

Shifting to a new paradigm takes commitment and hard work. It requires gut-wrenching honesty and the willingness to give up fear-filled control. [...] a new world view will challenge our old ways of imaging God. A little God—one concerned only for human beings who are like us or should be like us—will never do. The new paradigm includes all creation and is large enough to contain the immensities of the universe. In this new vision we are all connected, all part of the cosmogenesis that continues to unfold, even as you sit here reading these words. (14)

She goes on to say the following:

It recognizes the special significance of the human species as the consciousness of the cosmos, the universe having emerged in such a way that it is conscious of itself. Along with our consciousness comes the added responsibility to care for the Earth and creationkind. Knowing that we cannot possibly contribute to ongoing creation alone, we are empowered by the Spirit, mentored by Christ, and lavished with God's grace. (15)

I believe there is an innate, gravitational urge toward the divine that accompanies us at birth. How else could someone like Tim rise to the surface of his disaster-prone life to find freshness of meaning and purpose? Tim raised himself and understood what he must do to survive. He endured brutality, homelessness, extreme poverty, abandonment, betrayals, incarceration, and more. Yet, he believes and has great faith in the divine.

Because the critical first years of life strongly impact our personalities, you'd think Tim would be so psychologically stunted by lack of maternal and paternal bonding, love and affection, and security and trust that healing would elude him, not to mention the fact that he was alcoholic and drug addicted by the age of 10! No, Tim is a man who questions and tests, seeks and finds, that which makes sense to him. We might not all agree with his logic, but how can anyone fault his determination and his passion to find his place in the universe? Tim's interview helped to confirm for me Cannato's declaration that "we are the universe conscious of itself and that this capacity is not for our benefit alone, but for the good of all creationkind" (79).

Before recording his interview, Tim told me that he was indeed a *prophet* and had lots of wisdom to share, but "it takes money to be heard." This is sorely true as Tiny, aka Lisa Gray-Garcia, knows and speaks of in her book, *Criminal of Poverty: Growing up Homeless in America*: "Poor people are inherently denied a voice in the media, and they're also denied a voice in the creation of legislation and academic scholarship" (229). Through her book and Sisters of the Road's book, *Voices from the Street,* (culled from 600 interviews about the truth of homelessness from the people themselves), programs such as Write Around Portland[12], grassroots poverty newspapers like Portland's *Street Roots*, and other organizations appreciating and promoting scholarship among the poor and homeless,

---

12 Write Around Portland (http://www.writearound.org/) runs volunteer-facilitated writing workshops for people affected by HIV/AIDS, survivors of domestic violence, people in recovery from drug/alcohol addiction, people in prison, seniors in foster care, veterans living with PTSD, people with physical or mental disabilities, teen parents, low-income adults, and people who might not have access to the power of writing and community because of income, isolation, or other barriers.

these generally dismissed voices are slowly surfacing and being acknowledged. There's a long way to go, but with the tenacity of the ever-increasing numbers of social-justice activists, I pray that this trend continues the advancement of *"poverty journalism,"* a phrase coined by Gray-Garcia. Art, in any form, has always been an expression of one's heart both in anguish and elation, so why exclude anyone? It is through the expression of visual and written art that we leave our legacy. Yes, even the graffiti scrawled on the walls of our neighborhoods as well as the hip-hop dance steps of our youth are legacy statements. Through expressions of the heart, we find meaning and seed ideas with which to create a better world. Lisa Gray-Garcia, who founded *POOR* magazine, says the following:

> [...] From the core of my heart, I knew that everyone who wanted to write, who wanted to make art, who wanted to be heard but who didn't have the access to education, time and/or resources, should be given that space, that ability, that voice, so that they, like me, would be given some hope. (212)

Like Sisters of the Road, Gray-Garcia did her research, her homework with the people comprising her writing workshops. Below she discusses their process:

> We did extensive research on the issue, and together we developed several different templates for long-term change, culminating in what we proposed as a solution. Our solution to homelessness was Homefulness, which became the title of *POOR* magazine, Volume 1. The project that included a school for kids and adults,

available on a sliding scale depending on what you could afford, and providing everyone with that elusive thing that would ultimately take them out of homelessness on a permanent basis: equity. (213)

CHAPTER 8

Under The Bridge

...The very stuff that can destroy a person becomes the raw material for reclaiming the potential of one's life
—Gary Smith, SJ, *Radical Compassion*

R ain deluged Mike, who was enfolded in a threadbare blanket and newspaper under the Hawthorne Bridge. He liked that spot because it was away from the gangs that hung out around West Burnside; he felt safer there.

For nearly 20 years, his winter routine had consisted of sobriety, clean and sober hotels, and a few odd jobs. But, during the warmer months, he drank. Living as a wanderer and *canner* with a bridge or a cemetery bench for a rooftop. A *canner* is the name for people who collect pop cans for their deposits. It takes a lot of pop cans to survive on booze and food. Sometimes food is sacrificed. (I recall a saying in *The Wall Street Journal*: "You know you've hit bottom, when your behavior spirals downward faster than you can lower your standards.[13])

Mike's rotting teeth leached poison into his bloodstream. That summer, he was too ill to consider day labor, and there wasn't much chance of making it under those conditions, not at 45, he'd thought. In fear, he bolted upright, his makeshift shroud falling to the wayside. Other sleeping tenants cursed the disturbance produced by his shouts, "I'm too old for this crap! Too old!"

Thus, the elements jolted my kid brother Mike into sobriety, a feat we siblings failed to accomplish. Five years after his awakening, I received the telephone call that brought Mike back into the family's embrace. By then, he was living in the Mark O. Hatfield Hotel, a clean and sober SRO right across the street from the Downtown Chapel where I'd prayed for him for years. I found it strange that our paths never crossed during those five years.

"Why did you wait five years to call, Mike?" I asked. The last time we'd spoken, I told him that all of his siblings were letting go of him for the time being. "You know where to get help in Portland—shelter, food stamps, free meals—so call me when you're six months sober." It killed me to pull the tough love thing with him, but my brother Brian, my sister Gail, and I considered this our last recourse. We prayed that, one day, our tactic would save his life.

"Well, I didn't want to come back to the family without money in my pocket or some kind of a job. I didn't want to come back a victim." With these words, I knew Mike had a terrific chance at life beyond alcoholism. My own 12-step sponsor used to say, "It takes as long as it takes for people to let go

---

13 Beck, Melinda. *The Wall Street Journal*, "Are you an Alcoholic?" 8 January 2008.

of alcohol and drugs. People have different ways of bottoming out." In Mike's case, we thought his bottom was going to be subterranean, or death itself. From his phone call, however, he indicated it was time to grow up and get on with life.

Six years earlier, our brother Gary died of alcoholism, complicated by lung cancer. He died in a care facility shortly after he told me that he was going to have himself one last beer. Gary had no home, no money, only the clothes on his back when he died at age 59. As a child, my eldest brother had been my hero. In our family of five children, he was the first to fall prey to the disease of alcoholism, then Mike, and then me.

I thank God every day that I had experienced what 12-step programs call a *high bottom*. After 10 years of agonizing guilt and pain from drinking, I admitted myself into a treatment program. It was the right thing to do. It was the wise thing to do. Not everyone is so fortunate. Now at least Mike has a chance.

WISDOM WILL OF MIKE R.

Dear Friends and Family,

As you know, I was born in Portland, Oregon in 1951. During my sophomore year in high school, I began smoking pot. I turned into a little pothead, kind of a dropout thing for me. Later, when I was 18, I turned to alcohol. I never thought I had a problem with drugs or alcohol because everyone I knew was using. I continued smoking pot until 1969 and used alcohol for many years.

After high school, I went to work as a painter with my older brother Gary in California. He was also an alcoholic. We had various adventures, painting a few movie stars' homes. We lived in the Hollywood Hills and became active church members. Today, I don't drink, and I don't do drugs. I'm not interested in doing it anymore.

For more than 13 years, I was away from the rest of my family who still lived in Portland. I came back to Portland broke [*In fact, the day Mike came home was the same day I put our mother into an adult foster home, as she could no longer care for herself. Mom was bipolar, and she also suffered from obsessive-compulsive disorder. The decision to put her in an adult foster home was needed after she suffered a number of mini-strokes.*] After I came back, I had some bad times with family and with myself. I stayed at the family home for a while, but my siblings were selling the house, and they ended up tossing me out. At the time, I was still actively drinking and smoking in the house. They were afraid I'd burn it down, I guess.

Here in Portland, I was homeless for a while. A person can live out-of-doors fine in the summer. No problem. But when it gets cold and your resources go down, then you need to go inside for comfort, even if it means rock bottom at the Rescue

Mission. You can pretend to be saved or whatever to get a crummy little meal and a bed to sleep in. They throw you out at 4:00 a.m. in the morning. But the truth is at least it is a safe place to stay, if you can put up with all the forced religion and stuff.

On the street, I learned that when you're down and out, you have to be watchful. You can only sleep during the day because the cops hassle you at night. The homeless are considered trespassers on public property. You become really sensitive to sound and sleep with one eye open. A person learns to migrate to areas that are less of a hassle. I managed because alcohol helped me become numb.

With the aid of my sister Linda, along with some good friends, I went into recovery at the local detox center (Hooper Detox) and then on to treatment facilities. I went into treatment because using wasn't fun anymore. I couldn't remember the last time I'd had a good time drinking. The fun had turned into misery. Treatment included acupuncture, AA meetings, and group and individual counseling. I did all my amends work. My brother Brian hired me to work off the debts I owed him. For a time, I didn't want to go back to my own church because I had a lot of guilt about drinking. Eventually, I went there and just unloaded, like the fifth step[14] in AA, only deeper.

I have to say, a complete eight years dried out did me good. Today, I just don't need alcohol or drugs in my life, and I strongly suggest that no one else uses them. I know that kids like to experiment and act like adults, but using never works physically or mentally.

I've learned not to be prejudiced. I grant people the right to be. I don't think less of anyone because of color, race, or religion. I believe we are all beings driving around in our little

---

14 Fifth Step: "Admitted to God, to ourselves, and to another human being the exact nature of our wrongs." Catholics do this in the confessional.

bodies, but when we die, we shed them. I believe there is life after death. I'm sure there is a higher power for this universe. I'm not at the level where I know exactly what that is; however, I believe the Big Bang theory has big holes in it. Even if there was a Big Bang, who started it? Who put out the first thought? I believe we should help others survive, starting with our own family, our family in the community, and the animal community, as well as the entire planet. The whole idea of life is to assist in survival. If we don't help the least of us, that would be a serious mistake.

When Hurricane Katrina happened, I had an urge to help. I felt it was time that I gave something back to society. I went to my church and asked about it. The chaplain said they were sending a couple of crews to help the hurricane victims. I said, "Okay, I'm going." I dropped everything. I didn't have much money, but the church chipped in on the expenses. We got a new truck for the six of us on our crew. We went to Mississippi instead of New Orleans. We ended up at an elementary school. Some of the locals got left behind, so they confiscated the school for shelter during the storm. They started asking for assistance from the organizations that had come to help. My church group hooked up with a City Corps group. The Salvation Army and the Red Cross were there, too. A lot of guys in our denomination joined us from around the country, including a crew of about 40 Puerto Ricans.

We cleaned all the mud and debris out of the school gymnasium and cafeteria. We set up a store in two or three days for the stockpiles of goods that were coming in. We stocked, replenished, and kept the people in ice. The majority of the people were coming back because it was a rich, old, Southern community. The ones who got left behind, the poor folks, were helped, too. When some of these people came back, their whole house was gone. They were completely amazed by our readiness to help, coming all the way from Portland, Oregon, and Puerto Rico. The Puerto Ricans provided music and brought back some cheer and life to the community.

Our little crews joined with the Baptists, Lutherans, and other faith groups. We basically wanted to get the neighbors back in communication with each other so they could build a sense of community again. Even if one person's house wasn't destroyed, the next one might have been completely demolished. Everyone was in shock. We felt the best way to handle that was to get folks together to talk. One day, I went with the crew to cut out the mold in a home. I'd brought a bunch of tools with me because I thought they'd be needed. We cut down the drywall in an old gentleman's house, removed the mold, and then lifted trees off and out of his roof. He was so overwhelmed with gratitude that he invited us, and all 40 of the Puerto Ricans, to come stay at his house. He said he loved young people coming to help because it gave him some hope. He also said that he hadn't talked to his next-door neighbor in 10 years and that, the other day, they had a good *ole* talk. It made me feel good to hear him speak.

I just wanted to give back to people for helping me. I thought, *What if this happened in Oregon? What if Mt. Hood exploded or, BOOM, some city was bombed?* I'm survival trained, and this October, I'm continuing my education with training in emergency management, neighborhood watches, and methods for storing survival materials. This includes firefighting, CPR, and stuff like that. The training organization will authorize us to be first responders. I came home from Katrina feeling pretty good about what we'd accomplished there in terms of helping people. Every person we helped was grateful and thanked us profusely. My church crews will eventually go back to Mississippi to help some more.

These days, the church is on a big Interfaith Council, and we're working together with other faith traditions to get things done. We all have to keep our religions going because they are under attack more and more. Every religion is being smashed by various laws. Together, we are working to build an *interfaith mindset* to keep each other alive. Spirituality is far more important than anything material.

The other day, I was thinking, *I don't have any enemies anymore. I don't have anybody hating me or out to get me!* Today, I'm happy to be alive, dull as that sounds. I usually mention this when we gather in a circle at Christmas to pray at my sister's house. I might have been killed. I've been mugged before, out of sheer stupidity, like drinking in a bad area of town. Stupid. I went through the Rodney King riot and survived. I was living in Long Beach with the only white family for miles, right next to the tough neighborhood of Compton. I wasn't downtown when the guy [Rodney King] got beat up, but I saw a black lady bring her kids to a department store to loot after someone had already broken into it. She waited in the car. She'd get out of there before the police came to breakup one of the riots. Then she'd come tooling back and drop the kids off again to collect even more stuff from the store. That morning, we didn't know the riot was happening yet. On the fourth day of the riots, I had to go into Compton to catch the MAX train to travel 35 miles to downtown Los Angeles. I had a $12-an-hour job for the big Celebrity Center through my church. The crew working there said they wouldn't work during a riot. So my church brought in some heavyweight construction people. We had a blast. Helicopters were flying overhead. I had a good time doing something constructive when there was so much unrest going on.

Today, I'm happy, even if I don't look it. My life is simple. I've never been money-motivated. I love to work; activity with a purpose is always good. I could have worked harder or gone to school, but drinking got in my way. You can't really advise anyone not to drink, though. People are going to do what they do. Now, I'm totally against taking anything—except coffee, with lots of sugar.

In grade school, I thought I was a rebel; in high school, I was a radical. Today, I think I'm a pretty good Joe. There is something else I'd like to share: I try to learn one useful thing from every person I meet, including any enemies, if I have them. I think that's a good way to be. This is pretty much my story. I'll leave the eulogizing to other people.

With Love, Mike R.

The Mark O. Hatfield Hotel

Our parents are long deceased, but my two brothers, my sister, and I feel closer than ever. I'm usually the one who holds family get togethers, as I have the largest house. It feels so wonderful, so complete, to know that we are all safe now. Mike and I are free from the ravages of alcohol, but know better than to get too confident, in case either of us, *God forbid*, relapses. Mike is now sheltered from the elements, working and volunteering for his church. Our brother Brian is safe from his years in Vietnam, the memories fading. My sister Gail and her husband, Joe[15], enjoy retirement at the beach town of Waldport, Oregon. My sister survived an abusive first marriage, and her second husband was an alcoholic but now no longer drinks. We've all survived an unpredictable childhood due to the tragic mental illness of our mother. Back then, Mama was given shock treatments without anesthesia, which they now use. They stuck a wooden stick in her mouth to keep her from biting off her tongue when she seized and zapped her brain with electrical currents. Nowadays, treatment is more effective and less brutal. It's amazing how well Mom and Dad took care of us, considering her crippling depressions and manic highs. We were always fed and clothed, taken to doctors and dentists when needed, and introduced to God. These days, my siblings and I all have different spiritual paths, but we know the power of the divine and the grace that so blesses us.

---

15 Joe passed away in 2010.

CHAPTER 9

A Prophet In Disguise

Compassion—it is a word meaning to suffer with. If we all carry a little of the burden, it will be lightened. If we share in the suffering of the world, then some will not have to endure so heavy an affliction.

—DOROTHY DAY, *By Little and By Little*

I first met Glasker Rankin[16] at Sisters of the Road Café through my friend Monica Beemer, the director. She'd just featured Glasker on the front page of the Sisters' newsletter and suggested he meet with me to compose a Wisdom Will. His rap sheet as a hardened criminal was long. In his twenties, thirties, and forties he was in and out of jail, sometimes for years at a time. Three of Glasker's siblings and his mother died while he was in prison. By the time we met he had turned his

---

16 Glasker insisted that when talking about him I was to use his full name.

life around and was working as the cashier at Sisters. He had completed three years of sobriety from drugs and alcohol.

Glasker, as most of the prophets in this book, had meager material possessions and survived below the poverty level, so the prospect of gifting his wisdom to his sister and nephews excited him: "I want to give them my Wisdom Will for Christmas. God knows, I was a bad example to my nephews over the years. We used to drink and drug together, and now we are all in recovery. My sister will appreciate this, too." He beamed even before the interview began.

WISDOM WILL OF GLASKER RANKIN

Dear Family and Friends,

My background was sometimes violent. I was in and out of jail, on drugs, and I did a lot of rebelling in my life. I was at the point of not knowing any way to get along in life, other than what I was doing. I was pretty tough on the streets. I liked it then because I got respect from everybody. Now that I look back, it wasn't respect that I was getting; people gave me room because of my intimidation, my being a fool. I can recall someone saying, "Oh God, here comes that damn fool!" and it upset me. I asked myself why they would call me that. But I knew that's what I was. I acted just like a damn fool!

My turning point came after my last time in prison in 1996. I was in there for a parole violation and drug possession. I was seriously thinking, *Man, when is this going to stop?* I didn't know how to make it stop because I didn't know anything other than going to jail, getting out, and getting a lick—what I mean by that is getting some money to go do some drugs. So I sat back and I analyzed my situation. *Why am I always going to jail? Every time I go it's because of drugs, or if I do something, it's because I'm loaded.* I made a connection! Drugs were my problem! So I narrowed it down to this: If there was a way that I could let go of drugs and alcohol, I'd pretty much have it beat. I wouldn't go to jail anymore.

One more time in jail and I'd be labeled a dangerous offender, a habitual criminal. This was in 1983. My attorney once told me, "Glasker, I don't tell many of my clients this, but if you continue the way you're going and get arrested, or you get another Class A or Class B felony, the Feds will pick you up, and you'll go to federal prison for life![17] They'll never let you out! And if you get state time, it will be the same thing. You'll never see daylight again!" That was something for me to seriously think about. When he told me that, I was in my thirties. But I didn't seriously think about hanging up my guns and stopping doing my thing until I was in my forties.

There was a guy I'd known for years. He'd been in and out of prison. At the time, he had 12 years clean. I asked him, "Darryl, how did you get clean? How'd you do it? Show me how." I was afraid of rejection, and one of my reasons for not being clean or doing the right things in life was because I hated to put myself in the position that someone would turn me down and I'd be hurt again. I dared not ask. But I believed and trusted in Darryl, and I asked him for help. He said, "If you do what I did, you can get clean." He told me he'd gone to Stay Clean, a drug program in northeast Portland up on Alberta Street. So I went through the program. I didn't graduate because I was still in my rebelling mode, so I quit the program early. As soon as I did that I had a flash: *Wow, I finally have someone to believe in me, and I'm now getting to believe in myself. If I don't watch out, I'll be going backward.* I didn't want to go backward; I just didn't like Stay Clean. That very day, I jumped into another program, PCRP (Project for Community Recovery). I graduated from that one. From that point on, 1997 to 2000, I was clean. I liked most everything I was doing then. It was exciting to be clean. I was like a tiny child learning how to crawl, how to walk. But then I relapsed in the latter part of 2000 and was arrested again in 2001.

---

17 Under the lifetime criminal law in Oregon, if he were to be convicted again, he would be sent to prison with no chance of parole for the rest of his life.

I was in the backseat of a police car again. This time, I was smiling to myself. The cop asked, "Why are you smiling?" They thought I'd set them up because I wasn't sad for being arrested. I said, "I'm just sitting here thinking that I can go to jail now and get the help I need. It's over for me." I was enthused about this. I'd finally bottomed out. I was now willing to do whatever it took for me to get clean and stay clean. That was November 11, 2001. On November 11, 2004, I have three years clean and sober!

It's a struggle sometimes, but what keeps me going is remembering where I used to be, knowing where I'm at today, and knowing where I want to be tomorrow. I can never get to where I want to be tomorrow if I use again. The next time I use could be the end of my life. I might die.

The advice I want to give to my nephews is for them to think about things before they ever make a move or decide to do something. Think about it before jumping because there are consequences for everything, and they just may not want to face those consequences. Everything, good and bad, has consequences. In my case, because of my attitude, I encountered a lot of bad consequences. I would do things even knowing the price—do 'em anyway.

Before, I didn't have anyone to believe in me. I had a brother and sister die from drugs. My oldest brother died of cirrhosis of the liver from drinking. My mom and stepfather passed away. My mom and I were really, really close. I could talk to her about things that I couldn't talk to my stepfather about. After they were gone, I didn't have anyone to believe in me. I was orphaned, worthless, and abandoned, as though I wasn't a part of anything more. I just felt that, because each one of my family members died a couple of years apart, I was next. When, I didn't know, but I knew it was coming. I thought, *What's the use?* I continued to drink and drug and create problems for myself and others around me. I was setting it up to happen.

Today, I have faith. I believe in Jesus Christ with all my heart. I know God has a plan for my life. Me being clean today and being able to tell others where I've been is a testimony to God's plan. Before getting clean, I looked at people and said, "Better you than me," if someone got hurt. But, today, I pray for that person, wish them the best. I now have empathy for people, which I didn't have before. I also feel remorseful for a lot of things I've done. I can honestly say, today, I don't mind giving an apology if I'm wrong.

Pride is a dirty piece of armor, which is what I call it—*armor.* In myself, I had plenty of pride. I remember my mother and my father saying, "Son, you're going to have to stop that pride to keep on living, because that pride is going to get you into big trouble. You drop your pride, and you'll go a long way in life." That was me—*pride*, proud for being a big boastful person. I held onto it tight. I understand today what they meant, but back then, I didn't. It's a real good thing that I dropped my pride because being a prideful person only causes trouble for you. I have more understanding about right and wrong, do's and don'ts, than I had when I was hanging tight to my pride. It kept me in a state of mind to do something belligerent to someone—because I was proud, because I could, because I wanted to live up to the image. That's not the way to go. There's no enjoyment anymore in hurting someone, or even myself. I can think clearly today. I can now make honest and righteous decisions, which were impossible before because my mind was always cloudy. At the time, I thought I was making the right decisions. Even if I made the wrong decisions, it didn't matter because every decision was centered on drugs and alcohol. As long as I got my high, I was okay with it. Most of my decisions were wrong.

Sometimes, even nowadays, I say things that aren't kind. But now I stop myself and recognize them as stubborn thoughts. The first thing I do is pray to God to forgive me and my sinful thoughts about that individual or whatever it is. I try to watch what I'm thinking so it doesn't run away with me. Honestly, I'd like to say this world needs to become a bigger world, one where people pay attention. And, even when we don't pay attention sometimes, there is still something around that takes care of us. I like to think that it's my father, Jesus Christ, my higher power.

Walking into Sisters of the Road Café, where everybody welcomes me, is what makes me happy today. It makes me feel good because I can stop and talk to these people, the ones who come here, because they are my family. I can tell my story of where I've been and where I want to be tomorrow. My goal in life is to become a youth substance abuse counselor. I know a youngster is more vulnerable to making mistakes around drugs and alcohol. A youngster is easier to correct. If I'd had that correction or somebody in my life at the time, like a big brother figure, to point me in the right direction, I wouldn't have become the type of person I was. If I can help one youngster make the right decisions, I'd be the happiest man in the world. A youngster is like a ball of clay; you can mold him into any shape and form that he wants to be. We need to spend time to help mold young people into the right form. I've taken away so much from society that this will be my way of giving back.

Most of my life, I thrived on violence, fighting, and doing bodily harm to people. People would say, "That dude just laughed about what he was doing!" That was because I thought I was a tough guy. All I did was show people how sick I was.

One of my sisters died in 1990. Before that, in the 1960s and 1970s, she used drugs. She got arrested in 1967. When I was 13, my sister's kids came to live with us. My mom raised them, so my nephews are like brothers to me. There's always been closeness between us. We used to drug together; now we are in recovery together. I'd encourage my nephews to continue in that effort, and if there's ever a time they feel vulnerable and feel like using, I'd ask that they contact their support group, their sponsor, or just a friend who's in recovery and talk to them before making that decision.

I'd like to thank Gwen here at Sisters of the Road Café. I want to let her know that I love her from the bottom of my heart. She believed in me. She told me some things about myself that enlightened me. She saw strengths in me that I couldn't see. Gwen told me that I was an honest and trustworthy person. She's in recovery herself, so she understands my behaviors and motives and things that I would do. One time, when I got violent, Gwen fired me! My pride got in the way, and I wasn't going to go crawl back to her. What the hell would I want to do that for? But I got to the point where I continuously thought about what my mom and others had said: "You've got to drop your pride. That's what God wants you to do. There are people who you can help." I had to stop thinking about myself and start thinking about helping other people, quit being stubborn. Finally, one day, Gwen said, "Do you want your old job back?" I said, "Yeah." So she started me off with part time, and eventually, it turned into full time. The staff welcomed me with open arms. They made me feel not only like a part of the team that works here but also as part of a family. I have a bigger family than I could have ever imagined.

One of our employees left after relapsing, and it really hurt me. I just walked out the door a minute ago, and there she was volunteering to help out. Many people want to work here, and for me to be working here with these young college students, wow! If I'd gone through college and done what my folks wanted for me—graduate from high school and then go to college—I could have done more with life and gotten a really good job. But, if I'd done that, I wouldn't be here today helping out.

I want to thank Monica for pushing me. She says she wasn't pushing me, but I think she was. I'm glad she did. She interviewed me for the Sisters of the Road newsletter and now you. I'm in the paper, and things like that mean a lot. She introduced me to some people who helped me learn how to manage money. For the first time in my life, I started saving on a regular basis, thanks to her. My sister used to ask me all the time, "Are you saving any money?" I'd lie to her and tell her, "Yeah." Now, I'm really saving! I'm like a real human being. I'd like to thank everybody at Sisters of the Road. When I think about using again, not only would I hurt myself and take myself back to that road of hurt, but I'd also be letting everyone down that believes in me. It's a pretty big price to pay. Now, not only do I think about myself when thoughts of getting high come along, but I think about everybody else around me who cares about me. I look forward to continuing being that person who I'm supposed to be.

I'd like to be remembered as the Glasker who changed his life and got clean and stayed clean for a reasonable amount of time before he passed away, who started showing a lot of respect and empathy for others, and who continuously helped people in any way that he could and didn't mind doing it. That's something. That's what I pray for every morning before I continue on my journey. God put me in the position to help people, whether it's helping someone with information, or helping someone with bus fare, or giving someone 50¢ for a phone call. Just helping somebody, somehow, someway. When I help somebody, I don't do it for anything in return, not even a thank-you, because I believe in Jesus Christ with all my heart, so my thanks comes from him. My prayers for the world are as follows:

1. We all have a responsibility to ourselves to stay clean and sober and be accountable.

2. To my nephews and all other people in recovery, I'd say stay clean and sober. Under no circumstances should you let anyone around you make decisions about your sobriety. You weigh it out and make a choice for yourself. There's no situation where "getting high" is a solution. Be strong and continue to think positive. You have to have a higher power. If you aren't religious, which I am and my nephews are, you need to find something or someone to believe in to give you the strength to move on to the next level.

3. I honestly hope that the killing and the burdens people carry here in America cease.

4. I pray that they find places for the homeless and less fortunate people, places where they can live, not just in Oregon, but everywhere. With help, the homeless and less fortunate can stop using drugs and alcohol. They can do what I did—get clean and improve their lives. But it's not that easy for a lot of them. Many have mental problems and hang ups—disabilities that keep them from working. I think that's where the government should step in and help out. I just hope and pray that day will come.

I started working here in 1998, and now it's 2004. I've seen individual users who were coming here then and are still coming today. Many have changed, while some haven't. But not all change is meant to be. People can't help their situation all the time. People need to want the help, or we are being enablers.

One of the founders of Sisters of the Road, Genny Nelson, told me," We have a barter system here. People can work for a meal. This helps them to become responsible people." She said, "If you continue to give people free things, they don't learn. Let them work for it and learn how to be responsible." That makes a lot of sense to me. She doesn't believe in doing for people what they're capable of doing for themselves. So I tell people about the barter system, and some say, "I don't want to work." Then I say, "You don't want to eat, then. I'm afraid there's nothing I can do for you." I don't want to become part of the problem. I've done that before, and the person just comes back and comes back. Finally, I'd just have to tell them that I couldn't do it anymore. They'd get an attitude and not talk to me anymore. I knew I did the right thing anyway.

I'd like to thank Genny Nelson for instilling her teachings in me. In 1998 or 1999 meeting, she said, "What are some of the things that you do around here that are violent?"

The first thing that came to my mind was, "I don't hit nobody!" She taught me there are others things a person can do outside of the physical that hurt. Psychological pain is something that sticks with a person for life. I'd say number one is ignoring somebody. I don't like to be ignored Nobody likes to be ignored. Second is judging somebody. I don't like to be judged. Nobody likes to be judged. These things stuck. Now, when I'm talking to people, I try not to judge them. Anytime I catch myself moving away from someone when I'm working, I say, "Excuse me. Forgive me. I don't mean to ignore you, but I have to get back to work. Maybe we could talk on my next break." I really want to thank Genny for teaching me those things and many others. Her words have taught me how to be responsible. I was ready to learn. Today I am teachable.

With Love, Glasker

I finished transcribing Glasker's Wisdom Will and presented him with it in November 2004. It happened to be his 50th birthday. On February 10, 2005, a mere three months later,

I found myself sitting in a little church in northeast Portland attending Glasker's funeral! He died unexpectedly on February 7. At his funeral, the minister read part of his Wisdom Will, and while he was dying, Monica Beemer, the director of Sisters, tacked it to the wall of his ICU room for the staff and visitors to read.

Glasker exemplifies why recording our life story and wisdom is so important, no matter our life circumstances. It doesn't matter if we live on the streets or in gated communities. Glasker's survivors were uplifted in their grief by the legacy he left behind. Now, his memory will inspire his family and community for generations. This simple project becomes an important link for our survivors, something tangible they can refer to when overcome by grief.

My best friend, Mary Ellen, died in 1996. Her husband read and reread her journals seeking some mention, even a mere sentence, about him. There was nothing. Had she written a last letter, a Wisdom Will, a poem, or something intended for him personally, his suffering would have been greatly reduced. Written documents are so important to our survivors. I cannot stress this enough. The death of someone we love is a monumental emotional assault. We each have the power to assist our loved ones in adapting to loss if only we put pen to paper.

In her book, *Women's Lives, Women's Legacy's*, Rachel Naomi Remen, MD, observes the following:

> The beneficiaries of your spiritual-ethical will [Wisdom Will] are starved in ways they can't even imagine. Your legacy will nourish them; your words will fill the holes in their hearts and the gaps in their histories. Through your stories, they will know and remember

you. Your values will encourage and inspire them in times of cynicism, alienation, and hopelessness. Your blessings will teach them to love. When they are told that all truth is relative, they will find guidance in your honesty, courage and generosity. (239)

Authors Patricia O'Connell Killen and John DeBeers discuss the human drive for meaning in their book, *The Art of Theological Reflection*. We fulfill this urge through the process of reflection by taking stock of our feelings within our experiences. I found an enlightening statement in their book: "For human beings, the drive for meaning is stronger than the drive for physical survival" (20). What a powerful truth! Since this drive for meaning is so integral to human beings, I believe in sharing that meaning. Creating a Wisdom Will allows us to sum up our quest for life and document it. For people on the margins, it's an opportunity to see how far they've progressed. Most have survived unheard of trials and tribulations, many because of erroneous life choices, but now, they can reflect on what they've learned from the hard times. One of the women I interviewed repeated over and over again that she wanted people, especially her children, to never give up on themselves—never. She wanted her life to be an example for others.

She didn't give in to hardship, but kept placing one foot in front of the other, moving forward. Finally, in desperation, she reached out her hand, and to her amazement, someone took hold. The lesson is clear; we heal each other. We heal in community. Healing begins when we are courageous enough to admit that we need help. I believe one of life's difficulties is opening up to receive. In his seminal book, *The Tibetan Book of Living and Dying*, Sogyal Rinpoche says that if we hold a coin closed in our fist, our arm outstretched, fingers groundward, we must grasp it tightly or the coin will drop. This takes effort. But Rinpoche challenges us to turn our hand over and hold the coin skyward without grasping. With the coin resting naturally in our palm, there is room to receive. Both receiving and offering a handshake requires both parties to open their fists. I pray that more and more of us loosen our grip on our preconceived notions of what a homeless person is or is not. Instead, may we join our hearts and minds to end homelessness, and treat those less fortunate than ourselves with respect and dignity.

Portland Tribune's story, "Sisters [of the Road] turns cash into lifeline," Friday, July 27, 2007, reveals the following statistics:

> The National Alliance to End Homelessness said this week that Portland has seen its number of chronically homeless people drop from 5,103 in 2005 to 4,456 in 2007. That's a decrease of 13 percent and a dramatic reversal in what had been until 2005 an upward trajectory of homelessness in the city. The goal of Portland's Ten Year Plan to End Homelessness is to "end homelessness in the city of Portland and Multnomah County" by 2015. And National Alliance officials said the city was a great example of success nationally.

However, there were key trends revealed by the 2011 count in Portland, according to an article in the *Portland Mercury*, June 21, 2011:

One night a year, city staffers, social service workers, and an army of volunteers comb Portland's streets and shelters, trying to get every single homeless person to fill out a ten-question survey. The resulting **homeless census** is a lowball figure on the number of homeless people who live in Portland, but it provides a pretty clear snapshot of what their situations are like. Today, the numbers for this year's homeless census are finally in! And it's not so good. According to the housing bureau's strange **homelessness nutrition pyramid**, the number of people living on the streets, in shelters, and in transitional housing **grew eight percent** to 4,655 people [from 2009]. The number of homeless families grew by 35 percent.

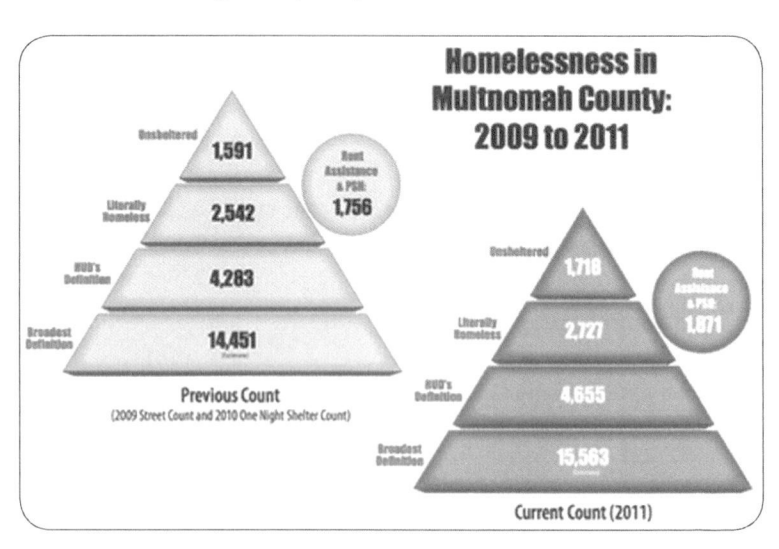

CHAPTER 10

Life In Reflection

When the act of reflection takes place in the mind, when we look at ourselves in the light of thought, we discover that our life is emblossomed in beauty. Behind us, as we go, all things assume pleasing forms, as clouds do far off. Not only things familiar and stale, but even the tragic and the terrible are comely as they take their place in the picture of memory.

—Ralph Waldo Emerson

*B*efore Christmas of 2007, I met Carl D., a case manager for Central City Concern.[18] Entering their drop-in

---

18 Central City Concern is not a religious organization. The mission of Central City Concern (www.centralcityconcern.org) is to provide pathways to self-sufficiency through active intervention in poverty and homelessness. It is the core philosophy of Central City Concern that in order for a person to successfully achieve self-sufficiency, they must not only have access to housing, support services, and employment

center, I'd felt a tinge of guilt for being overdressed: *I should have worn jeans and a baseball cap. Here I am in a pantsuit, for God's sake, and these folks probably just own the clothes on their backs. What was I thinking? I hope I won't make anyone uncomfortable.* It took a moment to remember that the visit wasn't about *me.* I'd come to learn something from Carl and others like him. So I left my narcissism on the sidewalk and entered. One of the loungers asked, "You here to see Carl, right?"

As I gazed around the cramped room, I suspected that the folks hanging out there were attempting to climb out of the abyss they'd dug themselves into or were testing the waters to see if there was any hope for them. I didn't know that for sure, though, and I didn't ask. Respect for confidentiality is integral to any helper or helping profession. Still, recalling one of the first rules of recovery (*showing up*), I smiled, praying they were heading toward a life free of addictions and finding shelter in affordable housing.

I offered Carl my hand. Immediately, I shared that I was more than 20 years clean and sober and that I had a brother living in the Mark O. Hatfield. This was my way of touching common ground with anyone living or working in the Old Town neighborhood.

Central City Concern's drop-in center is located next door to Sisters of the Road's offices. It's a cubbyhole space, but people manage squeezing in and out. Through the window, I often see groups of men playing cards at one of the tables, sipping coffee and chatting, or watching the antique television set. Carl endures an office without room to turn around. I noticed a swath of wrinkled and worn photos and papers tacked to the

---

opportunities, but also must be building positive relationships with those who have had common experiences and can offer support.

wall above his desk. The piles of folders surrounding him were stacked quasi-orderly. I knew that he was busy and overworked, which made his agreeing to see me and recording his story all the more generous.

WISDOM WILL OF CARL D.

Dear Family and Friends,

I was one of 10 children. My mom didn't have enough time to pay attention to all of us, so we learned ways to draw attention to ourselves. One of those ways was to steal my dad's cigarettes and his liquor. He was an alcoholic. I started drinking at about 10 years old. By the time I was 12, I was in reform school for car theft. My life started to snowball at a very young age. I was in and out of reform school from age 12 to 18 for different reasons—car theft, glue sniffing, all kinds of stupid stuff. Reform school wasn't fun. They treated you like a little animal. I spent a lot of time in isolation, and being so young, it really impacted me. I just wanted to get out and get even. I didn't know who to get even with or how to get even, but that's what I wanted. I ended up getting even with myself.

The drinking really took off around 18 years old while I was stealing wine and beer out of small stores around Oregon City, where we mostly grew up. Then, when I turned 21, I married my high school sweetheart. We started having kids, and I continued drinking. This was when I learned I could work a full-time job and sell marijuana on the side. I made a little extra money that way, and we had a good living. I got arrested in the 1970s for selling and ended up in Rocky Butte Jail, which is now a McMenamin's Pub/Restaurant. It was pretty scary in there. I only stayed a couple of nights, and then they moved me into a work-release program. After that bust, I took some time off and got in no trouble for a long time. Then, when my marriage went sour, I got divorced. I ended up downtown, where I worked at a galvanizing plant over in northwest Portland. Heavy drinking. Heavy drinking. Finally, I was introduced to cocaine, methamphetamines, and then heroin. This was in the early 1980s. From that point on it was downhill, with no turning back.

I was homeless and strung out on heroin. My ex-wife gave me the dog, my tools, my toy train set, and my van. That was it. I lost my three kids, who stayed with their mother. There hadn't been much parenting on my part during the addiction piece, anyway. I'd steal anything. I'd break the windows out of cars and take stereos, purses, or anything left on the seat. Or, I'd break into apartments. I started to meet people downtown who were doing the same thing, in the same predicament as me. For a while, I lived in my van. I still had my job and saved up enough money to start dealing drugs again. This time, it was methamphetamines. I had a little apartment up on Northwest Twenty-third Avenue, where I met a girl who was a heroin addict and prostitute. Everything went down the tube. I lost my apartment, lost my regular job, and lost my drug-dealing job. Again, I was on the streets. I didn't know what to do, so I started collecting cans for the deposit money and breaking into cars. The police got to know me pretty well. Every time they saw me, they'd search me, take what I had, and put me in jail.

Unlike most guys, I didn't live under any of the city bridges. There, everyone fights over the scavenged goods. Instead, I took the No. 20 bus from downtown out to Cedar Hills Boulevard in Washington County. I found a spot under an overpass to Highway 26. I kept a gun I'd found hidden in the rocks. No one bothered me there, and I felt pretty safe. At the time, I thought I was a pretty lucky guy and that my setup was a good one.

I'd get up in the morning and go canning. I'd cash in what I'd found and then go to a nearby Greek restaurant and lounge. I'd set my camp up right near a bunch of apartments. The folks

I met in the lounge just thought I was one of their neighbors. Sometimes, I'd get a free drink or even a meal. I was actually breaking into their apartments and picking through the apartment complex's dumpster. I went in and out of treatment—over and over and over again. I never stayed in any of the programs. The only person I was hurting was me.

One day, I was sitting in the Oregon State Correction Intake Center in Oregon City waiting to go to prison again. That's when I realized that all the people I was blaming for my problems weren't going into the cell with me. I understood that the only person sitting there ready to go to jail again was me! What a horrible realization. I was guilty of everything I was being charged with, plus a lot more. After I did the time in prison, I went into treatment. I thought, *What the hell, I've been clean for 60 days. I don't need treatment.* But I went to the Volunteers of America's program anyway, just to see what it was. Plus, I was sick and tired of my parole officer hounding me. I went there, and it changed my whole life! I'm now 10 years clean and sober!

This time, I graduated from the VOA's treatment program and went back to support the guys who were still there. I took them out to coffee, to support groups, and to 12-step meetings. The staff talked me into going to Portland Community College to become an alcohol and drug counselor. I took twice as long to get through the program as other folks because I only attended two classes at a time. My test scores going into the program were low, so I had to complete a lot of prerequisites. I succeeded in the program and earned my certificate as a certified alcohol and drug counselor (CADC). I'm also qualified as a certified mental health associate.

When the case manager's job at Central City Concern became available, I applied and got the job. I worked in the streets using a model called ACT (Assertive Community Treatment). We work with the homeless on the streets or under the bridges. Since I actually came from under an overpass, it was easy for me to explain that I knew how they felt. I showed people a mug shot of myself from jail. I keep the photo pinned above my desk to help others see me as one of them. I am not some snot-nosed college kid who went to school on my parent's dime. I can tell them that I struggled all the way through. I can also tell them that I have a wife and a nice apartment in a building that I manage. Most of the guys I work with here at Central City Concern are like the old me.

I love being down here on Northwest Davis Street because I actually know what it feels like being strung out on the streets. I have struggled with depression and post-traumatic stress disorder—not clinical depression, but definitely situational. I'd say most homeless people suffer from depression, grief, and PTSD. Part of the grief comes from loved ones and friends who no longer trust them or want them around, unless, by some miracle, it's to pay back money they owe.

I'm a Christian. I was raised in a Community of Christ Church. My mother was a church pianist. She didn't drink, smoke, or swear. My addiction pulled me away from religion for a good 30 years. I believe recovery is a gift from God. I believe God's help is available to each and every one of us, provided that we are willing to do the footwork. I showed up back at church about eight years ago. I've been leading a spiritual 12-step group since I went back to a church at Northeast Forty-eighth and Couch. The people there understand addiction and are open to helping folks help themselves, whether their addiction is alcohol, drugs, gambling, codependency, or something else.

One of the people who really helped me was Al F., who died earlier this year of emphysema. He was one of my counselors at VOA. Like other counselors, he said the same thing to me as I say to the folks here: "I've been there." At Central City Concern, I can offer folks resources beyond Alcoholics or Narcotics Anonymous. I can offer housing, mental health and medical services, alcohol and drug programs, and employment opportunities, if people choose to utilize them. The Community Engagement Program that we use is a housing-first program, followed by a list of other services. When I was out on the streets, I didn't know about any programs like this.

I believe that I'm here to help people. It's not always easy. But I try to go with the flow. In my last four years of home and street visits, I've found several dead people! I think it's something I'm supposed to experience, though. I don't know why. I just assume that it's part of my life work, my journey. I've learned how to accept people for who, what, and how they are.

I used to drive my custom Dodge van down Burnside, passing all the homeless folks and drunks. I'd say to myself, *That's never going to happen to me.* Well, guess what? Everything I said wouldn't happen to me did happen. It didn't just happen to me; it happened in the worst possible way! I said I'd never overdose. Well, I've overdosed and have been hospitalized five or six times. I said I'd never be homeless. I became homeless and lived in the same doorways as the folks I used to drive by. I've lived under bridges [overpasses] and everything else. It's made me humble. I'm grateful today that there are so many services at my disposal that I can present to others. Anyone can offer services to people, but many are too untrusting of the system to take advantage of them. That's when I might have to walk clients to their first appointment and show them no strings are attached. If they start on the right road, this program works miracles. People who no one else could deal with have come to Central City Concern and are now housed and doing well.

They aren't frequent flyers in and out of the emergency wards or the detox centers or the jails. Once people get into recovery, it's our responsibility to point out to them just how far they've come: "Wow, you've really made some progress here!" Getting a mentally ill person stabilized into recovery is a huge undertaking! There are certain ways to detox them first, stabilize them secondly, and then talk recovery. Some folks are hopeless; we can't talk to them or do anything with or for them. In the motivational-style interview, we use their progress to motivate them to continue in the right direction. If we can get them to stay in recovery on a weekly basis, we show them the leaps and bounds they're making. They don't often see it. Once they have a few months behind them, their progress becomes apparent as something phenomenal that they've accomplished.

All the years that I was out there, ripping and running, I never heard about recovery. I didn't know the word until 1997, when I went into treatment. I was 45 at the time and completely baffled by how people were getting clean and staying clean. There were AA meetings at the treatment center (VOA), but I couldn't figure out what those men were meeting for because it didn't have anything to do with the treatment I was receiving. I thought they must be homosexual, looking for men to pick up. It turns out that they were practicing the 12 steps of AA. Later, I got my sponsor and my support group from those same guys. The group thought my prior conclusion about their meetings was hilarious. They came together to share their recovery with the new guys to help us get clean and sober. When I think back on it now, I realize just how lost I was. Where once the word *recovery* meant nothing to me, today it's the most important word in my vocabulary and in my whole life.

I married a woman I met as a result of my addiction. She was in the women's Volunteers of American recovery program while I was in the men's. She now works for the VOA. We both sponsor people in AA and NA. We both take part in our own recovery program, but we don't interfere with each other's. We also have a program that we work together. I've reconciled with my three kids, so they are a big part of my life today. It took quite a while for them to trust me. I have two daughters, age 33 and 26. My son is 28. I wasn't a good example for him, and he's followed in some of my footsteps, like drinking. I hope, one day that he'll grow up and be clean and sober. One thing I want my kids, and everyone else, to know is that no matter what's been said, people *can* change. I'm a living example of such change. Even though the kids' mother is a late-stage alcoholic now, there's still hope for her.

In spite of my 32 years of drinking and using, here I am, now a counselor. I own a couple of cars and manage an apartment building. I have a wife and grandchildren. Throughout all those years of addiction, all the pain and suffering, I never gave up hope. I used to pray for heroin, and I used to get it. So I knew God answered prayers. I'm not so sure I was in search of a better life when I was using, but I ended up finding one. I loathe admitting that it was the Department of Corrections, the hated jail, which turned my life around! However, I'm happy that I went through yet another treatment program. Now, I know. I'd like to say to people who were as lost as I was, don't give up. A wonderful life awaits, and it's a surprisingly easier one.

Love, Carl D.

Like Carl, many recovering people I spoke to while working on this book shared experiences of post-traumatic stress disorder. The American Psychological Association describes PTSD as follows:

> Posttraumatic stress disorder (PTSD), a debilitating disorder involving intrusive thoughts associated with traumatic events, affecting millions of Americans. First known as "shell shock" and seen in WWI veterans, PTSD often involves flashbacks and nightmares following a traumatic experience, including traffic accidents. Many of these symptoms first surface many months after the trauma.[19] (1)

I believe this definition wraps itself around the homeless-poor, the addicted, and the alcoholic and that it intrudes, and may even exacerbate, when people enter recovery and find housing. Chapter 2 is evidence of how it affects many who finally have a roof overhead. PTSD pounces on its (formerly homeless) victims when they no longer live in hypervigilant states and are confronted with the first silence and peace they've experienced in years. It demands introspection, something hard to avoid when alone and safe.

Carl's abusive, traumatic experiences in and out of reform school as a youth as well as his crisis of divorce, the loss of his children, homelessness and addiction more than meet the PTSD diagnosis, in my opinion. Through each of the narrator's stories, we witness trauma. Suffering from PTSD makes recovery more challenging, as it influences recidivism. Many people interviewed are currently in counseling of one sort or another.

---

19 Copyright 2008 © by the American Psychological Association. Reprinted with permission. *Exposure Therapy Helps PTSD Victims Overcome Trauma's Debilitating Effects.* http://www.psychologymatters.org/keane.html.

Through extensive training, Carl D. has developed into a skilled listener. And although we can never truly know another person, nor integrate their experience into our own, we can empathize with and companion them as Carl does at Central City Concern. He recognizes and acknowledges people's brokenness, cheers their progress, and makes himself available by his presence and invitation to listen.

Listening isn't as simple as it sounds. Active listening takes practice. Mastery demands that we become comfortable with silence. Silence makes most people uncomfortable, and they rush to fill in the empty space with words and questions. Will Rogers once said, "Never miss a good opportunity to shut up!" I agree, and when I'm with someone, I do my best to regard any silence as sacred. It could be that the person is taking time to reflect and gather their thoughts before speaking. If I interject too soon, I might deprive them of a life-affirming insight. I'm nowhere near mastery of listening, but I keep practicing and encouraging others to do the same, especially in the presence of the bewildered, the fearful, the grieving, the remorseful, and the self-disclosing. When I truly listen, I know that I validate and affirm the other. This is what is called the gift of presence, which affirms their right to come to their own conclusions and insights. I don't have the answers for other people's pain, but I believe their *higher self* does. If I remain wordless, yet attentive, the other person might just hear that *still-small voice* of wisdom that transmutes the most grievous of pain.

CHAPTER II

The Face Of The Homeless

The poor teach me that serving them is not just some sort of Christian imperative. Rather, it is in serving them that I can discover, like the church, what is best in my own heart.
—GARY SMITH, SJ, *Radical Compassion (Chapter 7)*

My spiritual program requires serving. In this way, I discover, like Gary Smith, what is best in my own heart. I call it *prayer with feet.* For more than 10 years, I volunteered with hospice programs through two of Portland's hospital systems—Providence/St. Vincent's and Legacy Emanuel Visiting Nurses Association. Every week, I worked from two to four hours, either as a respite care volunteer or as a volunteer chaplain. The dying concretely taught me to live fully, to devour the preciousness of the moment, to readily reconcile any transgressions, and to love and thank people every day. But, more profoundly, they taught me about innocence.

Something happened to me whenever I was near the terminally ill and still does. It's as if their histories and transgressions dissipate. When I walk through the doorway to their room, I offer my hand to innocence itself. I recall one patient whose family revealed some of his most heinous behavior, including sexual abuse of one daughter. I'd listened to him review his life, sharing his Korean prisoner of war stories. We routinely prayed the rosary, and I brought him Holy Communion—all of this prior to the family's intimate revelations. After learning he'd abused his daughter, I recall hesitating before reentering his room. Trying to make sense out of what I'd just heard, I asked myself, *What am I suppose to do with this information?* While I hesitated, I heard that *still-small voice* of compassion say, "This man is the same man he was the last time you were in his room. He isn't his past behavior. In this hour, day, month of his dying, he is innocence itself." Smiling to myself, I proceeded to his bedside and sat with him in silence.

My spiritual mission is one of serving the dying and the marginalized, not about judging or directing. My caring must be bigger than someone's faults; it must be unconditional. I prayed for this man and his family, and ultimately, his abused daughter confronted him. As only God can do, they reconciled prior to his death.

Whether someone is terminally ill, addicted and living under a bridge, just moving into an SRO, or whatever laden position they find themselves in, I am reminded of their inner core—their innocence. When life beats us up and we are tossed out into the wilderness, we become vulnerable and frightened like children. Jesus said, "Let the little children come to me, and do not hinder them, for the kingdom of heaven belongs to such as these."[20] I

---

20 Matthew 19:14.(NIV)

believe it's in our nature to physically or metaphorically draw ourselves up into fetal positions when we are fearful, and this is the perfect position for God's enfoldment. This is when God protectively whispers in our ears, "Do not be afraid." If willing to receive, these can be times of awakening, of epiphanies—mini-glimpses into the shelter of the divine heart.

The stories in this book are a testament to the innocence at the core of each one of us and evidence of the indwelling divine spark. I believe it is this spark that ultimately drags us from the blackest, bleakest place into the light and points us in the direction of our highest good. We must, however, be willing to receive, or the opportunity for transformation dissolves. When we let down our defenses, only then can God enter. This is how Carl R. found a new life; he listened, received, and was blessed with a new, purposeful life in Christ. He turned his back on the past and never looked back, except to honor and bless it as part of his evolutionary process in becoming a wholly integrated person.

WISDOM WILL OF CARL R.

Dear Friends and Family,

I was born in Minot, North Dakota, in 1954. I loved the outdoors, where I learned to cross-country ski, snowshoe, and make snow caves. I also competed in Junior Rodeo. We lived near my great grandparents, whom I loved. My father was a jack-of-all-trades-master-of-none. He'd been a country western musician, and near the end of his life, he drove trucks. There were five of us—two sisters, two brothers, and me. One brother is deceased. I have a half brother that lives here in Portland, a sister and two nieces who live in Vancouver, Washington, and a sister and mother in Kansas, where many other relatives live.

At the age of five, I was taken by my father when he and my mother separated. He dropped me off in Grand Junction, Colorado, at my aunt Leona and uncle Carl's place. I was named after my uncle. For six months, I lived in hell. Both my aunt and uncle were late-stage alcoholics. While Carl was at the bar, my aunt used me as her sex toy. Looking back, I recognize that I am who I am because of my past—the good, the bad, and the ugly. Hardships provide great learning experiences and opportunities for my personal growth.

Six months after my dad dropped me off, my mom and dad reconciled, so he came to get me. He rounded us all up and took us to Troutdale, Oregon. We lived in a beach shack during the summer of 1959. Then we moved into a bigger place on 131st and Northeast Halsey Streets in Portland, Oregon. I went to Menlo Park Grade School. In North Dakota, at the age of five, I was in first grade, but the State of Oregon put me back a grade so I'd be with kids my own age. Naturally, I was the brightest one in class.

I was in a motorcycle accident at the age of 12. I died on the scene, until the paramedics resuscitated me. For two weeks, I was in a coma. I just found out two years ago that I've been living all this time with a broken jaw. From the time I was injured until now, I've been in pain. After the accident, I began acting out. I started smoking and drinking with the guys. In my sophomore year, my grades started dropping. I hung out with the wrong people and got into trouble. I believe the motorcycle accident threw the child abuse, and everything else painful, into my subconscious.

A year after the accident, I was in a football scrimmage where someone ripped my helmet off. I butted heads with a 250-pound tackle! I knocked him on his ass and made the first touchdown of my life! The coach told me to go to the showers. Halfway across the field, I collapsed. A week later, my mother rushed me to Providence Hospital with a case of spinal meningitis. They diagnosed it just before curvature of the spine could set in. I didn't have any control over my body, and I was vomiting bile. They gave me two spinal taps. Because of the head traumas and the child abuse, I didn't understand my behavior, or even who I was.

During his life, my dad suffered even more than me. My father was Scots-Irish and Dutch-Norwegian. He was also an alcoholic, always drinking beer. My grandfather used to beat my father with a tow chain. So he joined the Marines during World War II to escape the abuse. He'd rather go to war than stay at home and suffer the cruelty.

My grandfather on my father's side was Scots-Irish and Dutch-Norwegian. My grandmother on my father's side was Blackfoot, Sioux, and Crow. My great grandmother on my mother's side was English and Welsh, and my great grandfather was full-blooded Cherokee. My grandmother on my mother's side was German. So my mother is Cherokee, German, English, and Welsh.

During my high school years, I unwittingly let people use me. The motorcycle accident made me crave attention, especially love. There hadn't been any in the past, and I didn't understand why. My dad left for good when I was 10. My mother had a hard life raising us kids. During my junior year in high school, I decided to join the military. Because I was excellent at roller-skating, I originally wanted to become a roller derby star. My mom discouraged this, but strangely, she signed for me to enter the military. I never understood her logic. In 1971, at age 17, I joined the Air Force. Because of my physical education classes, I was in excellent shape. My father, who had been a Marine in the South Pacific during World War II, taught me self-defense and fitness.

My first duty station in the Air Force was Atlas Air Force Base in Oklahoma. In the Military Force/Security Police, we guarded aircraft and the perimeter. A couple of incidents in the military caused my drinking to escalate. One night, a buddy of mine, a sergeant in the 443rd Security Police Squadron, played Russian roulette and ate a bullet while I was at my duty station up the hill by the aircraft and he was at the guard shack. I watched him stumble out the door—brains everywhere. I was just 17 and had never seen death. The military put me on casual duty and processed me out of the military in 1972.

After I got out of the Air Force, I wandered up and down the West Coast trying to find myself. Like most young people, I experimented with drugs and alcohol. However, I ran into the right people at the right time, or I wouldn't be here today. Once, I sunbathed on a nude beach for six hours and suffered second-degree burns on 100 percent of my body. That night, I had fever and shakes. A couple of hippies pulled up in an old

Chevy pickup truck, and one guy said, "Wow, man, you look burned-out!" I was halfway gone on drugs when he gave me a tab of LSD. My mind went out of my body, and that's what saved me. By not concentrating on my physical condition, I was able to heal and not feel the pain.

That hippie saved my life! I never went to the hospital but rode with the hippies to Usaw Beach in the Boise-Cascade Forest on the California coast. It was just south of the Tree of Mystery. For two weeks, I kicked back with this bunch of outlaws, drug addicts, and alcoholics. I drank wine and smoked dope. My drug of choice was alcohol; I was never addicted to drugs. After two weeks, I went out behind a tree and, with the help of another guy, peeled off my backside in one piece!

I reentered the military from 1977 to 1986 via the Oregon Army National Guard. The first five years I was in the infantry with the Gresham Army National Guard. I was good at what I did—small arms expert, demolition, sniper. I was trained in all those areas. I was a good soldier. In 1986, during the Iran-Contra situation, I went to Honduras. I even ran into Lieutenant Colonel Oliver North twice—once on the breezeway and once in the mess hall.

Honduras was a cultural shock for me. The people lived in mud shacks with no windows and only dirt floors. They used donkeys for transportation and sold their goods at the front door. We brought in four C141s full of supplies and weapons. After three weeks in the temporary duty station, we came back to the United States.

All the while my alcoholism continued. I couldn't function anymore. I didn't understand why I was so emotional or why I couldn't act like other people. I was always drunk and then getting in trouble. I got my ass beat up in a lot of fights. With a glass jaw, I always lost. I sought help from our battalion chaplain. He suggested that I go to the Salvation Army and seek help for my alcoholism, which I did. I relapsed once and almost died of alcohol poisoning.

I lost a job because of it. While remodeling an old colonial house, I went to a bar on my first payday and spent my whole check getting drunk. I came back and slept in the house I was remodeling. When my boss showed up, the whites of my eyes were blood-red from alcohol poisoning. My boss said, "I can't use you anymore," and fired me. I went into the backyard, put all my gear under a sheet of Visqueen plastic, laid out my sleeping bag, and crawled in. For 24 hours, I detoxed. I went through DTs, hallucinations, shakes, shimmers, and lost 10 pounds. You could have wrung out my sleeping bag. That's when I hit bottom. I had a spiritual awakening. I knew that I'd either have to quit drinking or die. That was December 5, 1981. I haven't had a drink since the first five years I went to the Salvation Army. They put me in their Harbor Light dormitory, where homeless people stay. Since I'd relapsed, the captain was leery. He wanted to be sure I was sober and serious about entering their recovery program a second time. He let me in, and I finished the program and stayed clean.

For five years, I worked as a custodian at Harbor Light, the treatment and recovery center sponsored by the Salvation Army. Then, in 1986, I left for Kansas to be closer to my grandparents, who were getting on in years. I lived in Wichita for two winters and then moved to Des Moine, Iowa, where my sister lived. At the time, I didn't know she was a cocaine addict. With our Native American, Scottish, and Irish ancestry, we inherited addictions and aggressive behavior; however, I didn't get into cocaine, even though my sister tried to con me into using it. Instead, I worked a year in a plastics plant. Got my finances together. Bought a car. Everything was looking good.

I was clean and sober. At the end of the year, I decided to move back to Oregon.

On my way back, I stopped in Kansas to see my grandparents. By then my grandfather was dying of cancer. He was a very strong man, and he wanted me to continue my journey to the West Coast. He was more of a mentor than anyone else in my life. He taught me how to play golf. He taught me roofing, and I became a journeyman roofer. We were good buddies. After my motorcycle accident at 12, I had an out-of-body experience, floating above my body and watching while the paramedics worked on me. From then on, I knew there was a spiritual world. I experienced a number of spiritual epiphanies during my youth. So when my grandfather died, I knew he'd be okay. He was going to heaven. Once I went to an Apache wedding, used peyote, and had a vision of a Silver Phoenix. Owls and phoenixes sometimes mean death.

Sometimes, in my dreams, I talk with both my father and grandfather. My father died when I was 18. At the time, I was working on an oil derrick in Muskogee, Oklahoma. My uncle worked on the tower, rough-necking. One day, the driller came to work drunk, and the clutch and the brake slipped as well as the kelley, the machinery that forces the drilling pipe down. My uncle yelled to me, "Watch out!" I jumped out of the way just before the two-ton piece of machinery hit the floor deck! Again, I avoided death. The next morning, my uncle woke me up to tell me my father had died during the night. Coincidence?

I went back to Colorado after my dad died. The family was in chaos. Nothing had changed; it was the same dysfunctional family. My uncle Carl was still there, but my aunt Leona, who abused me, had died from cirrhosis of the liver. There was never a chance for me to make amends with my dad in any way or obtain his forgiveness. Because Leona had died, I didn't have the chance to confront her about the abuse or find closure. Later on, I wrote a good-bye letter to Leona and burned it, which helped.

Apparently, my father and the relatives on his side of the family weren't very well respected. After visiting my dad's grave, I went on up to the monument, which is a plateau above the Colorado River, just outside Grand Junction. There were about five pickups and cars up there. Some young men got out of the vehicles with guns. One of them put a .45 to my head and said, "You're going to get out of town, now!" My father's family owned a second-hand salvage company and had been ripping people off. I'm the spitting image of my father, so they thought I was him. I told them, "Yes, sir, I'm going." I confronted my grandmother about it, and she said, "It's none of your business!" There's a .45 to my head, and it's none of my business? So I left Grand Junction, Colorado, and I haven't been back since.

Later on, my father's brother Robert wrote to ask me for power of attorney because my grandmother had died. I had no problem with that at all. I didn't want anything to do with them. "All the money and the property—you can have it! I don't care." That was the end of my contact with my father's family. Everyone in Old Town, here in Portland, is more or less my family. I'm known here as Papa, Grandpa, Daddy, or Dad. I'm also considered a character, and I'm proud of that.

I first started going to Alcoholics Anonymous and then went to Narcotics Anonymous because alcohol is a drug, too. I completed the 12 steps. My counselor became my sponsor, the best sponsor I could have. The last time I used involved smoking a joint in 1991. I had to be honest about my recovery, so I got right back into recovery and changed my clean date to September 7, 1991. AA and NA changed my life. The people who came to the meetings, clean or not, became my family because I didn't have a family. I didn't know what love was.

I didn't know the difference between lust and love. I didn't know anything about unconditional love. I've never married nor had children, so I didn't understand what true love was. I didn't love myself. My parent's love meant being there for me financially and providing a roof over my head, but there was no kissing or hugging in my family, no saying, "I love you," or anything close to it. The people in AA and NA loved me when I couldn't love myself. They taught me that I'm not the problem, but I can be the solution. If I followed the steps in the book of AA and NA and gave my will and my life over to the care of God, then I'd be okay.

Today, I feel wonderful. I love myself. Nobody needs to fix me. Today, I enjoy friends whom I've seen grow from childhood to adulthood, and they love me. Some people, when they graduated from high school, have come to see me with their graduation photographs and big hugs. It's just like having my own big family. At Sisters of the Road Café, it's the same thing. There are a lot of men and women out there on the street who are still children because they didn't grow up emotionally. Since I was an abused child, I understand where they are coming from. When I learned self-love, I started to grow emotionally and spiritually by giving away what I have received. This is what I do daily. It's made me the man I am today.

I'm on Social Security Disability from my motorcycle accident at age 12. The injuries were reactivated when I was a body builder in 1996. At the time, I was working with the U.S. Postal Service and training to go to the Tri-County Body Building Championships. I would have shown first, second, or third because this was the master's division. There weren't any old farts out there that were as well built as me. However, I over-lifted on the shrug machine. I was working on my neck and shoulders, lifting 350 pounds. You could hear the snap in my neck clear across the gym! After the motorcycle accident, two discs were fused together in my neck. Lifting in the gym that day unfused them. Now I have degenerative disc disease in my neck and problems with spinal stenosis of the pelvis. I also have arthritis in my spine and many of my joints. I have hepatitis C from a one-time drug use with my little brother. He's deceased now. He died with a needle in his arm at age 35. He lived a fast life and died just as fast.

I didn't know much about grief before recovery because I didn't understand or acknowledge my feelings. I was blocked until recovery, when I gave my will and my life over to my higher power, who can take care of things. I can't.

It took four years to receive my disability pay. While I waited, I lived on nothing at the Sally McCracken SRO. That's when I first started going to Sisters of the Road and met Genny Nelson. She was a Godsend and an angel. I love her so much. After I was at Sisters for a few months, Genny asked me to be on the board of directors so I could help people. I was honored for the opportunity to look beyond myself and really help others.

I was on the board for three years; I worked on development and different activities of running Sisters of the Road. Genny is excellent at what she does, which includes starting Crossroads. This is about organizing people to cause systemic change for everyone's betterment, not just a few. Crossroads has defended and supported inclusiveness for many years now. Just recently, when Genny Nelson won a National Caring Award, she dedicated the award to all the people who work and volunteer at Sisters. That simple act boosted everyone's morale.

Now, I work as a member of the board of directors for the Old Town/Chinatown Neighborhood Association, on the Public Safety Committee. Sometimes I attend the Vision Committee meetings. What I do for Old Town/Chinatown at the neighborhood association meetings is to share my life experiences with those who are unaware of homelessness and addictions in order to encourage solutions. For instance, people who do not understand homeless people or people in recovery often fear them.

What I've done is sit across the table from people of stature and power in business, religious groups, and politics to let them know what a homeless person is. I am a homeless person. My persona, my soul, and my whole life is right in front of them. What I put out, people see. Their perception of me is what a homeless person or person in recovery is like. Not all are exactly alike, but I represent their face. Once a person understands what's occurring, they can't go back to ignoring it. For example, there was a lady I helped by letting her stay overnight at my place and use the shower to clean up. After taking a nap, she left my apartment with my whole collection of DVDs. She was still in her addiction. When I see her now, I don't have to say a word to her. I just look at her. Behind her eyes, I can see the festering of what she did. She does have a conscience—and so do the people I teach from across the table at the neighborhood association meetings.

My hopes and prayers for the future are for men to change from being good ole boys—only sissies cry—to being real human beings. I want both men and women to let children be children. Let them grow up and know what unconditional love is, without taking away their innocence, because this only perpetuates the abuse cycle. I never want to see another child go through what I did. That's one of the reasons I focus more on women, because a woman abused me. A gay man also raped me when I was 16, but that wasn't half as bad as the sexual abuse I suffered at five years old at the hands of my aunt. I lost my childhood.

I want to be known for helping women and children to love themselves so they can love others and for helping men get in touch with their feelings and open up. I'd like to be remembered as a caring person, who was a character and one who helped people get their lives back together. I want to be remembered as someone who taught others to love themselves and each other.

With Love, Carl R.

Carl is not the only veteran who has experienced homelessness. The National Coalition for Homeless Veterans note that on any single night there are nearly 68,000 homeless vets living on the streets. However, on December 13, 2011, the Department of Veterans Affairs and Housing and Urban Development announced that a new national report showed that homelessness among Veterans was reduced by nearly 12 percent between January 2010 and January 2011. The 12 percent decline keeps the Obama Administration on track to meet the goal of ending Veteran homelessness by the year 2015.

In a given year, 3.5 million people (1.35 million of whom are children) will experience homelessness. [21] Over and over, the people I talked with told me that most of us are just one paycheck away from taking up residence under a bench, in a

---

21 http://lahsc.org/wordpress/educate/statistics/ united-states-homeless-statistics/

building entrance, or in a car. Lack of jobs and poverty increase the chances of becoming homeless, especially among alcoholics and drug addicts.

Addictive disorders appear disproportionately among the homeless population, but by themselves, they don't explain the increase in homelessness. After all, most alcoholics and addicts are not homeless, though people who are both poor and addicted are at high risk. Low-income housing is scarce, which leaves those people suffering from addiction, disabilities, and mental illnesses more likely to lose out. They have no other option but street living.[22]

Carl calls himself the face of the homeless for the Old Town/Chinatown Neighborhood Association and the Public Safety Committee. He is one of the first formerly homeless people they've ever met. Simply by telling them his story, he awakens them to the reality of the poor, the homeless, the alcoholic, the drug-addicted, and the mentally ill who inhabit our streets. Through education, he humanizes his brothers and sisters. Knowledge is the beginning of our understanding, and when we understand, we can no longer feign blindness. Under the right conditions, this becomes the catalyst for change.

Carl is one of the prophets from skid row fighting for the rights of men, women, and children who face unimaginable tragedy, but who still deserve the opportunity for basic human rights and needs, including the kindness of strangers. I often see Carl outside of Sisters of the Road or in the area tooling down the sidewalk in his wheelchair. His mere presence commands respect. Carl *is a character* and one hard to ignore.

---

22 National Coalition for the Homeless 2201 P. St. NW, Washington, DC 20037. Website:
    http://www.nationalhomeless.org/factsheets/who.html

CHAPTER 12

Everlasting Friendship

> Compassion is not a relationship between the healer and the wounded. It's a relationship between equals. Only when we know our own darkness well can we be present with the darkness of others. Compassion becomes real when we recognize our shared humanity.
>
> —PEMA CHODRON

This chapter is dedicated to Don Looney and all the mentally ill people who live or have lived on the streets of America. Staggering numbers of the mentally ill are living on the streets, in part due to their deinstitutionalization, which began in 1955. In her *Newsweek* article, "A Secret Mission on the Streets,"[23] author Danielle Steel elucidates not only the reasons but the difficulty this poses for people with mental impairments.

---

23 June 23, 2008.

[…] The incidence of mental illness is extremely high, believed to affect 85 percent of the homeless population. Self-medication in the form of alcohol and street drugs is common. Programs that offer assistance are understaffed and underfunded. And for people already mentally disordered, filling out forms and wading through miles of red tape for benefits is not only daunting, but impossible. The wait for detox is long. Many of those people will be dead before they get in. It's a tragic reality on the streets.

As challenging as it was to live with a mentally ill mother, I often wonder what would have happened to our family if my father had died young, or even divorced Mama. We were already poor, and Mama was too debilitated for employment. My siblings and I may have ended up on the streets, just like so many other families today. Mama's brother Harvey was an alcoholic and lived on skid row in Portland for a time. Once, Papa said he saw him huddled up on a curb, nursing a bottle of booze from inside a paper bag. None of us kids ever knew him as our uncle, and at the time, we hadn't an inkling that our brothers Gary and Michael would follow so closely in his footsteps.

Even though, as a family, we escaped the streets, the de-institutionalization of the mentally ill affected us. After my father died and Damasch State Mental Hospital in Wilsonville, Oregon, closed, my sister and I carried the burden of finding help for Mama when she was assaulted by psychotic depression. When this occurred, Mama became immobilized with guilt and self-loathing. And even though we knew the events she reported were nonsense, they were very real to her. Sometimes, she'd think herself a murderess and that the police or FBI were seeking her. We often found scraps of paper stuffed into the pockets of her clothing with the suicide prevention hotline number written on them. Mama's fear of going straight to hell kept her from killing herself, but she was obsessed with the thought during unstable times. Mama sorely suffered, and witnessing it was incredibly painful.

At times, it took my sister and me 24 hours or more to find care for her. Each hospital required her to endure a complete physical. After its completion, they'd inform us they didn't have room for her in their psych ward, and they'd refer us to another hospital that embraced a similar protocol. On top of that, no one believed that we, her daughters, women who'd lived with Mama from birth, could accurately diagnose a psychotic depression. We knew Mama's only hope, or relief from the ferociousness of her disease, lay in the hands of competent psychiatric care. Getting her admitted was ever a challenge, but today, thinking about the obstacles the mentally ill on the streets must surmount to get proper care staggers the imagination. There are some wonderful advocacy programs in Portland, though—namely The National Alliance on Mental Illness (NAMI) and Central City Concern. And if the homeless find and link up with them, they do receive help and hope.

Unfortunately, my family hadn't discovered NAMI when Mama was alive. It would have been so comforting had we known about it. NAMI fights to improve the wellness and quality of life of mental illness sufferers. NAMI purports mental illness shouldn't be a hindrance to anyone in terms of living a full and productive life. This is a far cry from how mental illness is generally perceived in our culture, even today. With NAMI's expansive mission to bring understanding and improved care for those who suffer from mental illness, I believe the stigma worn so bravely by the mentally ill will one day pale.

I met Judy Redler Winter through my friend Mary Sue Richen, formerly of the Macdonald Residence. Some years ago, Judy came to the Macdonald Residence at the invitation of Mary Sue to speak about mental illness and to assist the staff and volunteers in providing the best care possible to the mentally ill residing at the residence and those struggling on the streets.

I met Judy at her Clackamas County Chapter of NAMI office to interview her for this book, but her preference was to tell the story of her mentally ill godson, Don Looney, and the impact he had on her life as well as many others. In the past, Don lived on Portland's streets. This is her godson's legacy story.

WISDOM STORY OF DON LOONEY (1961-2006)

As told by Judy Redler Winter

In God's mysterious and wise way, a desolate 38-year-old man discovered a nurturing woman old enough to be his mother. This convergence amazes me because he and I walked in such very different worlds.

Don L. began living on the streets at the age of 12, out of fear he might kill his father. The man was an alcoholic who raised his son on "the juice," beginning with a bottle of spiked formula when Don arrived home from the hospital. Don's father had a series of wives and stepchildren, all of whom he abused in various ways. Don's dream about killing his dad made him decide to leave before the dream materialized.

Life on the streets was not kind to Don. He fell into IV drug use and was frequently a victim of those pretending to help. Around age 24, Don's suicide rope in the Portland Park Blocks was too long. A passerby found him dangling, but not dead. He cut Don free and took him to his home to clean up and have a good meal. Then he proceeded to rape Don! Subsequent years on the streets were just as cruel.

As a young adult, Don managed to find work as a skilled cook and hairdresser. He even developed a successful routine as a female impersonator. Over the years, he made lasting friends, but alcoholism squelched all of his prospects. He began having delusions, and he agreed he could benefit from some mental health intervention; however, the clinic required him to clean up his addictions before they could help him. The addiction clinics labeled him mentally ill, insisting he get treatment for his condition before they would accept him for detoxification. What a dilemma.

Believing that he was imperious to death, Don planned to jump off the Burnside Bridge and become a spiritual being, immune to addictions. Since he wouldn't need his belongings, he loaded them into a shopping cart with the intention of donating them to the St. Vincent de Paul Society. At 2:00 a.m., before heading off to the bridge, Don proceeded to entertain the neighborhood with loud renditions of hymns. The Portland Police quickly deposited him in the Multnomah County Jail for disturbing the peace.

There, Don continued his loud serenading. The other inmates, wishing to sleep, complained, "Tell him to shut up." The jailers who were appreciative of Don's talent slipped notes into his cell with specific song requests. In a few days, the nurse, during a routine medical assessment, suggested Don take his medication. Don argued that he didn't take drugs for any reason. He didn't realize that they were offering him psychotropic meds. Finally, hoping that by complying with their requests, he would be let out of solitary confinement and given regular (not paper) clothes to wear, along with a blanket to keep him warm, Don took the meds. In a couple of days, they started to work, and Don awoke from a world of black and white to one of living color.

Unfortunately, lacking the stable housing and medical clinic connection to continue with his medication, Don soon resumed his addictions. In his late thirties, he entered the Hooper Detox Center. After he was stabilized, Hooper arranged for Don to stay at the Estate Hotel with his own room and bed. He rarely left the safety of that nest, fearing if he got locked out of his room, he would be back on the streets again.

One day, however, he did venture out, where he noticed a poster announcing tryouts for an experimental theater involving persons with mental illness as actors. Going to this tryout would at least provide him a little entertainment and distraction in his boring life. A number of street people were there reading lines and singing songs from *My Fair Lady*. Don enjoyed the process of singing at the tryout, but didn't expect to be selected.

Pauline Furness, a retired social worker and also a former NYC Rockette dancer, founded the theater featuring mentally ill persons. She had collaborated with the president of the National Alliance on Mental Illness in Clackamas County (NAMI-CC), who participated in the Portland Opera. They were assisted by me and a mental health worker from Clackamas County who had loved theater for years, a retired music teacher from St. Mary's High School in Portland, and a retired drama teacher from Portland Public Schools with mentally ill family members. Together, we formed In a Different Light Theater Group (IADL), intending for audiences to recognize the actors as talented individuals instead of mental patients, hence "in a different light."

Don didn't have a telephone, so Barbara Hollcraft, the director of In a Different Light, had problems contacting him. However, she finally connected with Don's sister, who brought him the message that he qualified for the lead role in the musical production. About that time, one of Don's old friends invited him to live with him in Oregon City. This friend had recently become a single father and needed Don to watch over his two young children while he worked nights. Thus, Don gained an "in-kind" job and a home all at once. He also became acquainted with Clackamas County Mental Health, who linked Don up to Social Security Disability so he could receive benefits. He was thus able to resume buying and taking his psychotropic meds. Life was finally becoming secure for Don as he attended rehearsals for In a Different Light and served as "mom" to his friend's children.

Shortly after the first successful production of In a Different Light,[24] I suggested to Don that he attend a training sponsored by NAMI-CC called In Our Own Voice: Living with Mental Illness (IOOV). People in this program who are coping with mental illness are trained to speak to the public about their journey to recovery. Don proved successful in telling his life story to audiences around the state.

I frequently provided the transportation and introduction for IOOV speakers, including Don. One night, on the way home, Don asked me about the Catholic Church, having noticed I was a member. During his years on the street, he had often taken refuge from the elements in Catholic churches. He admitted a secret desire to become a member of the church in which he felt God's warm, loving presence all those difficult years. I recommended he speak with the pastor at St. John's near his home in Oregon City. After he did so he began RCIA. He invited me to attend with him and to be his sponsor. I accepted with trepidation, realizing how different our backgrounds were and wondering what my husband, John, would think of the whole matter.

During the next eight months, from September through April, I picked up Don for the weekly classes at St. John's. I had converted 40 years earlier, when I married a Catholic. At that time, since the church was not offering a series of instruction classes, I had only a few one-on-one sessions with a priest, so this in-depth instruction at St. John's was proving very educational for me as well as for Don. When the *Catholic Sentinel* heard about Don's RCIA participation at St. John's, they did a front-page feature story on Don and me and our NAMI connection.

---

24 IADL performances were taken all over the state for a couple of years, then modified to talent shows that continued to travel.

Together, we grew in faith and in our relationship. By the time of Don's baptism and confirmation at the Easter Vigil Mass in 2003, each of us had found a personal, unmet need fulfilled in the other. Don had discovered the mother he never knew (his birth mom spent most of her adult life in mental hospitals). I was touched by Don's appreciation and his transformation into a devout Catholic. In turn, his enthusiasm inspired me to become a better Catholic.

Don continued to make many IOOV presentations. He also became a member of the board of directors for NAMI-CC and its state branch. In 2002, he, along with three other speakers, was awarded a scholarship to attend the national NAMI convention in Cincinnati, Ohio, where our local IOOV group was recognized for outstanding work. Previously that year, the national group had updated its information video, featuring Don as one of its seven IOOV speakers. So he was considered a celebrity by other IOOV participants in Cincinnati. Don's spirit lives on with each showing of the IOOV video. In it, he continues to reassure viewers that "we're not monsters, we're not killers, we are just ordinary people with a little higher hurdle to jump."

In addition to his instructions in the Catholic Church and NAMI work, Don was also attending Clackamas Community College to earn his General Education Degree (GED). Several NAMI leaders came to Don's graduation in June 2003, a very proud day for all of us. He was part of a presentation on drug and alcohol addiction given at the state NAMI conference in May 2003. In June, he presented at the National NAMI conference in Minneapolis as the NAMI consumer (person consuming MH services) representative from Oregon. I stayed home from that conference so my husband and I could complete a major remodel of our home.

Unbeknownst to any of us, Don was experimenting with "just a little" alcohol. This reality became apparent at the end of August 2003, when my husband was hospitalized due to an injury during the remodel. When I called Don from the hospital for support, I was dismayed not to reach him. The following morning, in route to the hospital to check on my husband, I stopped at Don's apartment. He was there, but behaving very strangely. I loaded him into the car and took him with me to the emergency room for assessment. That day, I tended to my husband in critical care and Don in the emergency room. At the end of the day, learning that Don's problem was extreme intoxication, I took him home while my husband was transferred to Emmanuel Trauma Hospital.

Sensing Don's increasing irresponsibility, his housemate asked him to leave. Don went to the apartment of another IOOV speaker-friend. When I brought them some food, I was shocked to see Don totally passed out. The new roommate couldn't stop him from sneaking out for beer. She and I began placing calls for assistance and learned that Don could be admitted into Hooper Detox at 7:00 a.m. the next morning.

Meanwhile, my husband was developing complications from his injuries, so I stayed at the hospital with him. Then the news came that John had suffered a stroke from a possible blood clot. None of my children were with me at the hospital, and I felt very alone. Glancing at the door, I saw Don standing there. How could it be? He was being held under lock and key at Hooper. I had to be hallucinating. But, no, Don was really there. He had requested a four-hour pass from Hooper and had taken the bus across town to be with his mom. Don was a great support during my hours of worrying whether John would be extremely handicapped or die.

After a few days, Don was released from Hooper. Having fully cooperated with the program, he was very sorrowful when others left before completing their detoxification. He vowed to come back and help others stay the course at Hooper. Back again at the Estate Hotel, he began an excellent recovery program provided by Central City Concern and the Community Empowerment Program (CEP). He spent his days receiving acupuncture, massage, medication review, and counseling while remaining in touch with me about John's recovery. During each acupuncture session, he silently prayed a rosary for John. A month after his fall, despite the extra prayers, John died of a staph infection.

John had met Don when he sang at my mother's memorial service and was very impressed by his singing ability, so I asked Don to sing at John's funeral in October 2003. In the weeks following John's death, my sons and I clung together and were essential to each other's survival. Don helped distract me by escorting me to plays and movies we both enjoyed. Don's sister, Lin, or his IADL play director, Barbara Hollcraft, often joined us.

Soon, Don qualified to move into the Mark O. Hatfield Hotel and then later moved into the Unthank Plaza apartments on Williams Avenue, near Barbara's home and her parish, Holy Redeemer. Once more, Don was featured on the front page of the *Catholic Sentinel*, as he participated in Holy Redeemer Parish's 100th anniversary. He and Barbara participated in the church choir together and in Saturday classes.

Don and I also attended the 2004 national NAMI convention in Washington, D.C., where he was sponsored by NAMI-Oregon as official consumer representative. We stayed a few days after the convention to see the sites, and Don realized a longtime dream of visiting John F. Kennedy's gravesite and viewing the Hope Diamond.

Don continued making presentations for IOOV. His favorite speaking engagement was for the Crisis Intervention Training (CIT). It was sponsored by the Clackamas County Sheriff's department for law enforcement training purposes on how to deal with mentally ill persons. The IOOV presentation was the highlight of the 40-hour training session. He frequently spoke of the six-foot-five deputy who came up to him after his first CIT presentation. With tears in his eyes, he hugged Don, saying how proud of him he was. In April 2005, Don was chosen by NAMI-Oregon to receive his training in St. Louis as Oregon's state IOOV trainer. This enabled him to be in charge of training other speakers.

Don's goal was to support himself without depending on Social Security checks. As a client of Working for Independence (WFI) in Oregon City, he received training to be a barista. While employed at the Clackamas County Administrative Office building, serving coffee, rolls, and sandwiches prepared by other persons with mental illness in the WFI program, he enjoyed connecting with his mental health professional friends. Ironically, with a 20-hour workweek, Don's meager income caused his apartment rent to rise and his food stamp benefits to decrease. In effect, he was working for nothing. So he chose to volunteer for IOOV instead of working to assist others afflicted with mental illness, loneliness, or whatever else was interfering with their happiness.

During his stay on Williams Avenue, Don established a NAMI support group at the apartments. As always, Don became fast friends with several of the other residents. By 2005, In a Different Light Theater Group advanced to scripted plays, and Don accepted a major role in Eugene O'Neil's *Fools*. In 2006, the troupe presented *Harvey*, with Don cast as Wilson, the orderly in the mental hospital. Life was good; Don was very productive and loved by all who knew him. At last, he was living out a line from one of the lyrics he used during one of his Salvation Army residence days: "To be understanding and to be understood."[25]

In October 2007, shortly after *Harvey* closed, Don presented his IOOV talk about his recovery process at the law enforcement CIT training. While he was entertaining the officers in the audience with stories of singing for the Multnomah County jailers at Multnomah County, I noticed something different about him. He actually fell asleep during the presentation. Later, Don passed it off, saying he hadn't slept well the night before. Two days later, Don did not appear at the graduation ceremony for CIT. He had a part in the role-playing during the final exam where the cops demonstrated what they learned during the training. On Saturday morning, I got a call from Don's sister, Lin, informing me that Don had been taken to the hospital after he was found unconscious in his apartment on Friday.

Although his kidneys were shutting down, doctors were able to reverse this within a couple of days. Soon, Don was talking with the many friends and family who visited him.

There was no consensus at the hospital as to what had happened to Don. Those caring for his diabetes and a heart condition thought he might have had a stroke or heart attack.

On Saturday night, Don had a wonderful visit with me, his sister, and a few other close friends. We discussed plans for his leaving the hospital and his aftercare. He gave Lin and me a wonderful hug and kiss as we left that evening. Sunday morning, Don's sister phoned to tell me Don had suffered a heart attack and was unconscious. Had a nurse not been present in the room, he would have died on the spot. Indeed, it took over ten minutes to resuscitate him and restore his breathing.

---

25 Taken from the Prayer of St. Francis of Assisi

Unfortunately, he had been deprived of oxygen for more than 10 minutes and had suffered brain damage.

Don never regained consciousness, even though friends hoped he was "taking a long rest" before awakening. After three days, his doctors suggested to his family that it was time to remove the breathing machines and let him go peacefully home. A group of longtime friends gathered with the family to make the final decision. The woman who worked with Don for years before as a nurse's aide recalled Don's concern lest patient's lives be prolonged in a vegetative state. In a way, Don had made the decision for himself. All of us gathered around his bed sadly agreed. We decided to talk and sing to him as the life support apparatus was removed. I led the group in reciting the Chaplet of Divine Mercy, which Don and I often prayed together on Fridays. This prayer is considered especially powerful when prayed in the presence of the dying so as to call down mercy from above. After a two-hour vigil, I had to leave, and Lin exited the room to go the bathroom. Just at that moment, Don chose to draw his last breath, sparing us the sight of his death.

We planned for a funeral Mass to be held at Holy Redeemer since Don was close to Father Joseph Corpora, CSC, the pastor there. He concelebrated with Father Ron Raab of the Downtown Chapel, who had recently served with Don on the Interfaith Council for Mental Health for the Archdiocese of Portland, under the direction of Dorothy Coughlin. Don's choir group, including Barbara, sang several selections. Barbara and I did the readings, which included First Corinthians Chapter 13, the passage on love, which was Don's distinguishing trait. One of the deputies of the Clackamas County Sheriff's office read her letter to Don while he was in the hospital. In it, she expressed her amazement at how he coped—no, excelled—with mental illness. She did not get through it dry-eyed. Don's picture placed beside an urn of his ashes and a large bouquet of red roses faced the congregation, a comfort to all of us.

Following the Mass, mourners gathered at a reception in the church hall. Thanks to Don's friends at NAMI, each person received a red rose in his memory. WFI supplied cookies from their catering service for the reception and then refused payment. A wonderful video, prepared by his IADL colleague, Don Moore, combined with snapshots and video clips with music were played. The most hilarious images were accompanied by, of course, melodies from *Looney Tunes* cartoons. This presentation was a comforting and fitting farewell to the man we loved and whom we'd adopted as part of our extended families.

Judy showed me the video about Don. It was so moving I wept. She told me that Don always said, "With a name like Looney, you need to develop a sense of humor fast."

These days, it is common to find bipolar folks living productively. They are just like the rest of us, trying to live out their lives with meaning and purpose. Bipolar disorder is sometimes called a "brilliant madness," because so many talented and brilliant people have endured its sting. In fact, actress Patty Duke wrote a book about her experiences with the condition called *A Brilliant Madness: Living With Manic-Depressive Illness*. Today, one rarely hears the words manic-depressive, as the most common name for it now is bipolar disorder.

As the scientific community develops new and more effective interventions, perhaps society will cease stigmatizing the mentally ill and will see them as people like themselves who just happen to have different health challenges. As Don Looney used to say, "We're not monsters, we're not killers, we're just ordinary people with a little higher hurdle to jump." And those suffering on the streets have even higher hurdles to leap.

All of us need to advocate for the care of the mentally ill, especially those who are homeless. Try to imagine how terrifying it would be living on the streets with mental illness. In so doing, you'll realize that Don's story is nothing short of astounding—one filled with hope for other homeless, mentally ill people. His story is proof that people can thrive in spite of their mental illnesses and that a productive, meaningful life can be found from the street up.

PART ii

CHAPTER 13 - 1970

WISH I COULD SERVE 'EM LIKE MY SISTER KATE

Before you learn the tender gravity of kindness,
you must travel where the Indian in a white poncho
lies dead on the side of the road.

—NAOMI SHIHAB NYE, *Kindness*

*I*n 2006, I was blessed to be embraced by the Sisters of the Holy Names of Jesus and Mary as an associate. I admire this order of Sisters because they are all-inclusive, considering everyone equal in the eyes of God. I love their work for social justice, especially their efforts to halt trafficking of women and children, and alleviate poverty and oppression. Time and time again, I am inspired by their life stories and the beautiful circumstances surrounding their deaths—"a birthing into God," as one Sister calls it.

At one point, I created a portrait of Mother Marie Rose Durocher, the foundress of the Holy Names Sisters. Her veil was collaged from photographs and symbols/images I found in the organization's newsletters and other publications. My favorite photograph, taken when the Sisters wore dark habits and veils, showed an elderly nun sitting down listening to a speaker and holding a three-pound barbell in her wrinkled and vein-riddled hand! This photo embodies the spirit of each and every Holy Names Sister I've ever met. The necrology of Holy Names Sister Phyllis Soreghan describes this spiritual director who, until her death in her nineties, continued working with clients. Students had to lie on the floor gazing up to receive wisdom from Sister Phyllis. She was restricted to a wheelchair because the extreme curvature of her spine forced her head to rest on her lap.

Another remarkable Holy Names Sister is Kate St. Martin. Her work in the 1970s and 1980s in Portland's skid row and Old Town launched many of the city's current services for the homeless, the poor, the addicted, and the mentally ill. I can easily conjure up the billowing dark habit and veil of Sister Kate as she scurried among this alien community. What a grace it would be if everyone followed the tenets depicted on a wall hanging from her office at the time. It read:

Love must be completely sincere.
Hate what is evil.
Hold on to what is good.
Love one another warmly as
Brothers [and Sisters] in Christ.
And, be eager to show respect for
One another.

—ADAPTATION OF ROMANS 12:9–10.

Sister Kate St. Martin

WISDOM WILL OF SR. KATE ST. MARTIN

Dear Friends and Family,

I was born in Winnipeg, Manitoba, Canada. We moved to Skagway, Alaska, when I was 10 years old. On July 4, 1931, we had a young, newly ordained priest, Father Salzman, over for dinner. He'd been ordained on Valentine's Day earlier that year. After dinner, my little brother Al and I went outside to play with sparklers. Mom said, "Why don't you light them outside the dining room window so that we can watch?" When I caught on fire, I crossed my arms and ran toward the back door. Al ran out in the street, yelling, "Fire!" Father Salzman grabbed a coat off the rack and rushed outside to smother the flames.

Crossing my arms had partially snuffed out the fire, but my chest was deeply burned, as were both arms from the wrist up. For a long time I couldn't open my arms wide enough to slip them into the sleeves of my dresses. My mother was grateful my face was spared, although my chin had been affected.

Within three years of this accident, Father Salzman was banished from his parish in Alaska for alcoholism. At the time, part of his therapy at the treatment center consisted of being dunked into ice-cold water. Father Salzman's plight was my first introduction to the disease of alcoholism. As a child, I added a litany of names to my daily prayers. My list included priests, alcoholics, convicts, the homeless, people of color, and drug addicts. Later on, I added homosexuals to my prayer list.

When I was 13, I felt called to become a nun. I spent my freshman year in Victoria, Canada, at Sisters of St. Anne's High School. I knew that St. Mary's of the Valley in Beaverton, Oregon, a suburb of Portland, accepted 15-year-olds into their convent because one of the Skagway girls was already there.

My mother and I spent five days on a ship to get there from Seattle. By the end of that first year in Beaverton, my father was transferred to Victoria, British Columbia. I never returned to Alaska.

At the convent, I just couldn't seem to keep the rules. The nuns warned my parents when they came to visit that they would ship me out if I didn't shape up. On April 14, they made good on their promise. I cried and promised to keep the rules. But it was a blessing that they sent me home. It gave me time to grow up. I returned to St. Mary's of the Valley when I was 19, and this time, I was obedient—well, mostly.

When I was in the novitiate, the mother superior asked me how I'd like to teach music. I said, "I wouldn't." She replied, "Well, you don't get to do what you want to in the convent. So you'll be taking college courses, preparing to teach music." I struggled through five years of instructing piano and some violin. After a while, I asked if I could go into teaching. I got that permission when a new administrator was hired, and I taught for some 20 years.

In 1965, the Maryville Nursing Home was built right behind the convent in Beaverton. Since I'd always wanted to become a nurse, I began working there. I remember reading a newspaper article with the headline "Priest Runs Skid Row Hotel." This was the Burnside Hotel on Northwest Couch Street, between Second and Third Streets in downtown Portland. I clipped the article out, and I thought, *Gee, I'd like to do something like that.* Later on, I had an office there in the Matt Talbot Center, named by Brother Fred Mercy after a drunken Irishman. After taking an oath to stop drinking, Matt prostrated himself daily in front of the church until the doors opened for Mass. Matt recovered the hard way. His biography really inspired me. At that time, the Sisters of the Holy Names of

Jesus and Mary sent some of their Sisters down to the Blanchet House, a soup kitchen founded by a group of students from the University of Portland, to hold sing-alongs. I thought, *I wish our community did things like that.*

So I entered nursing school with the intention to work on skid row. I asked the superior general at Maryville if I could volunteer there on one of my days off. She said that she'd have to ask the community. I waited and waited for an answer. Finally, I brought it up again, and she said, "Well, the community said we should ask Archbishop Dwyer." His answer came in three words: "Let her go."

I first started working on Tuesdays at the Blanchet House handing out vitamins, doing dressing changes, and giving health recommendations to the homeless. Some had massive, deeply infected sores caused by poor nutrition and neglect. Before long, I began volunteering on Friday, too. I'd walk the soup line handing out vitamins. Finally, the manager, Vern, offered me a little room next to his office for bandage changes or just to talk. When the men came in, I'd clean their wounds with hydrogen peroxide. This couldn't continue, of course, for the Blanchet House was an eatery, after all.

During the Vietnam War, I met a doctor from Beaverton who was a conscientious objector, and I'd ride with him downtown, where he maintained a little clinic on Second Street, between Southwest Ankeny and Northwest Couch. So I worked with him for a time. In those days, nuns wore a traditional habit and a veil. In the beginning, I felt uneasy because I didn't know how to respond to the street people. They'd say, "Hello, Sister Kathleen." And I'd avert my eyes because I wasn't comfortable among them. I became very comfortable as I began to visit the poor living in the Burnside Hotel, whose residents had to be clean and sober.

At the end of Couch Street was a tavern called Gus's Café. Above it was the Matt Talbot Center, where men could stay for 50¢ a night for as long as a week. My first introduction to housing for the homeless was the Holm Hotel, which most called the Chicken Coup Flop House, on Northwest Second and Burnside, right across the street from the Salvation Army. Inside the storefront entrance on the first floor was a ticket booth where the men checked in with the clerk. There were two floors above the entrance, where the men slept on cots with simple iron frames and mattresses. The second floor had an enormous green room divided into 6-feet-wide and 10-feet-long cubicles with ceilings of cardboard and chicken wire. The same was true for the third floor. A lucky few had sheets, but most just slept on bare mattresses. The chicken wire around the sleeping quarters served as protection from flying wine bottles. It also allowed more light and ventilation. The men were allowed to drink in the building.

One of the men became very depressed when his fiancée left him. One night, while drinking and smoking, he fell asleep. A fire started. The heat was so intense that part of his iron bed melted! Sadly, he didn't survive. After the fire, the Chicken Coop Flophouse was remodeled, expanding the sleeping enclosures to meet safety requirements. This, of course, limited the number of occupants, but created aisle space for quicker evacuation in case of another emergency.

At the Matt Talbot Center, people came to me for bandage changes for what they called wine sores. I first witnessed such wounds when I graduated from nursing school. In June 1969, I went to work at the county hospital. An African American woman was admitted with open wounds full of maggots! The doctors left them there because maggots clean up infection.

In 1970, I asked the mother superior if I could work another day on the streets. She took my request to the community, who promptly demoted me from charge nurse to staff nurse. Ironically, this allowed me an extra day. I wanted to live at the convent at St. Andrews Parish in northeast Portland because I'd taught school there in the 1950s and 1960s. Plus, it was much closer to downtown than my convent in Beaverton. Some Holy Names Sisters were living there, as well as Sisters from my order, the Sisters of St. Mary. Eventually, the community approved of my move. Later, I transferred from my order to join the Sisters of the Holy Names, who encouraged my ministry with the city's poor and destitute.

During my street experience, I met Michael B. Stream, a beautiful, young person who hated himself. Perhaps this was because he was gay or that his family rejected him. Michael was never comfortable around any of his family members. In his early thirties, he endured the scourge of AIDS. Once, he had a bad cold and was staying in an overnight drop-in center. But the thick cigarette smoke interfered with his recovery. So I invited him to stay in my guest room until he got over his cold. We would watch television and talk for hours. Michael was a clean and quiet person, as well as a wonderful cook. He even helped me organize my kitchen. What a loveable man he was.

I remember taking Michael to a "Mass in the Time of AIDS," held in a non–Catholic Church because the Catholic Church wasn't sympathetic towards homosexuals. As a result, Father Gary McGinnis said Mass at St. Stephen's Episcopal Church on Thirteenth and Yamhill Streets. After that, even though Michael wasn't Catholic, I took him to a Faith and Sharing Retreat at Mt. Angel. Everyone who ever met Michael liked him.

When Michael relapsed, he called me, sounding suicidal. I told him not to do anything foolish and wait until I got there. I found him sitting on a curb outside a convenience store. I sat down beside him and talked to him for a long time. However, Michael continued contemplating suicide as a way out of his distress.

Shortly after we talked on the curb, I asked Michael to drive me to Troutdale to pick up my new hearing aids. I noticed that he was exceptionally quiet. As I was getting ready to take him home, he asked if he could spend the night. I said, "Of course." The next day, I took him home, and when he got out of the car, he turned to me, gave me a big hug, and said, "I love you very much. I'll call you later." I told him, "I love you, too, Michael." For a moment after he said the words *I love you*, I felt a bit uneasy, like something was wrong. We didn't usually have such endearing exchanges. But I dismissed the feeling.

At 8:30 a.m. the next morning, I got a call from the medical examiner. A body had been found at the Estate Hotel. My heart sank! I said, "And the name?" And they said, "Michael B. Stream." When I went over to the hotel to pick up a couple of things I'd given him, his cot was neatly made. He'd been sitting on the edge of it. There was a chair next to the cot with a melted down candle resting on it. Michael had committed suicide by injecting himself with an overdose of heroin. Apparently, he had a second syringe waiting in case the first one didn't do the trick. He was not a mainstream drug user; alcohol was his drug of choice. I was simply brokenhearted. I said, "Michael, don't you miss me?" I missed him so very much. That event was the most difficult in all my years on skid row. Michael had shared with me that, as a child, he'd been sexually abused by a cousin, an uncle, and his grandfather. This made him see himself as a bad person and, I believe, ultimately led to his suicide. His mother and his aunt used to sit him down at the kitchen table and tell him how bad he was for allowing those things to happen. He was just nine years old! This is why his self-image was so damaged. Once, he said, "I hate my body!" But I told him what a beautiful person he really was.

The coroner asked me if Michael had any relatives. I gave them all my phone contacts, including Hooper Detox and OHSU (Oregon Health and Science University). Later that morning, Michael's sister called me. She shouted into the phone, "Why in the hell didn't he call me? He knew where I was." Inside, I thought, *Why didn't he call you? What did you people ever do for him except make him feel bad about himself?* But I kept my mouth shut. Michael is still very dear to my heart, and I look forward to seeing him again in heaven.

Jim Dunnelli is one of the first men I worked with who ever got sober and stayed that way. Father Gil Lulay founded the Burnside Hotel, and that's where I met Jim. When my cousin from Minnesota invited me to go with her to Hawaii for three weeks, I told Jim and the others. He said, "Send me a postcard." I said I would, and I did. That was the beginning of our friendship. At some point, Jim relapsed, and he came into my office. His shirt was wine-stained, and he was crying. He told me he was going to Seattle. I encouraged him to just go to detox. He said, "No, I'm going to Seattle on the freight," so he hopped onto the train and was gone for a year.

When Jim came back, I was in the soup line at Blanchet House handing out vitamins. The vitamins were a kaleidoscope of geriatric, pediatric, multiple, or any other kind I could get my hands on. I didn't recognize Joe since he'd altered his appearance somewhat and had shaved off his handlebar mustache. He'd told people, "Wait until Sister Kathleen sees me." I passed right by Jim, who said, "You don't remember old Dunnelli, do you?

Jim touched me with his loyalty. There wasn't anything he wouldn't do for me. I could always count on him. Jim went to stay at Harmony House, a halfway house on Southeast Twentieth and Taylor Streets. Two more Harmony Houses were opened back then, including one on Southeast Division Street and one in Oregon City. Each house could hold up to nine recovering people. I used to do counseling at all three places.

Blacky helped me in my early work at the Matt Talbot Center. When Blacky sobered up, he was a wonderful person. I brought him home once to my mother who lived in Tacoma, Washington. In his suit, Blacky looked more than presentable to mother. He even stood in for two of my volunteer staff members as their fathers, giving them away at their weddings. I felt so bad when Blacky relapsed after six years of sobriety. He fell, hurting himself so badly that he ended up in a nursing home for the rest of his life. Before his relapse, he told me he had been baptized Catholic, so when he made his First Communion, I was happy to attend the ceremony.

In the 1970s, when I began serving in Old Town/skid row, there weren't any recovery programs for the homeless-poor alcoholics and addicts, except the drunk tank at the city jail for 30 days. Once the men got out of jail, they went right back to drinking and using. I'd often see people lie helpless on the street, in doorways, on park benches, and under bridges. It touched me deeply to see them like that.

I have to say that the men I met respected women. Because I was a Sister and wearing a veil, they trusted me. I don't know how to explain why I did this kind of work, but I know, deep in my heart, this was where God wanted me.

Over time, other people showed up to help this marginalized community. Facilities such as Hooper Detox and DePaul

Treatment Center were opened, and the County Health Nurse saw to it that the men got their tuberculosis inoculations. Eventually, the Public Health Clinic opened down there, and other services became available, like halfway houses and SROs. Over the years, provisions became available for drop-ins so that people could find shelter at night. Then the city itself became more aggressive about safety requirements for groups in order to prevent fires like the Chicken Coop Flophouse incident. I worked as a nurse at the DePaul Treatment Center from 1982 to 1992. Hooper Detox moved to a new building, and I worked there as an advice nurse from 1992 to 1998. After that, I retired.

The Salvation Army, Portland Rescue Mission, and Union Gospel Mission existed from the beginning, but before they could eat supper or sleep there, the men were required to listen to what they called ear-banging sermons. The Portland Rescue Mission didn't serve food; they just provided beds, while the Union Gospel Mission and the Salvation Army offered both. The Salvation Army served a lunch where the men stood at rows of high tables to eat. Some who were employed there to do the cooking and cleaning were allowed to live upstairs.

As I reflect on my years working among the people on skid row, I am reminded of Mathew 25:35–56 (NIV):

> For, I was hungry and you gave me something to eat. I was thirsty and you gave me something to drink. I was a stranger and you invited me in. I needed clothes and you clothed me. I was in prison and you came to visit me. I tell you the truth, whatever you did for one of the least of these brothers of mine, you did for me.

From the beginning, these stalwart words influenced my ministry. Initially, my concern was for alcoholics, but before long, I recognized that when I worked with anyone on the streets, no matter their condition or challenges, I was working for Christ Himself. I was given the grace to see the face of Jesus in every person I encountered.

With Love, Kate St. Marin

In the October 1978 issue of the *U.S. National Catholic*, Roger Repohl, NSJ wrote the article "Wish I Could Serve 'um Like My Sister Kate." Repohl says, "Sister Kathleen is no prohibitionist or social reformer. She doesn't come on like Carrie Nation."[26] He quotes her saying the following:

> I don't make demands. But I do confront—like today. I was talking to a man who is just drinking and drinking. He told me he doesn't care. He's lost his will to live, so he wants to just go on blissfully drinking himself to death, and it should be nobody's business as long as he's paying his rent. He's 63 and he's got some money, but I guess he really doesn't have much to live for. I told him," Well, I'm going to keep seeing you and encouraging you to do something about your life."

26 Carry Amelia Moore (1846–1911), American temperance leader

[…] Most of the people I work with I've found to be gentle and very sensitive—yet there is just so much that they haven't been able to cope with, maybe all their lives. A lot of them started drinking after a real traumatic experience such as losing their wife and family. […] All in all, most of these guys are so nice you just can't help loving them.

Today, a different demographic resides on the streets than when Sister Kate was ministering there. No longer are alcoholic and drug-addicted men the primary homeless. Now, the streets are also occupied by families down on their luck, runaway teens, abused women and their children, drug addicts, alcoholics of both genders and of all ages, and a huge population of the mentally ill. There are few places that house the mentally ill for extended lengths of time. Only a few *safe* houses are available for women to escape their abusers with time-limited stays. There are, however, powerful people working in Portland to accomplish systemic change, people who envision the end of homelessness altogether in our city.

As I sat recording Sister Kate's story of her years on skid row, I couldn't help but imagine what this tiny woman was like in the 1970s. Once five foot two, but now four foot eleven, she is hard of hearing, endures macular degeneration, and has undergone hip and knee replacements. Still, today, Kate is robust enough to tackle anything she puts her mind to—just a bit slower. She doesn't whine or play "poor me." With a twinkle in her eye, she says she still hates to follow rules. Kate may lack her youthful vigor, but not her vibrancy. She reads large-print books and uses a magnifying glass or her Optelec machine to read everything else. Nothing keeps her behind the times. Even though Kate may have to steady herself when she rises from a chair, she volunteers one day a week at Our House, a center that assists people suffering from AIDS.

Kate is someone you can sit down with for hours of conversation simply listening to the wisdom and insight she's gained in her 86 years. She is grateful to reside in an assisted-living home because of her limited vision and unsteady legs. Kate's brother, Al, who witnessed her catch on fire at age 10, made her a crystal ceiling mobile. "When the sun's out, I come to my room just to see the rainbows dancing on the walls. It's so beautiful." From her windows, she enjoys a grotto in the backyard, with its statue of the Blessed Mother. Kate has a large collection of framed photos and a pile of albums that hold treasured images of her street friends. But most of these memories are held dear in her heart. From time to time, Kate takes them out and will happily share them with anyone who asks.

CHAPTER 14

Stars On The Sidewalk

> Whatever ordination is about, it cannot bestow any priest-hood higher than that bestowed in birth and interpreted in baptism; nor can it deprive a person of what birth has given and baptism shaped. In the fundamental and primary sense, laity and the clergy are priests together. Any lesser claim for the priesthood of the Laos calls the priesthood of Jesus himself, layman as he was, into question.
> —L. William Countryman, *Living on the Border of the Holy*

Roman Catholicism does not offer women ordination. If they did, I'd encourage Mary Sue Richen to go collect her priestly garb. Her spiritual caregiving for the residents at the Macdonald Residence, and its precursor in the basement of the Downtown Chapel, is pastoral in the truest sense. As a certified chaplain, Mary Sue is as close to the Catholic priesthood as she'll ever get, and that's fine with her. As for me, I consider her a priestess, according to the Order of Melchisedek.[27]

Mary Sue defines her religion as "God's Love." If all religions or spiritual paths abided by this definition and were truly guided by the commandments to love God and love one another, then the world would enjoy a sustained peace.

Mary Sue, before her retirement as spiritual director of the Macdonald Residence, guided nurses, caregivers, and students of social work through prayer and empathic listening. She taught them about feeding the hungry, housing the homeless, and spending time with the shut-ins and the mentally ill. Whenever she is encountered, Mary Sue glows as if she has just spoken with the Lord. Like Moses descending from Mt. Sinai, she's unaware of her radiance (Exodus 34:29 NIV). Even though, we don't see one another very often, I am honored to call her my friend and spiritual sister.

One of the mentally ill people Mary Sue continues to minister to is Paul. Every day, he phones her, even in her retirement, with the same question: "Mary Sue, am I going to be okay today?" Each time, Mary Sue replies, "Yes, Paul, you're going to be okay; everything will be fine." Then, together, they say the Lord's Prayer twice. At the end of the call, without fail, he proclaims, "Mary Sue, you are a credit to the human race and an inspiration to society!"

---

27 Jesus is considered a priest in the order of Melchizedek because, like Melchizedek, Jesus was not a Kohen, (<u>Hebrew</u> "priest," pl. Kohanim or Cohanim, a direct male descendent of the biblical <u>Aaron</u>, brother of <u>Moses</u>, and has a distinct personal status in <u>Judaism</u>), and thus would not qualify for the Kohanic (Jewish) priesthood under Torah Laws.

WISDOM WILL OF MARY SUE RICHEN
(Some names have been changed to maintain confidentiality.)

Dear Friends and Loved Ones,

As a child, we lived in Carmel, California, while my father was in the military there at Ft. Ord. Every night, I said my prayers beside my bed with my parents and sometimes my grandmother. My concept of God was simple and beautiful. One day, when I was three or four years old, I heard a woman's angelic voice coming from the other side of our backyard hedge. In order to find out who it was, I crept into a small hole in the foliage where I saw a pretty woman standing amidst her flowers. She sang as she tended her garden. I thought, *She must be like God.* I've never lost that early association of God with wonder and awe. Even as I've walked the streets among people in disheartening conditions, I've witnessed their promise. The sight of that beautiful woman singing behind our backyard hedge instilled in me a spark of divinity, a spark of healing, a spark of hope, causing me to believe in people.

Both my parents were sources of inspiration. My father was an orthopedic surgeon, and my mother was an educator. At the age of 18, she became a Catholic convert. She loved her faith as a positive rather than punitive or judgmental set of beliefs. My father was a cradle Catholic whose strict Irish mother prayed constantly. As a result, my dad's faith was practical, focused on beauty and holiness in ordinary experiences.

At my parochial grade school, I learned of Jesus, the commandments and sin, and the anchors of my faith. One day, after school, my dad announced, "I'm going to be the best man at one of my dear friend's wedding." The man wasn't a Catholic and neither was the church where the ceremony was to take place.

So I said to my dad, "But that's a mortal sin!" He looked down at me and said, "Horse feathers! It would be a sin not to stand beside people and support them on such important occasions. Horse feathers to that!" I've never forgotten that day, and I use "horse feathers" all the time. When I measure my decisions, I ask myself, *What is the highest priority of love here?* Then I choose.

I have always loved my faith. After attending St. Mary's Academy, I went to the University of Oregon and finally to the University of Portland, another Catholic school. My older brother, Dick, is a Catholic priest. My younger sister, Elizabeth, who lives on the East Coast, was afflicted with polio when she was seven years old. I was nine at the time. We'd always slept next to each other in our little bedroom and were very close. When she got sick, my brother and I were sent away for a month to avoid exposure to the disease. I tucked away in my heart the thought that she might die. I never faced the horrible fear that I might lose my beloved sister until much later in life, when I was mature enough to deal with it.

Elizabeth has been a tremendous inspiration and influence to both my brother and me. In the beginning, she couldn't move anything except her eyelids. For the rest of her life, she wore braces, used crutches, and sometimes wore casts. Now, she suffers from post-polio syndrome and is mostly confined to bed. However, she did marry and then raised five children. She also earned a doctorate in computer education. She helped people deal with their disabilities through adaptive education to become as independent as possible, like herself. My sister worked very hard to recuperate, and these days, they say that the ones who work the hardest are the ones who suffer most from post-polio syndrome.

In my senior year at the University of Oregon, I married a wonderful, wonderful man, who is an architect. I was attracted by his spirituality as well as his sense of beauty and wonder that I've always appreciated. We have three children and three grandchildren, all whom live close by and are a treasure to us.

I didn't finish my degree at the University of Oregon, so at the age of 40, with the encouragement of my husband, David, and my brother, Dick, I went back to school. Both of these men are gifted at rolling away stones from my perceived obstacles and allowing light to enter. That's what their encouragement did for me. I enrolled at the University of Portland, first completing my bachelor's degree and then earning a master's degree in theology. Later, my residency at Emanuel Hospital qualified me for certification as a Catholic chaplain.

For a while, I worked in the counseling department at University of Portland. One day, I heard about a job opening for assistant campus minister. I really wanted that position, but I didn't get it. I was so disappointed. It was a rainy day, and as I left the interview, I noticed a spilled box of gold and silver paper stars on the sidewalk. I took this as a sign that another door was about to open up, and immediately, I felt better, hopeful.

30 years ago, knowing my devotion to Our Lady of Guadalupe, my husband[28], David, took me to Mexico City to visit her shrine. For some reason, I was alone when I gazed at the tilma.[29] I felt God blessing me through Mary's loving gaze. Within my heart, I heard Our Lady tell me, "I want you to look at my little ones with all the love that I'm looking at you." Instantly, I felt a tremendous call. I didn't know how it was going to materialize in my life, but I had faith in this revelation.

---

28 The Blessed Mother of Jesus allegedly appeared to Juan Diego in Mexico City in 1531. For more information about the miracle of Our Lady of Guadalupe refer to http://www.sancta.org/intro.html.

29 A tilma is a type of outer garment worn by men at the time.

During my residency at Emanuel Hospital, I thought I was headed for hospital chaplaincy. When my supervisor said, "You've already had three units of Clinical Pastoral Education (CPE). However, during the summer, we only take people who can be ordained, and as you know, women aren't ordained in the Catholic Church. So we must ask you to skip the summer unit." I was really angry. I thought, *This isn't fair. I get a residency job for six months, and now, I have to wait until September to finish.* I mulled it over and decided to work for three months with my brother, Dick, who had just started his pastorship at the Downtown Chapel.

After I made the arrangements, my supervisor Reverend Bill Adix called me and said, "Mary Sue, one of the women in the program is very ill and won't be taking the summer training. Would you like to come back? It's too late for us to interview and assess a new student." I said, "Well, I've promised to work with my brother this summer." Bill said, "Maybe that's what God wants me to do, too! Let's start a street chaplaincy. This is new for me, but I know there needs to be a chaplaincy on the streets." So he incorporated the street program and visitations to residents in the SRO hotels as part of CPE training. My job was to mentor the student chaplains.

Bill was like a child with a new toy while working with the poor. He said, "I love the hospital, but this truly is a blessing. We are going where the people reside and feel comfortable. Since these places are their homes, as much as we consider them dark and gloomy, we need to reverence them." The words of my beloved friend Father Gary Smith come to mind: "The church is always at its best when it's with the poor."

After finishing my CPE training, I remained with the Downtown Chapel. I was the program director for the Macdonald Center, which my brother and I founded as a hospitality center operating out of the basement of the church. We began each morning with prayers, songs and storytelling, and sharing. Then we distributed food and clothing and visited the home-bound, sick, and poor in six or seven of the nearby SROs.

Nursing and social work students from the University of Portland, Clackamas Community College, and Linfield College all came to work with the marginalized here. Our goal was to break down the isolation people felt. We wanted them to feel that they are an important part of our neighborhood community.

While working out of the basement of the Downtown Chapel, nursing students who were visiting people at the SROs shared that they were finding many ill people who were unable to care for themselves. We knew that some of the folks chose to die in their rooms rather than being uprooted and sent to the suburbs, to neighborhoods where their friends wouldn't feel welcome. They'd rather die than lose their friendships and their sense of community in Old Town. It was obvious; we needed an assisted-care facility for those who couldn't manage alone. My brother, Father Berg, said, "Let's build one right here, in this neighborhood!" He worked for more than five years with the city council and commissioners to obtain permits, funding, and everything else that's required. The officials said, "You can't do it. There's no market for it. Taxpayers won't accept it." Father Berg forged ahead anyway. As I said earlier, my brother rolls stones away, transforming the impossible into the possible and real.

There was a vacant lot behind the Downtown Chapel, so Father Berg astutely crafted additional space by buying an adjoining piece of property. This expanded lot was large enough to accommodate the facility we wanted to build. Maybelle Clark Macdonald, a friend of our family, who dreamed of helping people with mental illness, had already contributed monetarily to the hospitality center. Now, she gave even more to the establishment of the care center. My brother, Dick, created a place where we could hold one-on-one conversations with all who open up the gospel for us, those poor among us who teach us about the heart of God. For this reason, one of my heart mantras is, "We need to go to the poor to get the good news!"

One night, as I was getting ready to go home after work, a Native American man, who'd recently lost his wife to breast cancer, came in with his eight-month-old baby. "Would you hold my baby boy?" he asked. "He's used to having a woman hold him." I reached out and took the infant. I felt him snuggle close to my breast, and I wondered if he missed his mother's voice. Of course he did. Did he miss the way she held him and looked at him? Of course he did. I prayed for God to bless that baby and help him know his mother's face again, even though it wasn't physically possible. I turned to the weeping man and said, "Please tell me about your wife." As I held his child, he shared stories about her. I asked, "How will it be for you with your wife gone?" He told me that he was on his way to the reservation. "They always, always take care of us. We will be well provided for." Fortunately, our center provided him with transportation money.

Later, on my way to the bus stop, I encountered a man I knew who lives on the streets. He was sitting on top of a nearby stone wall. As I approached, I heard him singing, *"Jesus's love never fails you. Jesus's love never fails me. Jesus's love never fails us."* Tears came to my eyes as I recalled my earlier experience. The man on the wall looked right at me, saying, "Sister Mary, Jesus's love never fails you. You remember that." That's how divine grace surprises me—at the most appropriate, yet unexpected times. This obviously tipsy fellow was singing his blessing for whoever cared to receive it. Thankfully, it was me!

In my first years at the Downtown Chapel, before our wonderful Macdonald Residence was built, I volunteered during my lunch hours at Sisters of the Road Café. The employees were people who lived on the streets. They both trained and monitored my work. My assignment involved some table bussing. Mostly, I was in the back cutting the cornbread. Next to me was a man doing an incredible job of washing dishes. I said to him, "I'd like to know who you are since we're working side by side. My name is Mary Sue. What's your name?" And he said, "My name's Meathead." I took a rather long pause, thinking, *Lord, what am I going to do with this?* Then I asked, "What did your mama call you?" And he said, "John." So I said, "Would you mind if I called you John?" He said, "Well, okay." Then he pounded his fist on his head and said, "I'm called Meathead because it's all gristle up here!" *How sad*, I thought to myself. *He's gone through life thinking he has gristle for a brain. And God knows how many years he's been called "Meathead."* John and I became great friends. During the years we worked together, he relapsed into drug abuse. Occasionally, I'd see him on the street, and he'd lower his eyes. I respect people enough to honor them when they don't want to engage. At times when John didn't, I sent him love through my glances. As he went in and out of addictions over the years, we laughed, shared, and renewed our friendship.

A friend of mine, Rosella,[30] has been part of the Macdonald Center Volunteer Program from the beginning. Now, she lives at the Macdonald Residence. Rosella was born with cerebral palsy and is confined to a wheelchair. At times, her speech is difficult to understand. Rosella doesn't let that stop her from visiting folks in the SROs or from helping with orientation of

---

30 Rosella was instrumental in obtaining the dips we find placed in sidewalks making wheelchair access available to the handicapped.

new volunteers. She's done this for over 20 years. She challenges us to look at others, not at their job, their appearance, or their disability, but for who they are as human beings. "People first" is her policy.

Another person in Old Town who is very dear to me suffers from mental illness. I've known Paul for many years. One day, while attending Mass at the Downtown Chapel, I sat in front of him. When it came time for the Greeting of Peace, usually expressed with a handshake, I noticed a newcomer to the chapel. He approached Paul with an outstretched hand. Paul turned to him and said, "I'm sorry, I don't shake. But I love you!" In this way, Paul expressed his truth about the boundaries he maintains in order to feel safe; however, there is no boundary to Paul's love, no boundary at all.

One dark night at the bus stop, I fumbled in my purse for my bus pass. All of a sudden, a man in a wheelchair approached me. Both of his feet were bound. I looked at him and said, "Oh, John, I've been trying to find you! Where have you been?" When he said, "I live over at the Holm Hotel," I asked, "How do you manage? There's no elevator there." He looked at me and said, "You know, the vets want to put me in their home, but I don't want to go there. I'll never go there! My feet and my legs hurt like hell, but I wheel up to the bottom of that huge stairway at the Holm Hotel. No matter how bad I hurt, I bump my way up to the top. And, you know, Mary Sue, someone is always at the top waiting for me. A friend is there who understands and knows me."

I continued fumbling in my purse while he talked. Before I knew what was happening, John reached into his pocket, then asked me, "Need a little change for the bus, Mary Sue?" I looked up. "Oh, John, I love you!" I opened my arms, and we shared a tremendous embrace.

It's so important for people to be willing to receive gifts from others. I've also discovered that the other side of compassion is letting them know we need them. My gift that night was reconnecting with John and exchanging warm hugs. This is another way I know God reveals his grace to me.

The Macdonald Residence opened in September 1999. Its 53 rooms all include a bedroom, bathroom, and windows, which allow light to fill the rooms. In this assisted-living facility, residents receive the help they need to stay independent. A nurse and a caretaker are available 24/7. In addition to visiting in our Macdonald Residence, many volunteers also visit the residents in the SROs. Afterwards, the volunteers are debriefed so we can keep track of the people in the hotels, on the streets, and in the neighborhood. Volunteers freely share both their frustrations and their blessings. We want to make sure they are supported and encouraged in their work.

One of the first tenants at the Macdonald Residence was so afraid of his large quarters that he slept on his closet floor before adjusting to sleeping in a bed. When we opened our doors, many different kinds of people were brought together. In the beginning, residents didn't know each other. They were a group of strangers thrown together. As they developed friendships, a lovely camaraderie happened. Now, they all share great pride in their home. Through the years, a strong sense of hospitality and ownership has grown. All who step inside the door mention the same thing: "There's something different, something gracious about this place." Our residents deserve acceptance, beauty, and reverence in their lives, and here they can experience it.

Once, I sat with a gentleman who was dying and said to him, "I know that you lived in a number of the SROs and were homeless before that. What was that like for you? He said, "I want to stop you right there. Don't go any further. The truth is I never had a home until I felt the love, the respect, the wonderful sense of community, and the caring that I've felt here at the Macdonald Residence. This is my first real home."

The caretakers, the med aides, the dietary aides, and the janitors all have felt a calling of the heart to serve with us. They understand the residents. They understand what it's like to live in poverty. They understand what it's like to be frightened, wondering what's going to happen next. They understand not having security. They know how to listen within their own hearts as they listen to others.

In my early years, the mentally ill were dropped off downtown, along with bags full of their medications. The institutions that provided long-term care had all closed their doors, leaving the mentally ill to fend for themselves. These days, the SROs do the best they can, assisted by agencies like Aging and Disability Services, Cascadia, Project Respond, and other havens for people to find food, clothing, and shelter within a caring community.

Here, I will share the story of Padu because he is always in my heart. Padu lived in a dinky hotel room the size of a parking space. Padu came from Haiti and struggled with the English language. However, he'd pull out his little guitar and sing to us all the time. Padu used to kneel beside me, look into my eyes, and sing his songs with a gorgeous smile. After he taught me the lyrics, I sang with him. Besides being very, very poor, Padu suffered from major mental illness. Sometimes his eyes widened when he'd hear a strange noise or someone's footsteps coming down the hall. Padu needed constant reassurance of his safety.

One Christmas season, Padu asked if I'd come visit in his room. He met me at the door with a beaming, yet mysterious smile. He raised both closed fists to my face and said, "Which hand, Mary Sue? Which one do you want?" I pointed to the left hand. Inside his palm was a $20 bill. He said, "It's for you, to help people you work with, like me. I want you to help them because you've helped me so much. My sister gave me the money for my birthday, and I don't need it. You can give it to people who are sleeping on the street." I said, "Oh, Padu, you know that your sister probably wanted you to buy something special for yourself." He said, "Look!" as he opened his refrigerator. "I have everything I need in here." I saw a loaf of Wonderbread and some Coca-Cola. Then he opened his cupboard, showing me six cans of vegetables. Next, he drew me to his closet and said, "Look at all my clothes!" There was one jacket, a sweater, two tee-shirts, two pairs of underwear, and a pair of pants. "I have more than enough!" he said. Tears welled in my eyes as I thought of myself—my overflowing refrigerator, my stuffed closets, and my large home. Padu continued, saying, "You know what, Mary Sue? I want somebody else to have as much as I have." Before I accepted the money, I thought, *Dear God, how am I going to accept this?* But I knew I had to. This was a gift of his heart, and he would have been heartbroken had I refused it. I closed my hand around that $20 bill. The joy in his eyes when I received his gift blessed my soul.

My walk from downtown Portland State to Sixth and Couch, where I worked, involved 20 minutes of healthy exercise. One morning during Advent, I was struck by the beauty of the sun rise on my way to work. The narrow necks of the street lamps glowed in the street like sanctuary lamps. I considered myself as walking on holy ground. I noticed two men ahead of me sitting on a park bench, and I prayed: *Dear Lord, I'd love to wish those guys a Merry Christmas, but you know, Christmas is such a difficult season for some people. I'm afraid if I say anything, I might upset them by dredging up sad memories. So, instead of speaking, I'll give them the gift of my smile. The rest I'll leave up to you, Lord.* As I approached the bench, I smiled. Both men immediately stood up. They said, "Do you know how much God loves you?" I melted. *Who said Merry Christmas to whom, Lord?* "You two helped me realize how much God loves me with your sweet greeting. You reverenced me by standing up and delivering God's message. God's love grows every day for me because of people like you." I mentioned how I'd hesitated to wish them both a Merry Christmas for fear of inviting sorrow. One of the men smiled and then said, "My name's Henry, and I was born on Christmas Day. It was a merry day for my mom, I know that!" I spent 10 minutes reflecting with them on how God was working in our lives.

That Advent couldn't have been more memorable. On a shivering December morning, those two men reminded me of the depth of God's love for all human beings—every day, every hour, every minute, amidst the tears, amidst the laughter and the warmth, amidst the questions and the mysteries of life. When I'm with those who are poor and disadvantaged, I think, *How can this be, Lord? How can they summon the strength to get through the day?* Today, I'm happy about the many agencies in Old Town caring for God's "little ones," who teach us about acceptance, compassion, humility, courage, generosity, hope, and especially, love.

With Gratitude and Love, Mary Sue

There are no huge barriers to cross when speaking to the homeless community. They are psychologically naked. Life has shredded their emotional, protective gear. What you see is the *real* thing. It is representative of all suffering humanity. I believe the majority of people who negate the homeless do so from fear. I am reminded of one of Dr. Seuss's children stories about fear being an empty pair of green pants. I call it a frigging collection of what-ifs! One of my mentors taught me, "When we live in the past, we live with guilt for the things we did and didn't make right. When we live in the future, we live in fear of what might happen next. And so we can only deduce that the safest place to be is in the here and now." That has to be one of the hardest things on earth to do, but we can start a few moments at a time and build on it. That's what a good advocate does. Presence is everything.

So many people I've met from the streets carry a huge sense of shame with them, just as John does when Mary Sue encounters him during a relapse. She notices it when he averts his eyes from her. She is kind enough not to intrude upon him, but still, she silently prays for and sends him love.

It's difficult for recovering people to understand the difference between guilt and shame. I believe that guilt means I've done something wrong, but there is a way out because I have the opportunity to correct my mistake and make amends. I view guilt as a burden I create inside myself when I know I've done something wrong.

Shame, on the other hand, seems to shout, "I am *that* something wrong, and therefore, I'm irreparably ruined!" I believe shame is something put on us from early childhood. I can still see its wagging finger. Can you? It's much more difficult to unpeel the label of shame. That's where people with compassion like Mary Sue and other street advocates come in. They validate not only the homeless but everyone they encounter. It's part of their modus operandi. They listen deeply and feel with the person. They let their love and their constancy show. Mary Sue never gave up on John nor did she quit loving and praying for him. He felt stable with her, perhaps for the first time. And they renewed their friendship in and out of his recovery process.

At our core, I believe we are all innocent children of God. And, yes, there are exceptions, and evil does exist. But, for the most part, we are innocent. Perhaps we've lost our way, but every one of us is just trying to feel better. Whether we do it in skilled or unskilled ways, our aim is the same. Everyone deserves second chances and thirds and fourths. I seem to remember some prophet saying that we should forgive not 7 times but 77 times. With every opportunity to forgive someone, we hold out hope for them, and we replace what could become a festering resentment within ourselves with love. Forgiveness doesn't mean we agree or accept the other person's infraction; it means we forgive the person for whatever made them commit it in the first place, and we're willing to put it behind us and move on. When our wounds are from heinous acts like the sexual and physical abuse we've seen in earlier chapters, it takes a long time to forgive and often must be done at a distance. There are some relationships that are healthier when abandoned.

In an August 2, 2008, talk in Denver called The Banquet of the Faith, Elizabeth A. Johnson, CSJ, PhD (distinguished professor of theology at Fordham University and author of numerous books on theology) said this about forgiveness: "Forgiving does not mean condoning harmful actions or ceasing to criticize and resist them. But it does mean tapping into a wellspring of compassion that encompasses the hurt and sucks the venom out so we can go forward making a positive contribution, without hatred. This is the work of the Spirit, reconciling at the deepest level, so that community coheres and witnesses in a grace-filled way."

CHAPTER 15

Cups Of Mercy At The Downtown Chapel

Some of us see this invisible underground [of the homeless] as a pestilence among us. And some of us see their haunting presence as the failure of a society, of institutions, of policies gone wrong. We see heartbreak personified.

—GENNY NELSON, *Voices from the Street* (XIX)

When I returned to the Roman Catholic Church after a 20-year absence, I adopted the Downtown Chapel of St. Vincent de Paul as my parish. Some of my Catholic friends challenged my attendance there, saying, "Why go there? It's full of alcoholics and the mentally ill. Don't you find it depressing?" I go to the Downtown Chapel for many reasons. For one thing, this church resembles the original communities formed after Christ's death. People gathered in one another's homes, sharing meals and discussing Christ's teachings. Together, they built a viable community, including outcasts—the widowed, the orphaned, the homeless, and those without a family or a family name.

Digressing for a moment, I'd like to mention that these early home churches gave people the assurance of honorable burials when they died. Prior to the formation of Christianity, those who died without families were the ones tossed into common graves, their bodies to be incinerated—an ignoble way of handling a person's remains. These seeming misfits found family in the community of Christians, in the community of the Church. By pooling their funds, early Christians buried one another respectfully.

At the Downtown Chapel, I feel comfortable and at home. I came from a family with a mostly absent father, a mentally ill mother, four siblings, and the scourge of alcoholism. The congregants at this Catholic parish are my family, my tribe. After going to Mass there, I feel as if I've just experienced a lovely dinner. Because of its simple sense of Communion around the altar table, I feel as if I partake right along with the apostles and the prophets of old. I step back in time to join the original Christians. I love and wholeheartedly embrace this urban community standing on the border of the holy.

The chapel, with its box-shaped threshold, is located on the corner of West Burnside Street and Sixth Avenue. A statue of Christ the King (a discard from another parish) juts over its portal. When I attend Mass, it is not unusual to step over someone on the sidewalk, sleeping rolled up in his or her belongings, just to get to the chapel doors. Recently, I encountered a row of six or seven sleeping-homeless stretched around the corner of the chapel. Road construction, with its noise and noxious fumes, prevented traffic from disturbing them. One Sunday, a group of men and women sat in their bedrolls chatting and enjoying breakfast. A toothless, smiling woman offered me a bite of her pancakes. I declined, wishing her a good morning. I walked away wondering, *Who brought the pancakes?*

Father Ron Raab, CSC, is the chapel's assistant pastor, a compassionate and loving priest, a prophetic speaker, and my friend. Father Ron has created numerous programs for the church, including the Brother André's Institute, which offers a prayer and support program called Nothing but Hope for people experiencing depression. The institute also sponsors a Personal Poverty Retreat, and every Friday night, there is a meal served on the street for the poor and homeless, which they call Brother André's Café. I asked Father Ron to share some details about himself and the marginalized congregation he serves and loves.

WISDOM WILL OF FATHER RON RAAB, CSC

I am a Holy Cross priest, and I've worked at the Downtown Chapel of St. Vincent de Paul for six years. As a rule, we associate pastors stay at a parish three years, but I just recently renewed my contract for another three. Because this is a small parish for two priests, only one is usually assigned here. So I'm keeping a rather low profile because I don't want to leave.

Most of my life, I've done parish ministry or directed a retreat center at Notre Dame in Indiana. What I really wanted to do was work with the marginalized. It's a simple act of grace that I find myself at the Downtown Chapel, where I'm able to implement many ideas I originally had for the retreat center.

The Downtown Chapel is where the Church (Roman Catholic Church) can fulfill its *real* mission. In general, I think the Church struggles to serve the world today, but we've forgotten the core focus of the gospel. I think we need to learn from the mentally ill, the addicted, the poor, and the homeless— marginalized folks in general—about how to be the Church, about how to live. This was Christ's mission on earth. In the Church today, we have a tendency to want to fix people. The work here at the Downtown Chapel is not about fixing people, not at all. It's about learning from people, learning the real stuff of faith, about how to direct one's entire being toward God. Most of our parishes are full of people who are numb to life and to one another. Collectively, people seem to be more about protecting the parishes and themselves than about living fearlessly in the world with faith and hope. For me, the Downtown Chapel is a place where the Church can learn about how to *be* in the world.

I tell people they don't know what they are missing by not belonging here. When I first arrived at the chapel, I had perceptions about who I was, what I was about, and what was important; however, my ministry at the Chapel has propelled me into a deeper maturity and a much broader view about God and life in general.

Today, I'm not so focused on the rules and regulations of the Church. Working with the disenfranchised forces me to let go of a lot of things because so much of what I deal with is mental illness, depression, drug and alcohol abuse, childhood abuse, and other things that beat people down. The staff and I concentrate on allowing folks to feel God's inclusion and love. It's a lifelong journey. The Downtown Chapel is a place of raw evangelization—speaking God's love and allowing folks to open their lives to that love. I think I've learned more from our heroin addicts than I have from many of my ancestors in the Church. They've taught me how to believe and to live a life of freedom and goodness free from self-deception and free from lying and all the games that make addicts go back to using. It is a great honor and joy for me to watch recovering people discover their strengths and develop a strong faith in God.

Every day, I hear peoples' stories, and they continue to teach me how to be a real person. Before my mother died, I took a short leave from the parish and went back to Indiana to spend time with her. While I was gone, Father Bob mentioned at Mass where I was and what was happening, asking for prayers from the congregation. When I came back the following Sunday, a homeless person came in and sat on the floor. His clothes were drenched from the rain, his hair was long and greasy, and he reeked. Just as I was about to say to him, "You have to go," he looked up at me from his place on the floor and said, "How's your mother?" Situations like that force me to be authentic in relationship to others. Another time, the staff and I were cleaning the lobby after our morning hospitality center closed.

A young man, obviously very mentally ill, was sitting out on the sidewalk in the middle of the foot traffic. Even though the church doors were closed, I could see through the windows that he had a cat with him. A woman came along carrying a briefcase. She wore a gray suit, looking very professional. I watched as she shook her finger at the man and scolded him. Finally, she came inside and said to me, "That guy out there is really mistreating that cat." I said, "No problem, I'll take care of it." After she left, I turned to one of the staff people and said, "I just ache for the day when someone comes in and says, 'We have a homeless, mentally ill man sitting on the ground. Couldn't we act together to do something about that?'"

The Downtown Chapel has allowed me to see things that I've never wanted to see before. I've learned that people are people; it's just that some people have more stuff! I've also realized the folks with the most possessions are the most ungrateful and unhappy people in the world. I'm not trying to glamorize the poor, but I think when we live with less, we become more grateful for what we do have. The stories I hear continue to teach and open me up to the reality of my humanity. I can't fix people or judge or label them. I can't make them be more than they are. But I can just *be* with them. The goal here is not to fix people but to be in relationship with them.

Once a year, we bring folks who want to join the church through the process of the Rite of Christian Initiation (RCIA) program. I also conduct a Personal Poverty Retreat for groups of six to eight people. Both of these programs draw people to connect with us in some way. The response has been pretty amazing. I remember a gentleman who joined one of the small retreat groups. A month later, I received a thank-you note from him. He said that he went back to his home parish and somebody asked him, "What did you learn about homeless people?"

He responded, "I didn't learn anything about homeless people; I learned everything about myself." I've been asked at these mini-retreats, "Why don't the homeless just go out and get a job?" I have to admit that even if we handed the disenfranchised a new life on a silver platter, it wouldn't work for more than a day. People go back to what is familiar, unless they undergo some kind of transforming experience.

Our services at the chapel are not about resolving poverty but about looking into our own lives to confront our own personal poverty, our need for God. We create connections between prayer and service, between people and God. When I speak before groups, I emphasize that Jesus asked us only two things: 1) to learn to be loved by God and 2) to learn to love other people. This is how we can live truly Christian lives. Our difficulty with the first thing—being loved by God—is the impetus that compels us into service.

I live upstairs over the church, and one Friday night in 2004, I awoke around 3:00 a.m. to what I thought was the sound of gunshots. I said to myself, *Surely, I didn't hear gunshots from up here in my bedroom. It can't be.* I fell back to sleep. About 10 minutes later, I was convinced that I had heard gunshots. By the time I came downstairs, the police had arrived. The front door was already yellow-taped, but I pushed through it and mentioned to the police officer that I'd heard five shots fired. He said, "Well, Father, you slept through the first four!" A young man, just 19, was shot nine times right out in front of the chapel. The murder has never been solved because no one has dared come forward with information. This incident created a need in me to do something to honor the memory of the victim, Daniel, and his family. He was an African American young man from northeast Portland. When the *Oregonian* ran a story about the murder, I asked the reporter how I could contact the family. He gave me their phone number. After calling to offer condolences, I invited them to a street prayer service, a memorial for their son at 3:00 a.m. on a Saturday morning, the same hour Daniel had died in the street. I also invited people from the Downtown Chapel, everyone including the mentally ill, elderly, insomniacs and gay people. The reporter who'd written the account of the murder asked if he and his photographer could record the event.

The *Oregonian* featured an article on the memorial, which ended up in the national press. Our local church newspaper, the *Catholic Sentinel*, picked up the story as well. Now, whenever there's a murder in the neighborhood, we go out as a community after Mass to the place where the murder happened. We conduct the same kind of prayer service as we did that Saturday morning at 3:00 a.m. for Daniel. His murder got me thinking about how we could move out of our sanctuaries and into the ministry in the street. I use a litany form to name the evils of our neighborhood and to connect as a church community:

Street Prayer for the Murdered – Father Ron Raab, CSC

Response: "Save us, O God"

1. From the brutality of murder and violence...
2. From the hardship of poverty and loss...
3. From the addiction of drugs and alcohol...
4. From the fear of isolation and worry...
5. From the evil of war and hatred...
6. From the corruption of sin and darkness...
7. From the terror of gunshots and stabbings...
8. From the suffering of illness and disease...
9. From the coldness of loneliness and self-pity...

10. From the bitterness of homelessness and empty pockets...
11. From the need of prostitution and pornography...
12. From the snare of mental illness and all discrimination...
13. From the desperation of pride and jealousy...
14. From the silence of apathy and neglect...
15. From the wounds of sexual molestation and abuse...
16. From the deserts of ignorance and suffering...
17. From the arrogance of racism and greed...
18. From the burden of grief and despair...
19. From the torture of broken promises and empty commitments...
20. From the doubt of selfishness and insecurities...
21. From the web of egoism and self-centeredness...
22. And from all evil...
23. And from all evil...
24. And from all evil...

I believe the meaning of life is to fall madly in love with God. As an instrument of God compelled beyond ourselves, we can use our gifts and talents, and strengths and weaknesses for God's purposes. Many obstacles stand in the way of our feeling loved by God. We think we can live and sustain ourselves by our own power. We give importance to our monetary possessions. I believe that our arrogance, ignorance, and attachments come from a place of fear.

We live in fear 90 percent of the time. Most of our parish communities want to self-protect, want to protect their children, and they don't want to lose their belongings. It's difficult to break out of a culture of fear because no one wants to admit that fear is the motivator.

I've learned so much from people's struggles. Mental illness in our society is a huge problem, as is our own mental health. I don't have all the answers yet, but I keep looking. I keep believing. Working here at the chapel helps me expand my believing, giving, and receiving.

Often, when speaking to groups at different parishes, I begin by asking them, *What are the most important things for you at this phase of your life?* People will mention love, family, freedom, and so on. However, when I ask that same question here at the chapel, the answers are: a clean pair of underwear, a shower, and a dry place to sleep tonight. These concrete, real, immediate needs indicate survival is most important here. Living in this environment forces me to focus on folks' raw and present needs. They are just trying to make it through one more day.

As a staff, we do what we can to avoid burning out. Every third month, as a group, we receive spiritual direction. We have two spiritual directors who listen to us process our daily challenges. This year, we've worked with a psychiatrist. He constantly tells us that we, as a staff, have something to offer the disadvantaged that other places can't. We can offer a place for people to feel safe and to be who they are without fear. This past year, the staff received an educational grant to study addictions and mental illness. Also, we go on overnight retreats together. I don't know of another parish that offers these benefits to their employees.

One of the questions I keep asking is, *How do we deal with inconsolable suffering when all we do is stand there open-handed? We have no answers; we can't change people. How do you deal with the inconsolable suffering of life?* I think the answer lies in remembering that the best effort we can put forth is our faith. Our faith says to us that we must enter into Jesus's passion, death, and resurrection. That is the place where a whole new life can be born. If we are going to find new life and resurrection, we must also follow Him into the passion and death. Here, we achieve that through the real presence of the support staff and volunteers, through prayer, and through the Eucharist.

The stories we hear can depress anyone, but some stories also inspire us on our journey. It's not all bleakness. As a staff and a people, we must take a posture of standing open-handedly in God's presence.

When I think about leaving here, I realize that I'll miss all that keeps me grounded in my faith and maturity. The chapel teaches me more and more about being a real person, an authentic person. That's what I'd miss the most—the constancy of this lesson. This place has given me a spiritual authority no one can take from me. I can speak with a much more prophetic voice than ever before because of my experiences here. I believe I have an obligation to speak to the Church on behalf of the mentally ill and marginalized. Acknowledging and recognizing my obligation is what I find life changing and energizing.

People who want to work with the homeless and the poor must be willing to be changed. Volunteering is about other people, not about oneself. Volunteering, here at the chapel, means developing a deeper sense of faith. It involves letting go of all the things once considered important, as well as all the preconceived notions about the disadvantaged. Volunteers need to discard their desire to change or fix people. The only situation we can control is our own transformation. I often say the last thing the Church needs is another "do-gooder." What we do need are people who have found God's love propelling them into doing something good. That's a huge difference. Being a "do-gooder" is about the good deed, not relieving suffering. We must remember that real service is helping the *other*, not just ourselves.

Were I to die tomorrow, I'd like to be remembered as a spokesperson, an advocate for the marginalized. I'd like to be remembered as a person who personally invited people into God's love and taught them that God's love was accessible, no matter who they were.

Love, Ron

Helen Keller once said, "I long to accomplish great and noble tasks, but it is my chief duty to accomplish humble tasks as though they were great and noble. The world is moved along, not only by the mighty shoves of its heroes, but also by the aggregate of the tiny pushes of each honest worker." (Optimism: An Essay, 1903).

Many prophets walk through the doors of the Downtown Chapel. One gentleman, Mary Sue's friend, Paul, inspires all of us attending Mass that God answers all our prayers—big or small. Paul suffers from schizophrenia, but his loving devotion to God, to prayer, is a beacon of light. On occasion, he shouts out, "I love you, Father Ron!" During Prayer Request time at the weekday service, Paul makes mighty his desires. "Jesus, please, please, do not jerk me around today! I want to get my new underwear, and I want to be able to get the cap off the damn shampoo bottle!"

Sally is the front desk person, the face of the Downtown Chapel. Sally shows up every day, not espousing to be a miracle worker, but as one of those who moves the world along with her tiny pushes and her willingness to be real. Any day of the work-week, you can find her just inside the vestibule doors, either behind a sliding glass window that opens into the business office or out in front serving someone hands-on. Sally shared the following story of a man's humility, which she found remarkable:

> A gentleman happened to catch me as I was returning from lunch. He stopped by the building. We hadn't seen each other in quite a while. We were chatting, and I asked how he was doing. He said, "Well, I'm doing okay." He had his sign, and he was going to place it by the interstate to ask for money. He said, "You know, Sally, my son thinks I come downtown to work in a flower shop. For the past 20 years, he's believed that's how I make money. The truth is I come downtown and humiliate myself. That's how I can provide a home for him." Those words, "I humiliate myself," just struck me in the heart. He wasn't sad about it; he was matter-of-fact. It takes a tremendous amount of humility to ask for what you need and to say, "I lack. This is what I don't have."

Sally also shared a story with me about a woman who taught her a new method of praying the rosary:

> There is a woman who became quite known to the community. Her name is Barbara, and she was living at our chapel doors for most of the winter. I spent a lot of time with her, as did the rest of the staff. She was really a part of the community. One of the things I learned from her was how to pray—pray about everything, pray for everyone. She loved to say her version of the rosary. Barbara said a prayer intention on each rosary bead.

She prayed for everything—for her kids, for safety, for peace, for chickens, for smiles, for gloves, for anything she could think of. I learned that nothing was too small to pray for and that every day there was something to be joyful about.

I never got a clear understanding of her story because she changed it so often. Barbara lived with mental illness, quite a big burden on her life. I only knew her two or three months. During that time, I witnessed great joy from her. Here was a woman without a place to live, enduring confusion, feeling fearful, and being vulnerable. Still, with all of that, she had such a sense of happiness and delighted in a cigarette or a pair of gloves; nothing was too small to enjoy. Barbara left once and then came back. Then, around the New Year, she left, and we haven't seen her since. I'm not sure where she went. I miss her.

Sally continued to talk about how difficult letting go is for her when she gets attached to someone. When they leave, she has no way of knowing where or how they are:

The nature of this work is throwing out a lot of fishing lines and letting them sit. Some of them come back, and some of them stay; some of them break, and some of them disappear. The coming and going of it all can get to me at times, to not have a chance to say good-bye to someone who might get sick, or go to the hospital, or might have to go to jail, or wherever. That constant not knowing is so much a part of the lives of the people we serve. None of them have steady ground to stand on.

I've met lots of prophets and learned a lot about faith and what it means to have nothing other than one's faith to be able to hold and know and share. People literally rise up from the pavement every morning to wait in line to eat, to use the phone, to use the bathroom, to find shelter. Most people seem hopeful, even if they aren't smiling. Their lives seem tremendously difficult. Just think what it must be like waking up at five in the morning on the sidewalk and finding a reason to say, "Yeah, my morning's been good." Coming from their position, to be able to say that just blows me away.

Before we leave the staff of the Downtown Chapel, I want to introduce one more of its employees, Andy, a young man finishing his master's degree at Notre Dame and recently married. He is a pastoral associate of the Holy Cross and is remarkably wise for his years. Like everyone I've found working in the impoverished community of Old Town, Andy feels he was led there.

It wasn't strength or power that brought me here, but a need for deepening my relationship with God and God's people. Becoming grounded was what I sought. I wanted my faith to be something tangible. That's what led me to working here in Old Town. At the time, I'm not sure I was conscious of what I sought, but through my experiences here, I recognize my mission. Today, I associate people with *suffering* rather than labels. The prophets we speak of are the people we serve who freely open their lives and experiences with us. They ask nothing more of us than to listen or to pray for and with them. They just ask us to be present to them. I've learned that I'm not here to fix anyone or to solve problems. I'm here to be in the moment with people and to open my heart. In this way, we both receive. There are times to celebrate here and times of real disappointment—disappointment for someone who's relapsed or has everything stolen from them, which forces them to live back on the streets. It takes time to acquire a new birth certificate and personal identification, as well as recover what's been lost so that they get housed again.

The people I learn from most are those suffering from mental illness. Since their reality is different than the rest of us, their voices aren't heard. They ask more patience of me. I visualize one low day when a person burns all their bridges. They can be healthy and well functioning for three months and then have a bad day, are unbalanced, or off their medications. In one full swoop, they can burn every bridge, every support system.

I think the work here is all about relationships. It's about building bridges, supporting each other in transitions. I use the word *transitions* in a broad sense, whether it is how we are going to recover or find peace. It's all those things. We are here on this corner of a Portland street to give some foundation to the person who's right in front of us, who we are serving. We want that person to move forward in their day with the ability to advocate or take some positive action for themselves, even if it means just doing their laundry or approaching a caseworker.

I ponder whether we are here to help alleviate the issues that people are experiencing, such as homelessness, addictions, mental illness, or whether we are looking at systemic causes. Are we looking at the situations that brought people to their current predicaments? I think we are always here for the immediate needs, but we need to address what is bringing people to us. There must be a balance between addressing basic and immediate needs with advocacy for the marginalized. Something I've learned from the people we serve is that it's easier for me to make a phone call to inquire about someone's benefits than it is for that person to make the call themselves and be on the receiving end of insensitivity. Negative responses to their needs could cause them to go deeper into depression, or even give up hope.

When I first arrived here, over three years ago, one of the first people I got to know was a gentleman fresh out of prison. He was a sexual offender. I spent days with him, talking with him about how he was going to reintegrate himself into society. He started with so much hope and positive outlook and then, over the course of two or three weeks, became very cynical and feared that the best place for him was back in prison. He couldn't find a way to get back into living with the barriers before him as a sexual predator. Somehow, this man did retain hope. He looked forward to the time we spent together because I wasn't judging him. The truth is this was a new experience for me. I'd never had a face or a name to attach to a sexual offender. Spending that time with him made me drop the last of my labels for people. He came to me so open, with his regrets, his hopes, and his dreams. I haven't kept up with him as he's moved on, but overtime, he did find a place to live, not in Portland, but in a nearby city. He did stop by once to see me and to let me know that he was moving in the right direction. We never know where people's stories end or where they could go. My experience with him was a real gift. When I came here, I was thinking I'd meet people who fell under that big, generic, meaningless word—*homeless*. That word doesn't have much meaning for me anymore.

We have volunteers here who are also homeless, who are seasonal. They may leave Portland at the end of the summer and then come back in the spring. There is always this hope to see them again, but there is also hope that we don't. In the community, where we focus on relationships and build them up, it's tough to let go of people. When I see someone again and they are still on the street, my first reaction is, "It's so good to see you." But then I have to realize that I'm seeing that person again because of a relapse, or their housing has been lost, or they've come back to town and are still in the cycle of homelessness. I find this emotionally difficult. I don't know what change I expect for them, but I do hope for something better in their lives.

We all yearn for that place where we are loved, validated, and treated with respect. Many people I know have sought housing in other parts of Portland. Since they don't know anyone there, they end up back with us in Old Town. Their friends are here. They enjoy the supportive community at the Downtown Chapel; however, it isn't always the best situation for them. It may be the place where they are the most vulnerable regarding their addictions and other temptations. How do you tell someone not to come back to the one place they are accepted? It's tough terrain to navigate.

In regard to sex offenders, such as the one Andy speaks of above, I was quite taken aback with a 2007 report from the Human Rights Watch regarding sex offender laws in the United States. We need to understand the whole picture before making blanket assumptions about people who end up in this ostracizing category. The Human Rights Watch article disclosed some points for us to consider.

- People children know and trust are responsible for over 90% of sex crimes against them.
- Sex offender laws are predicated on the widespread assumption that most people convicted of sex offenses will continue to commit such crimes if given the opportunity. In fact, most (three out of four) former sex offenders do not re-offend and most sex crimes are not committed by former offenders.
- People who have not committed violent or coercive offenses may nonetheless be required to register as sex offenders and be subject to community notification and residency restrictions. For example, in many states, people who urinate in public, teenagers who have consensual sex with each other, adults who sell sex to other adults, and kids who expose themselves as a prank are required to register as sex offenders.

I have no idea what type of offense the person in Andy's story committed, but I think it's important, at least for me, to keep the above statistics in mind before launching folks into categories of gross generalizations.

In her book, *The Cup of Our Life: a Guide for Spiritual Growth*, Joyce Rupp interprets Matthew 20:22: "Are you able to drink the cup that I am about to *drink?*" The symbol of the cup is equated to Christ's suffering, passion and death. Rupp points out that, "There is a consequence if you make a choice to be with me (Christ). If you want the glory of being with me, you'll have to take the suffering too" (93).

So many people inhabiting the streets know what suffering is and need all the acknowledgement, encouragement, and hope we can give them. Somehow, we must assure them that, beyond suffering, the peace of God awaits. We need God. We need not wait until our suffering runneth over. Daily, I want to present my cup of tears to God to drink. When I do that, I am better equipped to inspire others to follow my lead.

In 1 John 1:5[31], it says that in God, there is no darkness at all. When we shine light on our difficulties, the darkness dissipates. I honor all of those who work and volunteer for the Downtown Chapel, Sisters of the Road, Macdonald Residence, Central City Concern, Transition Projects, Volunteers of America, Outreach in Burnside, Hooper Detox Center, DePaul Treatment Center, Street Roots newspaper, the National Alliance on Mental Illness (NAMI), and all the other helping agencies in our city. Each offers an effulgence of light to the afflicted, urging them from darkness to fuller lives on the other side—lives filled with hope, meaning, and promise.

---

31 The light shines in the darkness, and the darkness has not overcome it.

CHAPTER 16

How Are We Being Together?

We have all known the long loneliness and we have learned that the only solution is love and that love comes with community.

—DOROTHY DAY

*I*n my view, the first contributing factor to finding meaning in life is honestly accepting our humanity, the darkness and the light. The second is letting go of our expectation that everyone conform to our ideals and ways of being. Wholeness is an expedition, and as tough as it gets, we need each other to traverse the rocky terrain. When we accept ourselves as fully human, we have a better chance to squelch the friction that sets ablaze individuals and countries. Embracing and forgiving our imperfections enables us to do the same for others. No longer separate, we understand that wholeness is doubtful and world peace impossible unless we work together.

In my early recovery, I sat silent in 12-step meetings, spending my time listening to others speak. As they let loose the stones of their misbehavior, I heard their grief and guilt. Before long, I recognized parts of my own story intertwined with theirs. The nakedness of self-disclosure exposes only one story of humanity. We are more alike than we care to admit.

Sisters of the Road Café is located a couple of blocks from the Downtown Chapel. Its mission is one of breathtaking compassion.

> Sisters of the Road exists to build authentic relationships and alleviate the hunger of isolation in an atmosphere of non-violence and gentle personalism that nurtures the whole individual toward changes that will reach the root of his or her homelessness and poverty and end it forever.

Sisters caters to people down on their luck—the homeless, the poor, the mentally ill, the addicted, and others. I purchase their lunch coupons from time to time, which I use to offer hot meals to homeless folks instead of cash. Patrons pay with cash, food stamps, and gift coupons, or they barter for meals. There's truly no free lunch at Sisters, but what is there is far greater.

The café is not just a place to eat. Within an atmosphere of peace, acceptance, and safety, patrons build community. Additionally, Sisters lends its address, telephone number, and message board to customers. Monica, the director, introduced me to Glasker Rankin and other individuals whom I've tape-recorded and written about in this book. With the unflappable stamina of a Mother Teresa, Monica seeks God in many disguises. Monica is one of the most joyful and centered women I've ever met. She understands that loving oneself precedes loving others. Monica is consistent in her journey of self-discovery and growth, as you will see in her Wisdom Will below.

WISDOM WILL OF MONICA BEEMER

Dear Family and Friends:

Every day, I try to *wake up*, meaning to work on healing myself so that I can be present every moment, with intention and love. These are the standards that I weigh my life against. If we are kind to each other, we can change life for the better. I believe the small things are more important than the huge ones. Sisters works toward some pretty profound goals, like ending homelessness.

Sisters is a great place to work. I'm really lucky to be part of it. The organization recruited me through friends who hung out with Sisters for many years. At the time, I was taking a six-month break to paint my house and rest. Social work can be pretty overwhelming at times. As a workaholic, I was hoping to change my habit. I wanted my world to slow down. Since that six-month period, time has never gone by that fast again. During my sabbatical, Sisters was looking for another codirector; however, I wouldn't have accepted this job if I hadn't unlearned a lot about work and learned how to *be*.

At Sisters, we sit in a circle every morning and check in with one another. This ritual reminds us every single day why we're here and what's most important. At Sisters, the indicator for success is how well we know each other. How are we *being* together?

When I went to work at Sisters, I left behind a large salary, and still, it was the best decision I ever made in my life. When I look at our society, I wonder, *Who is really disenfranchised? Who really needs to be changed in this society?* So many people have the power to create a different world, but they don't participate. The paradigm of nonviolence at Sisters truly changes people. When we look at the margins of our society, we see the injustice in the world. However, I'm not sure who are the real disenfranchised persons—the poor and homeless or ourselves? Certainly, it's painful to be oppressed, poor, mentally ill, hungry, and homeless. Living in a society without a vision of life is a real disenfranchisement in itself. The philosophy at Sisters changes me every day. I'm happy about that because my waking up is a daily process. It's just like the goal of nonviolence at Sisters. It involves trying to do the right thing. Here, we have a saying, "Everyone is our teacher." I believe this to be true; it's also a state of mind.

Glasker was one of the teachers who came to Sisters and volunteered. He was then hired as a cashier. He was special because he'd gone through so much in his life—hard, terrible addictions. Glasker was such a mean guy when he was using. He said he was addicted to everything. He was also a dealer. A person can come out of that kind of despair and be either more hurtful or more helpful to people. The result is profound either way. Someone told me a story once about a guy who had been hit by lightning and was suffering. He went to a hundred doctors, and the hundredth doctor acknowledged that his condition was actually a phenomenon. Everyone else told him he was crazy. This man could have either chosen to be super pissed about consulting a hundred doctors before getting a diagnosis and an acknowledgement of his injuries, or he could have used the experience for good. The man chose the latter. He created a website to connect with others who have also been struck by lightning.

I'm amazed by the people I meet who share the wisdom gained from their experiences. Many tell me terrible stories about the police. They've been hurt by the very people that society looks to for protection. I try to listen, even though it's tough. The street prophets are the ones who share their stories with openness and truth. It's not about letting go of all that and forgetting about it when life improves. No one can do that. Hopefully, people can come to a place of peace without destroying their spirit. I'm incredibly moved by these people and thankful to hear their stories. They remind me that Portland is not a great city for everyone. We have a lot of work to do here, but we can do it.

Someone complained to me about people camping in the parks, and I said, "Maybe the parks could be good advocates for affordable housing, then." People are sleeping in the parks because they have no other place to go. It's pretty hard to work on advocacy when people are blaming the poor and disdaining them for their poverty or mental illness. One of the customers at Sisters has kept her indignation, and I think it's awesome!

She identifies what's wrong and speaks out. It's hard because sometimes she gets angry with us, but sometimes it's right on. I don't know how she does it when she's humiliated every day. When a person is homeless, her day-to-day experience of things not being right can cause her to lose her anger about it. I'm proud of this woman because she can still express her anger. The street prophets are the people who trust enough to share their stories and are confident you'll believe them and give them some hope. She's one of the prophets; she reminds us when things aren't right through her anger. It's an absolutely appropriate response. Once, she came in after she'd been humiliated at Burger King one more time, and she was pissed. She wanted to use the phone to call a lawyer, so I helped her. It's amazing that she hangs on to what's right.

Sometimes, I ask people if they're scared, and they reply that they are so used to danger they are numb to it. It takes them time to normalize back into society once they get housed. When C., one of my favorite people, got housed, she fell into a deep state of anxiety and depression. A couple of months later, I helped her furnish her apartment. It took her that long because everything she wasn't able to deal with on the streets [suppressed feelings] came rushing at her. Her meltdown really was a good thing because she was processing and letting go, doing her grief work. She's remarkable. Like Glasker, where everything came from his heart, C. zaps you in the heart. She helps folks understand her experience. She's able to size-up a situation and explain why things are the way they are. C. is extremely intelligent, fascinating, and willing to share what life on the streets is like. It's a gift to talk to her. C. was housed after 20 years on the street. 20 years of hypervigilant existence! Her stress is huge due to the change. One woman in our book, *Voices from the Street*, said she'd rather be raped than homeless! She acknowledged that women can actually fear something worse than rape or being beaten up, and that's homelessness. Men and women are fearful on the streets, but women, in particular, dread the dangers.

I define spirituality as getting to know myself more in order to become more of whom I really am. In the process, I also get to know more about what I call God. I become more aware of the energy that's all around us. Being at Sisters keeps me awake because Sisters' philosophy is not to overwork but to know each other, to be open-hearted, to deal with conflict without getting too stressed. Because I'm working in such a diverse environment, I am constantly aware of when I'm present and when I'm not. It's a privilege and an opportunity to serve people society ordinarily would prevent me from knowing. I'd be living in a different area and never come into contact with the street community here. Sisters challenges me. It offers constant reminders. Its philosophy of nonviolence, community organizing, and gentle personalism makes me feel really blessed. I have a great home life, a great partner, a great family, great friends, and a great community. My spiritual practice is very helpful to me.

Sisters' goal is to be aware of how spirit is working within each of us all the time. One of the ways I get reminded, besides talking with people, is to go to Subud House and practice Latihan. It's a worldwide spiritual practice that is nondenominational, nondogmatic, and founded by a Muslim man from Indonesia in the 1920s and 1930s. Latihan simply means spiritual exercise, combining a social or dharma component of doing good works in the world. My partner and I go to Subud House once or twice a week. We practice it at home, but community is encouraged. Latihan's prayer involves surrender to whatever a person needs to receive. This has been my practice for eight years, and I've found it fits right in with the philosophy of Sisters.

At Sisters, when an issue comes up, there's no blaming. This is very healthy. When things have been tough at Sisters, we use a great process, including consensus, to make sure we're doing the right thing. We invite as much input as possible, doing "go arounds," where everyone has their say. Regarding our goal of nonviolence, we ask ourselves, "What would love do in this situation?" That doesn't mean it isn't stressful sometimes. It might mean that we need to continue what we are doing, even if we aren't saving money—like we had to do when working on *Voices from the Street*. I just pray that we're doing the right thing and that my angels are watching out for all of us. When we do what's right, they are, and powerful things happen. We basically spent our reserves to finish *Voices from the Street*. It was after the crisis of September 11 in the United States, and we questioned ourselves, "Do we stop this project when no one else has ever asked homeless people what's needed? Do we stop when we are halfway done, or do we keep going and pray?" We had to lay off a few people, but we did make our payroll. When times are difficult, we can always learn from experience in order to do better the next time.

If I had to leave Sisters tomorrow, I'd really miss how all of us here work to reach an agreement and treat each other well. This doesn't mean that we're nice all the time; we can say the hardest things to each other. Part of the process is being honest with each other and to continue working on ourselves. At Sisters, we avoid scapegoating. I've never been the scapegoat; I'm always the super hard worker. Watching how other organizations blame people is so difficult to watch. Here, we feel like we are part of a culture change and a revolution. We've just started conducting nonviolence trainings for KBOO [local nonprofit radio station], with over 500 volunteers and an amazing staff. Working together in community in a non-blaming way involves an absolute culture change, because in our society, when we make a mistake, we're bad. However, that's not true. We make mistakes all the time; the truth is we are more than our behavior. The mistakes we make are opportunities to tell each other what we need, to work on it, and to say, "I'm sorry."

We need to be accountable and loving to each other and ask for what we need, without saying, "You're bad." Instead, we can say, "I'm going to tell you this because I believe in you."

Gandhi would say absolutely *no* to violence in any form or any form of humiliation, sexism, and racism by which we hurt each other. Part of the process means knowing each other, believing in each other, and never giving up on each other. In our culture, we give up on each other too easily. If I left Sisters, I'd lose what everyone loses when they leave Sisters—a place where people are challenged to be the best they can be, are loved in spite of their mistakes, and are not in denial about their shortcomings. It's the same for the customers who come to Sisters. It's a place where they can do dignified work in exchange for good food and a choice of entrées, where someone knows their name. Sisters means more to the customers than those of us on the staff because the customers have fewer places like Sisters. It's a living room for folks. Our customers say that Sisters brings out the best in them by loving and challenging them.

For would-be volunteers, I'd say open up your heart and share yourself. Remember, you're getting changed as much as the people you are helping. Try not to think that you're the helper and the customer is the helpee. Transformation happens within all of our hearts. That outlook is the most therapeutic part for the customers and ourselves. I'd also say that it's really natural to feel many different feelings, so be honest with yourself and work on them. We all learn a bunch of stereotypes about people who are experiencing homelessness. Sisters can help recognize our prejudices about the poor: *They're all lazy; they're all scary.* They're scary because we've put people out on the streets with extreme mental illness. Yes, they have erratic behavior; they have schizophrenia! Can you imagine sleeping on the street while enduring a mental illness? We need to be honest instead of blaming or fearing the mentally ill. It would really be great if the park system could get to the root of why people are sleeping in the parks and recognize why veterans with post-traumatic stress disorder can't sleep in quarters with 150 people because they get too triggered. Lack of public bathrooms is another problem. We get mad at people for peeing or defecating in public. Yet, what are you suppose to do if you're homeless and there's no bathroom available? Imagine getting a ticket for that and having to go to court? We need to accept reality and do something about the problem.

The explosion of homelessness began in 1979, when the city government made major cuts in affordable housing. These cuts run parallel with homelessness. Let's wake up! What are we doing blaming individuals? This is not a DNA thing. If it is, we are blaming 40 percent who are children of the homeless. Let's look at solutions. Let's build affordable housing. It's not that hard. We know what to do. So let's do it.

The other day, Genny Nelson said, "I'll never ever stand in line again for the funds. When I see how much money is spent in Iraq, we could have ended homelessness and hunger in the United States, and probably ended homelessness itself three times over!" I'm not going to wait in line any more, either. I'm going to stand up and say that I know the money is there.

I see funds go to blow up children and innocent civilians! I'd much rather feed and house people in our own country. I know it's my tax money and that I absolutely have a role in the solution. When are we going to get so pissed off that we take to the streets every day to protest homelessness? I hope we'll soon move out to the streets and hold hands around Pioneer Square to make our voices heard. As a people, I think that we have lost our indignation!

It's not so important that I be remembered for what I've done, but rather for how I've lived my life. The other day, my partner said that she liked the wrinkles I'm developing because she thinks they are all smile wrinkles. I'd like to die knowing I did the best that I could to work on healing myself and that I made a difference because of who I was. Plus, I had a good time doing it. My mother wore a big smile on her face when she took her last breath. It was so profound for those of us watching her. I'd like to be remembered as a person who had a lot of fun and helped others to have fun while being myself and helping others to do the same.

Love, Monica

In Luke 12:48, it says, *"To those who have much...much is expected."* It takes so little effort to help another human being, to make life just a tad more comfortable. Most of us have more than enough to share and to spare. I think Monica challenges us to contemplate our blessings. Daily she is faced with those who are *without*. And, yet, are they truly without? Many of them have a clearer understanding of what "much" means than the rest of us. All of the prophets in these pages expound upon the riches and blessings in their lives since sobriety, and society could still look upon every one of them as being *without*. Yet, they don't hold back. There is no hoarding of their time, talent or dollars. I learn so much from their example.

I read in the *Oregonian* newspaper the other day that Portland has the highest number of hungry children in the country! Children with food anxiety, not knowing when they are going to eat again! How can that be in America, the wealthiest country in the world, a place touted as offering the greatest opportunities for a better life? What a shame it is on our state to have such publicity.

As a people, I think we care, but we're too harried to do anything about it. What are a few cans of food, a couple of hours of volunteering a month, a donated monthly bus pass? It's about consciousness. It's about recognizing the overabundance of blessings we each have, and our willingness to share with our community. I believe that Sisters of the Road, and all the other advocacy programs in Portland and other cities, challenge, not only themselves, but everyone to answer the question, "What can I do to make today a better day for someone else?" *To those who have much...much is expected.*

Monica Beemer with the author.

CHAPTER 17

A Missive From Genny Nelson

The greatest challenge of the day is: how to bring about a revolution of the heart, a revolution which has to start with each one of us.

— Dorothy Day

U p to this point in Part II of the book, I've gone in a chronological order, starting with Sister Kate, who, in 1970, took her black habit and veil to the streets to alleviate as much suffering as she could. But I wanted to end the book with the wisdom of one of Portland's greatest women. Her wisdom is as much a beacon for the homeless and disenfranchised the world over as it is a summons for the rest of us to follow suit. On Sisters website (www.sistersoftheroad.org), there's an article about Genny receiving an award a few years back. She stands alongside some great Americans.

Genny Nelson, who co-founded Sisters in 1979, won the 2005 National Caring Award. Given by The Caring Institute, the award honors the ten most caring men and women and five most caring young people in American as selected by a prestigious panel of judges each year. Genny traveled to Washington, D.C. to receive the award. Past recipients of the award include President and Mrs. Jimmy Carter; Millard Fuller, founder of Habitat for Humanity; and Mary Jo Copeland, founder and driving force behind Caring & Sharing Hands, an organization that provides food and clothing for the homeless.

WISDOM WILL OF GENNY NELSON

Dear Family, Friends, and Community:

In 1972, at the age of 20, I found my work. I was a third-year student at Portland State University. I asked the work-study office if they could find me a job in my major, sociology. As a result, I was hired by Burnside Projects. I worked at the Everett Street Service Center, an all-night shelter for folks on the street.

Two significant things happened the first night. A number of conscientious objectors to the war in Vietnam were doing their community service there. They introduced me to the work of Dorothy Day and Peter Maurin. Dorothy and Peter were founders of the Catholic Worker Movement. These conscientious objectors also introduced me to community organizing. Both experiences changed my life and how I do my work forever.

The philosophies of nonviolence and gentle personalism practiced in the Catholic Worker Movement are the bedrock of all my work. Not many administrators and line staff of non-profit agencies share power with their customer base, genuinely and mutually tell each other the stories of their lives, or refuse to do something for someone when the person can do it for themselves, which are all tenets of Community Organizing.

I didn't know in the beginning how fortunate I was to find my life's work at such a young age. I came to understand that most people struggle with this journey. I was also not aware that I'd found my soul-work, something many people discover and/or implement in their retirement. In the last few years, I've come to realize that my work is God's gift to me. Sometimes, I have brought my own neurosis to the work, something I am not always proud of. But I'm humbled by the opportunities I've been given. I was born and raised Roman Catholic. For a time, I was a member of the Catholic Workers in Portland, Oregon, a community based in hospitality and direct action. Now, instead of connecting with a church, synagogue, or mosque, I have strengthened my personal relationship with God, and that has sustained me. My church is Sisters of the Road Café. It's where I go to break bread. It's where prophets walk in the door. It's where God is strongest in my life. This community is not one-denominational; it extends across faiths.

While working with the Portland Catholic Worker at Emmaus House of Hospitality, I got the chance to walk my talk. Dorothy Day was still alive at the time and writing in the *Catholic Worker* newspaper. I was surrounded by other dedicated Catholic Workers who taught me the art of opening my home, alongside my family, to people who needed a place to stay, sometimes for a night, sometimes for a couple of years. For five years I did that. Then my marriage ended. Thinking about what I was going to do next, I went back to where I'd started— Old Town/Chinatown, which was Portland's skid row. In 1979, I was hired again by Burnside Projects and returned to the same shelter I'd started at. That shelter led me to serve women in the Burnside neighborhood.

In 1970, Portland opened its first domestic violence shelter, the Bradley Angle House. Like other cities around the country, Portland was seeing more and more women on skid row who were escaping violence at home. By the late 1970s, the message, "There isn't any truly safe place for them on skid row," was being circulated by a group called Women on Burnside.

As members of Women on Burnside, Sandy Gooch and I staffed Boxcar Bertha's, a federally funded information, referral, and advocacy project for women fleeing from domestic violence, dealing with homelessness, or simply on the road.

While working there, we witnessed firsthand the calamities confronting women on the street. Unfortunately, by the fall of 1979, the federal funding ended for Boxcar Bertha's. Sandy and I canvassed the neighborhood speaking to both women and men about the issues they faced on the street. We asked what they considered the most important need at the time. Again, we were using a community-organizing model, not presuming two white, privileged women knew what was best for this neighborhood. At their request, we spent hours experiencing the soup lines and the missions, where people showed us a real need. They wanted an alternative where they could dine with dignity, where they could barter with their labor, where the food was recognizable on the plate, and where they could gather together in community. Most homes have living rooms, but people who live in SROs often lack any such gathering space.

The women in the neighborhood named Sisters of the Road. Boxcar Bertha, who lived during the 1930s, advocated for the rights and protection of women on the street at the time. Her biography is called *Sister of the Road*. So the women in the Burnside neighborhood named the café in her honor. On the day we opened, someone drew a circle with chalk on the sidewalk outside the front of the café and added three Xs inside it. This old hobo symbol means "good food, nice hospitality inside." We started with a $10 donation from John Curry of the Downtown Chapel and bartered for the rent.

At the time, St. Vincent de Paul was leasing the building and running a Meals on Heels program on the weekend. Unlike other neighborhoods, where meals are delivered in cars, they are walked from room to room in Old Town hotels. We agreed to manage the Meals on Heels Program on the weekend for St.

Vincent de Paul in exchange for use of the property by Sisters of the Road during the week. After nine months, St. Vincent de Paul moved out, and we arranged a lease with the current owners of the building.

Sandy used to say that she brought the restaurant know-how, and Genny brought the philosophy. And that's the absolute truth. I wasn't a good cook back then, and I'm still not. However, Sister's is so much more than just offering people a meal. I brought the philosophies of nonviolence and gentle personalism I'd learned from the Catholic Worker to Sisters of the Road. The community-organizing paradigm we instituted in Sisters charged us to go to the root of the problem, not to expect Band-Aids to change things.

When hunger and homelessness were no longer problems, we would happily focus on the goal of being the best coffee-house in town. Until then, we would greet people dealing with hunger and homelessness with gentle personalism and nonviolence, teach them how to organize their community, and always focus on a systemic approach.

The first tenet of nonviolence is not to humiliate anyone. We have practiced that radically in our organization from its very first day over 28 years ago. News went out quickly in the neighborhood about our attitude toward visitors to Sisters:

> You're wonderful, for just walking through the door of the Café. However, if you humiliate yourself or someone else, we're going to call you on it. We're going to name that behavior; and explain why it's not appropriate at Sisters. Then, we're going to ask you to change it. If you can change the behavior, you're welcome to stay. Otherwise, we will set a proscribed time where you can

> return for conflict resolution and be welcomed back in the Café.

We don't have a big rule book because we evaluate policies on a regular basis. Circumstances create the policies. If those circumstances change, we often discard the outdated policies. People who live on the street know that Sister's is fair. We've tried to be really consistent by making sure that people are treated the same way.

Peter Maurin coined the phrase "gentle personalism" after being impressed with the Personalist Movement in France. He's credited with bringing that philosophy to the United States and teaching it via the Catholic Worker Movement. Basically, Sisters says to people, "We don't need a government at any level to tell us how to be good human beings and do the right thing." That's a personal responsibility. We need to stand up for each other's freedom. Someone might come into Sisters saying, "I had this happen to me, and I don't know what to do about it." We sit down with that person and help them create a strategy. We don't do the work for them, but we serve as their ally. We support and encourage people dealing with homelessness, many whose family relationships have deteriorated. We create family together.

We listen carefully to our customers. Back in the early 1980s, many of them told us their food stamps weren't very useful. Sisters could accept stamps from the elderly and disabled, however, our homeless customers, who were not elderly or disabled, were not allowed to use theirs in exchange for a meal. Since they didn't have a place to live, they didn't have a refrigerator or stove. They asked, "You can accept food stamps in exchange for a meal from these other two groups of people, so why can't you take them from us?" We studied the dilemma and recognized that the issue was worthy of investigation. It took about two years. We got help from former senator Mark Hatfield. He attached a food stamp amendment to the drug bill signed by then president Ronald Reagan. Ultimately, for the first time, homeless people from across the country could use their food stamps in exchange for hot, prepared meals in nonprofit dining facilities. Sister's was the first in the nation to do this.

Community organizing is part of the bedrock that makes Sisters effective. After years of "experiments in truth," to quote Gandhi, we have learned a lot. Our Civic Action Group (CAG) is comprised of folks with direct experience of homelessness. Our community organizer was without housing for eight years. On weekends, when our café is closed, CAG uses Sisters' space for organizing their community. It is where they get down to the business of implementing their campaign.

It's amazing. I'm like a proud mother. Wow! CAG held a truth commission on the effects of the Sit-Lie Law[32] on Portland's homeless community—just one of their tactics. People who've experienced homelessness firsthand are the best ones to organize themselves. No one else is going to be as invested as they are. They need to train their leaders, and that's what they're doing. Organizations need to listen closely, be accountable, and get out of the way. We can offer them friendship, mentoring and training when requested, space, resources, and opportunity.

Initially, Portland's Ten-Year Plan to End Homelessness involved customers from Sisters of the Road. The National

---

32 Sisters of the Road started a postcard campaign to fight ordinances that make it illegal to sit or lay on city sidewalks during business hours. Along with *Street Roots* newspaper, they also worked to repeal the anti-camping ordinance, which they believed was being used to sweep homeless people from the area. On June 23, 2009, a Multnomah County judge ruled the Sit-Lie Law was unconstitutional.

Alliance to End Homelessness website notes that the majority of the 10-year plans were created without any input from people who were dealing with homelessness. One of the successful features about Portland/Multnomah County's Plan to End Homelessness is that Sisters stood up for the right of people who've actually experienced homelessness to represent themselves. Sisters worked diligently to ensure that the views and wisdom of homeless people were included. We submitted all kinds of data about the barriers that keep people on the streets.

Sisters of the Road, from fall of 2001 to spring of 2004, conducted two-and-a-half-hour interviews with 600 people who were without housing currently or in their past. We encouraged them to identify in detail the causes and multiple calamities of and the solutions to their homelessness. Visit Sisters website (www.sistersoftheroad.org) for information about how to access this tremendous amount of data.

One of the outcomes from our research was the publishing of *Voices from the Street: Truths about Homeless from Sisters of the Road*. Most of the credit goes to the 600 individuals who narrated their life stories in scenarios like the following:

> I'm a veteran and homeless.
> I grew up homeless.
> I'm a woman who was a victim of domestic abuse and landed on the street
> I'm dealing with mental illness, and I'm on the street.
> I have a physical disability, and I'm on the street

The book is a tribute to Sisters that people felt safe enough to share the depth of their lives with us. We wanted peoples' stories based on their candid experiences, not just their answers to yet another survey.

From the beginning, we have practiced nonviolence and gentle personalism with the police department as well as our customers. Generally, when we have raised questions, the officers have given us respect. We stand up for our customers when other people don't. We tell the truth about police brutality if we see it. We work to build a rapport with officers on the beat and in command because it's important to us that we challenge our perceptions of each other. Gandhi talked about transforming the perceived *other* into an ally. Talk about a daily experiment in truth for all sides.

Years ago, Central Precinct sent over an officer who proposed that we take photographs of any drug runners, users, and sellers coming into the café and then keep them in a designated album. Additionally, he proposed that Sisters refuse entrance to anyone in the photos. He said that many neighboring social services had agreed to this recommendation. I was outraged! I said, "Why would we even remotely be interested in doing this?" I immediately wrote a letter to the commander at Central Precinct. The commander called a meeting of social service providers in Old Town/Chinatown to which one of Sisters' board members and I attended. There, I explained Sisters philosophy about drugs in the café

> You know it's inappropriate behavior to sell or use drugs in Sisters of the Road Café. We're vigilant all of the time. In fact, we've posted a three-minute limit on the bathrooms to deter people from using them to shoot up in. We have explained our policy to our customer base, so they know how seriously we take these behaviors.

I explained Sisters' process for remaining vigilant and added, "You wouldn't ask any other restaurant in town to take photos of people and then refuse them service. So we're not going to go along with such a practice, either."

At the end of the meeting, the commander agreed with our board member that, indeed, Sisters rows a different boat; however, he added that we were successful in deterring drugs in our organization. He acknowledged that Sisters would not be participating in the proposal.

Sisters has a well-known reputation for *watching* when police are arresting someone. We don't interrupt the process, but we observe to make sure that the interaction is appropriate in every way. We encourage others to do the same. By this check and balance system, we're saying to everyone that we are all accountable.

Sometimes, prophets walk through the door at Sisters of the Road Café. One of the most profound compliments we receive from our customers is, "I am not invisible in Sisters," which is the reason a prophet can be detected. The prophet is the older fellow who stopped by the table where I was having lunch and handed me his prayer for the insane world we live in before he even introduced himself. It was a healing balm in two lines. The prophet is the barter worker who wrote and sang his enchanting songs like an angel while pearl diving in the café's kitchen.

Jesse is one of these prophets, too. In the early years of Sisters, we already knew that we needed to expand, since there were only 20 seats in the original café. Breaking down the wall of the adjoining storefront wasn't an option then. We were seriously looking at moving to the east side of the river and housing our operation in part of the square footage belonging to another nonprofit. Jesse dealt with tremendous mental illness. Her favorite mantra was, "It's horrible, just horrible, everything's horrible." Yet, she was the one who saw the truth. "You can't move!" Jesse said. "You've proven to the neighborhood that you aren't a fly-by-night." She was referring to organizations that boasted great things for the neighborhood, yet folded in less than a year. Jesse challenged us to rethink this move and continued to challenge us as we began initial preparations on the site. Jesse was absolutely right. We ended up not moving. Just as we were getting used to the idea of staying put, the storefront next door became available. The rest is history. Today, we can seat about 40 people. If we pay attention, we'll recognize the prophets. They're always around us. We just need to quiet ourselves and listen.

Years ago, there was a homeless artist who would come in and order up a cup of coffee. He painted his pictures in the basement of the Butte Hotel, below the café. He played the best blues guitar rendition I have ever heard of "I'm Confessing That I Love You." I never missed a chance to ask him to play it again. He would smile at me with a cold stogie hanging from his mouth and then reach for his guitar. His gift would mesmerize everyone fortunate enough to be in the café.

Watching people transform is amazing. That's the magic at Sisters. People come in, and they notice something different happens inside the place. They watch staff work at telling their truth. If somebody who's relapsed comes into Sisters, we understand that it's part of recovery. In recovery, a person needs people in their life who will tell them the truth. So many times, people hear, "Oh, it's good to see ya," and leave it at that. When we know someone well enough, we can say, "It's good to see ya, and why the hell are you here?" At Sisters when they say, "Well, I relapsed," we ask, "What are you going to do about it? Can I be your ally in some way?" Not an enabler, but an ally. Then you hear later from people, "You know what? You asked me the hard stuff, and that's what helped me get back on track. You didn't pretend everything was just fine. You also didn't get upset or punish me. You didn't reject me because I'd started drinking or using again. When I get dismissed like that by a person, I feel like they don't like me. But when you say, 'You know what? You're under the influence, so we can't hold a real discussion because it's only going to be one-sided. But I'll check in with you later, and we will have this conversation,' then I know you care."

People remember this and say, "Genny's not saying she hates me or that I'm bad or ruined in her eyes. She still believes in me." I don't think we realize how easy it is for people to return to some dark and distraught place, feeling destroyed and worthless, or how easy it is for us to be there for someone in such a way that they avoid that place.

I possess an infinite passion to help change the world into its most loving possibilities, but I am a recovering workaholic. After 35 years, the majority of them at Sisters, my body's well-being was banging at the door of my life. I had to answer with more than excuses or worn-out time lines: "I will start taking better care of myself as soon as…" I was way too tired to ignore my truth.

I've been diabetic since I was eight years old. From age 20 to 40, I ran a race with my life based on my doctor's belief that I would die in my forties due to complications from having this disease. In 1972, I told myself, *You have less time than most to get your work done.* Consequently, I've lived with a fair amount of depression. Practicing nonviolence and gentle personalism in my life, as well as in my work, has strengthened me.

I don't think a person can grow up with a chronic illness without needing to be in a fair amount of control. That became a way of life for me. As my role in Sisters of the Road changes, I am now faced with learning how to let go in some pretty profound ways. I am grateful for my personal relationship with God; it is the richest part of my faith.

I have worked closely with people who are raw in their addictions. Years ago, part of my spiritual program included attending Al-Anon. I was a significant other for many of our customers. Al-Anon helped me learn where I could stand with them and what was detrimental to my health. I learned not to be an enabler and how to set fair boundaries. Knowledge of the 12 steps has helped me encourage people to accept responsibility for their actions and, maybe for the first time, know the power of forgiveness.

For decades, I've had conversations with God. When I pray, the philosophies of nonviolence and gentle personalism are my spiritual checks and balances. When I die, I hope I am remembered for who I was, not what I did.

With Love, Genny

Genny was influenced early in her career by Dorothy Day and Peter Maurin, founders of the Catholic Worker Movement. Like Day, Genny's pacifism is a way of life. In the Gospel of Matthew 26:52, Jesus says, "Put your sword back in its place, for all who draw the sword will die by the sword." Genny expounds upon the definition of violence so that it includes negative speech. Within the confines of Sisters of the Road Café, people sense something different. There is an aura of peace, acceptance, and of course, sustenance that the homeless rarely, if ever, find in other city establishments. There is a feeling of neighborliness, of welcome. Around the lunch hour, the Personalist Center shields a long line of hungry bellies. These people are Genny's friends, who she enjoys a meal with, prophets who often set her on the right path, and every one of them feels her love. Everyone I interviewed espoused great affection for her.

Mother Theresa endured dark nights of the soul and depression and, like her, so has Genny. However, it hasn't halted her propulsion to live and serve the oppressed. Genny knows that every small act of loving kindness counts—"by little and by little," as Dorothy Day would say.

CHAPTER 18

Do Not Be Afraid

> We must learn how to look into our fears because we cannot let ourselves be controlled by fear. [...] if we can't look death and failure in the face, well, then we can never live because to live means to risk to do things.
>
> —JEAN VANIER, FOUNDER OF L'ARCHE

During Advent, Father Ron often preaches to us about the birthing of Christ within us. "Do not be afraid," he says. This phrase comes from the Gospel of Matthew 1:18–24, where an angel appears in Joseph's dream to inform him that Mary has not been unfaithful, but is carrying the Christ child, the messiah of whom the prophets spoke. "Do not be afraid," the angel said to Joseph. Father Ron adds the following:

> Every time Jesus is about to do something incredible— every new move, there is this phrase—*Do not be afraid.* [It is a Biblical warning that] God is going to do

something incredible and all heck is going to break through. Not just in the past but right now in us, but only if we are willing to face our fears. Advent is about waking us up from a slumber that covers and blinds us to the needs of people.

God created us as receptors of divine light, and as such, our mission is to take care of one another—feed the hungry, nurse the sick, and provide food and shelter for the homeless and abandoned. As light bearers, we are the one's to fight for systemic change in the world. The struggle is daunting when looking at the plethora of pain in the world. But, as Mother Teresa taught, each person can make a difference by helping one person at a time. Is this not the birthing of the Christ within?

If I let go of fearing what I don't understand, if I let go and surrender to the Will of God, won't I open a space within myself, a womb in which the Christ light can dwell? Today, I ponder this place within myself, imagining the laser of God's light purifying and widening the opening so that I might harbor Christ daily in my heart and express loving kindness to all I meet. These are contagious acts. One by one, light bearers grow in number, and one by one, we hold each other up.

Do not be afraid. It's true; everyone fears what they don't understand. If we've never been desperate, hopeless, and homeless, how can we understand? I've discovered that by putting myself in the company of those struggling with survival amidst great odds, I can easily empathize. I've found that I'm more alike than different from most people, no matter their neighborhood or station in life. One way we alcoholics learn this is in our Alcoholics Anonymous meetings. After hearing the testimonies of others, early recovering people soon realize that they've all made similar mistakes, and if there are some things they aren't guilty of, it's probably because they failed to think of them. Falling down is part of the human experience, but so is rising again.

There is no escaping our oneness—whether broken or whole. We are all more alike than we are different, and that's what I've wanted to express here on these pages through the stories on the streets. In *Radical Amazement*, Judy Cannato explains how analogous we all are.

> We are not so different from other species as we might think. Recent genome research has concluded that of the 30,000 genes in the common house mouse (*Mus musculus*), ninety-nine percent have direct counterparts with the human species.[33] Despite appearances, we all share essential components of life that make us more similar than different. (58)

> We are the universe conscious of itself, and we are about using our consciousness to reflect, to know, and to make choices in behalf of the whole. Rather than being a process that degrades human status, evolution allows us to glimpse a profound mystery, one that reverberates all the way back to the ancient mystics who say, "We are all one." (66)

Cannato confirms my belief that every human being brings something to the table, and when we reject their gifts, we negatively influence everyone on the planet. When I judge, fear,

---

[33] Quammen, David. "The Evidence for Evolution Is Overwhelming." *National Geographic.* p. 6, 206. November 2004.

or shun the disadvantaged, I deprive myself of a learning experience, and I don't feel good about myself. Jean Vanier, the founder of L'Arche, an international network of communities for the mentally disabled, bravely faces his fear when sharing the following self-evaluation:

> I discovered something which I had never confronted before, that there were immense forces of darkness and hatred within my own heart. At particular moments of fatigue or stress, I saw forces of hate rising up inside me, and the capacity to hurt someone who was weak and was provoking me! That, I think, was what caused me the most pain: to discover who I really am, and to realize that maybe I did not want to know who I really was! I did not want to admit all the garbage inside me. And then I had to decide whether I would just continue to pretend that I was okay and throw myself into hyperactivity, projects where I could forget all the garbage and prove to others how good I was. Elitism is the sickness of us all. We all want to be on the winning team. That is the heart of apartheid and every form of racism. The important thing is to become conscious of those forces in us and to work at being liberated from them and to discover that the worst enemy is inside our own hearts not outside! (19)

Perhaps the greatest fear each of us has is confronting ourselves and embracing both the light and the dark side of our humanity. I find when I do that it is easier for me to accept others for who they are, avoiding the projection of my ideas of right and wrong. In 12-step programs, self-examination is encouraged as well as self-forgiveness. Both are part of my spiritual program.

Only when I can identify my own elitism can I hope to assuage it.

My spiritual director, Cecilia Ranger, SNJM, PhD, advises me when I'm challenged by moral conundrums. For instance, if I reject every person living on the street or in dismal poverty, she'd describe my reasoning as a "casuistic moral theology," error thinking, thinking in black and white. There is always tension between reason and emotion; there's no getting past it. When I use either-or reasoning, I fail to consider countless elements. I believe that anyone's judgments or generalizations about the marginalized or others renders them sightless. And there is no room for reconsideration or for new information.

I admit that having had two abjectly poor, alcoholic, and often-homeless brothers, my tendency is toward compassion. I see my brothers in the faces of street dwellers. I see, as Mother Teresa acknowledged, "*God in God's many disguises.*" Still, I teeter on the border of self-righteousness and unconditional positive regard. Walking in Christ's footsteps is an enormous struggle. I'm not certain I've budged at all. I keep trying. I keep showing up. I believe these are requirements for spiritually awakening.

Every recovering person you've met within these pages keeps trying, keeps showing up. They've risked life itself to discover who they really are and have journeyed beyond incredible grief and fear to find wholeness, to find God. They've died to themselves, reawakening to God's embrace. No one has more courage, in my opinion, than the poorest of the poor who face the demons of homelessness, mental illness, and addiction. Paradoxically, every person within these pages embraces their disease because it's brought them back to the lap of our all-loving, all-forgiving God, even though God, as is said, wasn't the one who moved in the first place.

Every person's story is an asset. Without stories, we would have no history. There would be no measurement to calculate our development as humans. We would have no sustenance to draw from. We learn from the social communion of our ancestors who wrote the preamble to life as we experience it today. We are the writers of future history, and through one another, we can influence the outcome of tomorrow. Author Margaret Silf wrote an article in *America Magazine*[34] titled "Between Yesterday and Tomorrow." In it, she spells out why it is important to share our life stories with loved ones and community:

> What is true for a city is true for every person too. Our history matters—our collective and our personal stories. When we listen to our memories, we expose hidden layers of who we are. The memory-keepers (which means all of us) have a sacred duty to share their treasure with those who follow. To fail to do so is to risk becoming one dimensional beings with no depth beyond the immediate impulse, no hinterland to lend perspective.

In *The Gift of the Jews*, the biblical scholar Thomas Cahill gives his definition of history:

> We normally think of history as one catastrophe after another, war followed by war, outrage by outrage--almost as if history were nothing more than all the narratives of human pain, assembled in sequence. And surely this is, often enough, an adequate description. But history is also the narratives of grace, the recountings of those blessed and inexplicable moments when someone

---

34 March 26, 2007. pg. 8.

> did something for someone else, saved a life, bestowed a gift, gave something beyond what was required by circumstance.(Cover page.)

Cahill challenges our responsibility as earth citizens:

> God does not control the future because it is the collective responsibility of those who bring about the future by their actions in the present. For this reason, the concept of the future—for the first time—holds out promise, rather than just the same old thing. (131)

In 2007, the National Alliance to End Homelessness reported that, on any given night, approximately 730,000 men, women, and children are homeless in the United States. Between 2008 and 2009, they reported an increased homeless population of approximately 20,000 people (3 percent). Over the course of a year, between 2.5 and 3.5 million people will live either on the streets or in an emergency shelter.

It is true that some of our street dwellers are there because of their own poor choices, but even more are there because they've fallen victim to calamitous events in their lives. All deserve to be heard. The people within these pages are a modicum of the fortunate few who have managed, thanks to divine intervention, to shimmy up the rope to recovery and end their homelessness. This book is a testament to them. They have much to teach us about living beyond mental illnesses and addictions. They have much to teach us about living in the moment. They have much to teach us about hope. And they have much to teach us about love and community. I want to end this book with the engendered wisdom of Genny Nelson:

I learned something early on, and it has shaped the language that Sisters uses; you really can't say someone is dealing with homelessness. What they're dealing with are the calamities of homelessness. It could be just one, such as divorce or losing a job, or it could be a combination of things—but it's never just homelessness. It's hard luck, it is bad decisions, and it's all of the above.

We need to preserve the insights of the homeless, poor, mentally ill, and recovering addicts so future generations can benefit from their experiences. Perhaps by sharing one another's stories and the lessons learned, we can heal the fragmentation occurring in our society today.

> Let us pray
> For those who are blamed
> For their homelessness and
> Criticized for being poor.
>
> Let us pray for the addicted, the mentally ill
> The abused, the forgotten, and ignored.
> May they find peace.
>
> For this we pray to the Lord.

(Adapted from Prayers of Faithful Sunday, September 15, 2011, Downtown Chapel)

APPENDIX I

Disenfranchised Grief

Disenfranchised grief is the grief that persons experience when they incur a loss that is not or cannot be openly acknowledged, publicly mourned, or socially supported. The concept of disenfranchised grief recognizes that society has sets of norms—in effect, grieving rules—that attempt to specify who, when, where, how, how long, and for whom people should grieve. (4)
—Dr. Kenneth J. Doka, *Disenfranchised Grief*

Without numbing substances, addicted people's brokenness is exposed. Unrequited losses become whirling dervishes, ever-taunting them. During the state of bereavement, we grieve our losses. The greater our attachment, the more difficult our grief work. When people find themselves addicted, poor and/or homeless, they lose many things they once held dear, some of which are their faith, family, and friends; peace of mind; self-esteem; and health. I believe the greatest of all losses is that of their humanity. When people are ignored or dismissed by others without even so much as a glance in their direction, this is surely hell on earth.

Letting go of addictions involves tremendous losses. Writing as a thanatologist, I consider grief work a requirement for the treatment of alcoholics and addicts. Speaking as a recovering alcoholic, I once based my survival around my drugs of choice—alcohol and cigarettes. I forgot what a clean and sober life was like. I couldn't imagine it. Before I quit, I remember telling my husband, "If I let go of alcohol and cigarettes, what's left *for* me?" At the time, so wrapped up in my addictions, they were my identity. At a deeper level, I believe I actually meant, "What's left *of* me without them?" I couldn't imagine being exposed and vulnerable. Letting go of them plunged me into a profound state of grief. Alcohol and cigarettes were my means for coping with any stressors, good or bad. At the same time, they suppressed the anguish and pain in my life.

In the beginning of my recovery, I recall both anxiously pacing and moving robotically. Bereft of any filters, I suffered stimulus overload and insomnia. I thought I was going crazy. My journal entries were frantic, as if my life depended upon them. My blood sugar level nose-dived because I wasn't eating properly. I felt panicky day in and day out.

At the same time, I was shedding my alcoholic self, but I wasn't quite ready to accept the clean and sober me. I couldn't focus at work. With my job performance compromised, my boss sent me to the beach for a week to get "straightened out." She had no idea about the symptoms or dynamics of recovery from addictions. The addict's grief process is not acceptable to society, so their mourning is misconstrued as laziness, slacking, orneriness, victimhood, and insanity—even by those recovering themselves. Both physical and psychological symptoms were present during my recovery work, and much of the work involved grieving the many losses in my life, not just the ones caused by my drinking, but all the way back to childhood, when I felt bereft of my mother through her mental illness and abandoned by my father because he worked out of town.

When people are recovering from any addiction, all the hidden, discounted, and traumatic events in their life rushes forward, seeking the light. I heard author Wayne Dyer say once that "You cannot bury a worm." All alcoholic and addicts suppress their past traumas as a matter of course through their addictions. But, in recovery, like the worm, they continue to surface until they are resolved. Every person in this book, including the advocates for the poor, has endured the stigma of disenfranchised grief.

According to society, recovering from an addiction is not a credible reason for grief. People in recovery do not construe it as legitimate, either. All the substance abusers I've known have experienced emotions related to grief: shock, denial, anger, guilt, sadness, depression, loneliness, hopelessness, numbness, and more. In his book, *Grief Counseling and Grief Therapy*, William Worden suggests four tasks necessary to resolve grief, which I believe apply to anyone stepping into recovery work (the bracketed comments are mine, not Worden's):

1. *__Accept the reality of the loss.__* [The death of our using self, and the love vs. hate relationship with our drugs of choice. We must bury our desires and acknowledge that we are addicts, which is the death of our denial. We feel bereft of our *crutches*, naked, exposed, and vulnerable. There are other deaths, that of our drinking or drugging friends who must be dead to us for the sake of our sobriety.]

2. ***Process the pain of grief.*** [Processing the pain of our withdrawal physically and psychologically. We mourn the loss of our addictions.]

3. ***Adjust to the world without the deceased***. [Learning to live without negative crutches. We must replace the time we used drinking and drugging with positive habits, exercise, meditation, prayer, hobbies, reading, etc.]

4. ***Find an enduring connection with the deceased in the midst of embarking on a new life.*** [While this step doesn't exactly work with my analogy; we can say that the connection to the death of our dependencies is *enduring* because we must never forget that we have the disease of addiction. Without vigilance, it can rear its ugly head again, no matter how many years of sobriety we may have behind us.

   As in saying good-bye to a loved one or a dependency, there is a big hole in us. To fill the hole and prevent relapsing, we must develop activities that enhance our recovery, staying away from those who are using and investing in relationships with people who don't use or are in recovery programs. We can then embark on a new life of giving back and sharing the grace that we've been given. We need to use the time we spent drinking and drugging to invest in—as recovering folks say—*the next right thing.*]

My husband, David, a recovering alcoholic, knows the devastation of grief. His only son, Jeremey, died when he was just four years old. David also understands the grief involved in letting go of alcohol. When I asked him to describe the connection between grief and recovery, his words were profound.

> When we let go of drugs and alcohol, we grieve the death of ourselves. Everything we were ceases to be. With the learning aptitude of a young child, we must consciously recreate ourselves. We must give up all the people we thought were our friends and our support system. Drinking and drugging took 24 hours a day. We were either looking forward to our next drink, actively using, or suffering from the effects. Once we're sober, what are we suppose to do with the time that we formerly occupied abusing? We have to replace it with something.
>
> We grieve the active part of drinking/drugging. When hungover, one is less apt to spend time in self-reflection. When actively drinking, we projected our craving on to the next time. We were always planning when and where. This also leaves little time for self-reflection. Grieving the rituals of addiction is tough, too. We spent time courting, anticipating, raising the glass, and feeling its effects, but now that time is empty. The hard part is, we're left with ourselves, and we can no longer avoid introspection.
>
> It's difficult because it is not our standard operating procedure to live a day at a time. This is something we must learn. Once we're sober, we're way down the road thinking, *Oh my God, I can never have a drink/drug for the rest of my life!* What a grief that is! It takes a tremendous amount of support and effort, and all the strength we can summon, physically and emotionally, to see ourselves through the initial part of sobriety.

Not only that, when we've been sober for a while, we expect life to get better. In many cases, it gets worse because we are engaged again. We are forced to self-reflect. Grief is not something we choose to do, but it's no longer optional. When we were drinking, we could always drown the thoughts. Sober, we are catapulted into self-loathing, regret, grief, and fear. We become self-reflecting 24/7. There is no escape from it. We lack an identity. That's big.

Until we deal with our feelings, we can't begin to heal and build the self-esteem we lacked in the first place. We must build our emotional house on rock rather than on our drugs and/or alcohol. Even regret has some choice involved depending on our worldview. But grief comes no matter what. No one escapes grief. It's right up there with love and hate. It's universal and comes from a multitude of losses, not just the death of a loved one.

Ritual is a sacred part of grief work. We may choose to select our caskets or buy urns. We make arrangements for funerals and memorials so the community can grieve with and support us. We mark holidays and anniversaries by placing flowers on graves, lighting prayer candles, and creating memory altars. We join support groups or seek individual grief counseling. We write journals and even publish books about our loved one or our process of losing them. Likewise, 12-step programs provide the recovering person with rituals and guidelines to follow, meetings to attend, prayers to recite, and AA phrases to chant. By attending support group meetings with people who share our experience, we feel acceptance, empathy, compassion, companionship, and hope, all of which helps us to open up and share our own stories.

Eventually, in 12-step meetings, we voice our grief and shame, and our love and gratitude. We can measure our progress by celebrating milestones along the way with 30-day coins, 90-day coins, one-year coins, and so forth. We celebrate 12-step birthdays (sobriety anniversaries) with our families and friends in recovery.

As recovering, addicted grievers share their histories and stories in meetings with others of similar experiences, they learn they aren't much different from one another. We all make mistakes. We all suffer losses. We need reassurance that there is life after loss, human or otherwise. We need to reinvest our energy into a life without the presence of our loved one or abusive substance. It is then, and only then, that we reap the benefits of peace of mind, clarity of vision, and optimism for the future and can begin offering our services to our less fortunate brothers and sisters.

> Perhaps all the dragons in our lives are princesses who are only waiting to see us act, just once, with beauty and courage. Perhaps everything that frightens us is, in its deepest essence, something helpless that wants our love.
>
> — RAINER MARIA RILKE

APPENDIX ii

Writing Your Own Wisdom Will®

Those who do not have power over the story that dominates their lives, power to retell it, to re-think it, deconstruct it, joke about it, and change it as times change, truly are powerless, because they cannot think new thoughts.

—SALMAN RUSHDIE

Passing life's wisdom, values, beliefs, and blessings to future generations[35]

*D*o you ever wonder what you'll be remembered for when you die? If you want to leave behind a legacy of your wisdom, values, beliefs, blessings, and prayers for loved ones

---

35 Many of my ideas in this chapter were adapted from Dr. Barry Baines. See Bibliography.

that will last for generations, you'll want to write a Wisdom Will. Someday your words may be just what someone else needs to move forward, be rejuvenated, or find hope.

A Wisdom Will is an ancient tradition renamed. It began over 3,500 years ago as a Jewish commandment, or mitzvah. It was called an ethical will. In ancient times, the patriarch gathered his sons around his deathbed to bless and give them advice and instructions. People nowadays compose these legacy documents at turning points throughout life, such as births, baptisms, graduations, bar/bat mitzvahs, confirmations, weddings, before or after major surgery, or anytime it feels right. Wisdom Wills are less daunting and more manageable than full memoirs.

People prepare legal wills, trust funds, and living wills when they do their legacy planning. I suggest they include their Wisdom Will along with the other bequests. Before you start writing your legacy document, you need to be aware of a few challenges, which might include the following:

1. The discomfort of confronting your own mortality.
2. The danger of revealing your perceptions of family members that might be hurtful to them.
3. The risk of deceiving yourself and others about who you are—your beliefs, values, and convictions— just to look good.
4. The temptation to consider a Wisdom Will as an instrument for controlling people from the grave.
5. The tendency to blame and unload resentments.
6. The potential for tapping into unresolved grief and conflicts, thus creating discord instead of the peace that comes from writing your Wisdom Will (In this case, I recommend seeing a grief counselor or other therapist to work with your issues.)

WISDOM WILLS ARE POSITIVE DOCUMENTS, MEANT TO UPLIFT, ENCOURAGE, INSPIRE, AND PROVIDE A BIT OF SOLACE TO OUR SURVIVORS. ANYTHING LESS WOULD BE UNETHICAL.

Getting Started

Start with an inexpensive composition book/notebook, which will serve as your wisdom journal. Use your journal to practice the following writing exercises prior to compiling the finished document.

1. <u>Create a list of</u>:
   - Meaningful, personal, or family stories.
   - Lessons learned from personal or family experiences/people.
   - Your fondest memories of childhood, school, and growing up.
   - People who inspired you.
   - What you learned from your mistakes—the wisdom they taught you.

2. <u>Create a list of</u>:
   - Personal values and beliefs—what got you through the tough times. *When times were tough I…*
   - Your proudest achievements/times. *I'm happy that I   I feel good about myself for…*
   - Spiritual/religious values and beliefs. *I believe that… My spiritual values and beliefs include…*
   - Expressions of love and gratitude. *I'm grateful for my son, John because…   I love my family who have always…*

- Reconciliatory thoughts/words. *Some things that I regret are... Please forgive me if I've...or for... I forgive you for... and release you to...*

3. <u>Create a list of</u>:
   - Blessings, dreams, and hopes for present and future generations. *May you always... May God answer your prayers for... May you experience the blessings that God has granted me, such as...*
   - Advice and guidance. *I hope that you learn.... Please remember that... My advice/hope for you is....*
   - Requests. *Please take care of... Pray for... Remember...*
   - Organ donation requests and living will/funeral plans.

TIP: Look through old photo albums to stir memories.

TIP: Meet with old friends and siblings, cousins, aunts, uncles, etc. to reminisce.

TIP: Look through old-era magazines or on the Internet for what was happening at the time of your birth and the years following. Who were the popular stars from radio, television, or music? What products were on the market? What did you enjoy doing, buying, or using. All of these activities will spur memories.

MORE PROMPTING IDEAS/QUESTIONS FOR WISDOM WILLS

<u>Exercise:</u> Write at least one or two sentences for each of the following questions in your wisdom journal. Select and expand on the ones you feel strongest about.

- Talk about pivotal points in your life or peak experiences.
- When did/do you feel most alive?
- Are there specific things that you want your family/ loved ones to know about you?
- Talk about your most important roles (e.g., family, educational, employment, vocational, community service, religious, spiritual, etc.) you have played in life so far.
- What makes these roles so important to you?
- What are your most important undertakings, and which of them are you especially proud?
- What are your passions and talents?
- What have you learned about life that you would want to pass along to others?
- How were you brought up in terms of religious or spiritual traditions?
- How have your ideas about religion/spirituality changed over the years?
- Talk about your beliefs/or lack of them in terms of God, the divine, a higher power, etc.
- How would you describe your relationship with God, the divine, etc?
- Write about a time you felt close to divine.
- When do you feel closest to God these days?

- How do you communicate to God or your higher power?
- What words of guidance or advice would you like to pass along to your son, daughter, husband, wife, significant other, parents, friends, etc.?
- Are there any words or instructions you would like to offer?
- Are there particular things that you feel still need to be said to your loved ones or things that you would like to take the time to say once again?

By now, you have garnered more than enough material to write your Wisdom Will letter. Some people like to start with a personal statement of how they've tried to live their lives, for example: *I've tried to live my life as a loving and compassionate person*, or *I've tried to live an authentic and truthful life.*

In the last paragraph of your Wisdom Will, I suggest people write about how they'd like to be remembered. This is a wonderful way to reflect on their sense of accomplishment in life. We've all accomplished some good things as friends, parents, siblings, grandparents, aunts/uncles, churchgoers, employees, employers, artists, writers, homemakers, gardeners, pet lovers, hard workers, educators, students, addicts/alcoholics, survivors of many difficult times, and so on. Every person accumulates many roles over a lifetime, and self-acknowledgement is important to our sense of well-being and peace of mind.

APPENDIX iii

Bibliography

Alcoholics, AWSI. *Alcoholics Anonymous*. New York, NY: Alcoholics Anonymous World Serve, Inc., 2002.

Anthology, PACP. *Doing Time: 25 Years of Prison Writing--a Pen American Center Prize Anthology* (First Ed.). New York: Arcade Publishing, 1999.

Baines, MD, Barry K. *Ethical Wills: Putting Your Values on Paper*. Cambridge, MA: Perseus Publishing, 2002.

———. *Ethical Wills: Preserving Your Legacy of Values*. 3 August 2003. http://ethicalwill.com/. 2003.

Borchard, K. *The Word on the Street: Homeless Men in Las Vegas*. Reno, NV: University of Nevada Press, 2005.

Brokering, H. *I Will to You: Leaving a Legacy for Those You Love*. Minneapolis, MN: Augsburg Fortress, 2006.

Byock, MD, Ira. *Dying Well, Peace and Possibilities at the End of Life*. New York, NY: Riverhead Books, 1997.

Cannato, J. *Radical Amazement: Contemplative Lessons from Black Holes, Supernovas, and Other Wonders of the Universe*. Notre Dame: Sorin Books, 2006.

Cahill, T. *The Gift of the Jews: How a Tribe of Desert Nomads Changed the Way Everyone Thinks and Feels*. New York, NY: Nan A. Talese Doubleday, 1998.

Corpus.Org, *Writing Ethical Wills: I Wanted My Kids to Know Me*. http://www.corpus.org/. 2006.

Countryman, L. W. *Living on the Border of the Holy: Renewing the Priesthood of All*. Harrisburg, PA: Morehouse Publishing, 1999.

Day, D. *By Little and By Little: The Selected Writings of Dorothy Day*. New York, NY: Alfred A. Knopf, Inc., 1983.

Doka, K. J., ed. *Disenfranchised Grief: Recognizing Hidden Sorrow*. New York, NY: Lexington Books, 1989.

Duke, Patty. *A Brilliant Madness: Living With Manic-Depressive Illness*. New York, NY: Bantam Dell Publishing Group, 1999.

Dyer, Wayne. *Change Your Thoughts, Change Your Life: Living the Wisdom of the Tao*. Carlsbad, CA: Hayhouse, 2007.

Eslinger, Richard L. *The Web of Preaching*. Nashville, TN: Abingdon Press, 2002.

Fleisher, Mark S. *Beggars & Thieves: Lives of Urban Street Criminals*. Madison, WI: University of Wisconsin Press, 1995.

Foundation, H. *The Dual Disorders Recovery Book*. Central City, MN: Hazelden Educational Materials, 1993.

Freed, R. *Women's Lives, Women's Legacies: Passing Your Beliefs and Blessings to a Future Generation*. Minneapolis, MN: Fairview Press, 2003.

Glasser, I., and Rae Bridgman. *Braving the Street, the Anthropology of Homelessness*. New York, NY: Bergheim Books, 1999.

Gray- Garcia, Lisa. *Criminal of Poverty: Growing up Homeless in America*. San Francisco: City Lights Foundation, 2006.

Hendricks, Jon, ed. *The Meaning of Reminiscence and Life Review: Perspectives on Aging and Human Development*. Amityville, NY: Baywood Publishing Company, Inc., 1995.

Hurmence, B., ed. *Before Freedom, When I Just Can Remember*. Winston-Salem, NC: John F. Blair, 1989.

Lopez, Barry. *Crow and Weasel*. North Point Press, Sunburst edition, 1998.

McCord, B. *The Gift of You: How to Tell Your Loved Ones Who You Really Are*. Chicago, IL: Chicago Review Press, 2004.

Miller, Henry. *On the Fringe: The Dispossessed in America.* Lexington, MA: Lexington Books, 1991.

Morrell, J. P. *Voices from the Street, Truths About Homelessness from Sisters of the Road.* Portland, OR: Gray Sunshine, 2007.

Muller, Wayne. *Legacy of the Heart: The Spiritual Advantages of a Painful Childhood.* NY, NY: Simon & Schuster, 2005.

Northrup, C. *Mother-Daughter Wisdom: Creating a Legacy of Physical & Emotional Health.* New York: Bantam Dell, 2005.

Pelaez, PhD, Martha and Paul Rothman. Southeast Florida Center on Aging. Florida International University for Hospice Foundation of America. 2001. 1-800-854-3402.

Remen, MD, Rachel Naomi. *My Grandfather's Blessings.* New York, NY: Riverhead Books, a member of Penguin Putnam, Inc., 2000.

Riemer, Jack, and Nathaniel Stampfer. *So That Your Values Live On: Ethical Wills and How to Prepare Them.* Woodstock, VT: Jewish Lights Publishing, a Division of LongHill Partners, Inc., 1991.

Rinpoche, S. *The Tibetan Book of Living and Dying.* San Francisco, CA: Harper San Francisco, 1992.

Schachter-Shalomi, Zalman, and Ronald S Miller. *From Age-Ing to Sage-Ing.* New York, NY: Warner Books, Inc., 1995.

Scott-Maxwell, Florida. *The Measure of My Days*. New York, NY: Viking Penguin Books, 1968.

Smart, Ninian. *The Religious Experience*. Upper Saddle River, NJ: Prentice Hall, 1996.

Smith, G. N., SJ. *Street Journal*. (3rd printing). Kansas City: Sheed & Ward, 1994.

Smith, G. S. J. *Radical Compassion: Finding Christ in the Heart of the Poor*. Chicago, IL: Loyola Press, 2002.

Smith, G. S. J. *They Come Back Singing*. Chicago, IL: Loyola Press, 2008.

Spence, Linda. *Legacy: A Step-By-Step Guide to Writing Personal History*. Athena, OH: Ohio University Press, 1997.

Stroebe, M. S., and Robert O. Hanson, Wolfgang Stroebe, Henk Schut, eds. *Handbook of Bereavement: Consequences, Coping, and Care*. Washington, DC: American Psychological Association, 2001.

Swanson, Linda Ross, MA, CT, SNJMA. *Wisdom Wills: A Legacy of Wisdom & Values for Future Generations*. Marylhurst, OR: Marylhurst University, 2005.

Vanier, Jean. *From Brokenness to Community*. Mahwah, NJ: Paulist Press, 1992.

White, J., and W. Richard. (1992). *Rude Awakenings, What the Homeless Crisis Tells Us*. San Francisco, CA: C.S. Press, 1992.

Wolch, J., and Michael Dear. *Malign Neglect, Homelessness in an American City.* New York, NY: Josse-Bass, 1993.

Wood, Robert E. *Life's Footprints, Inc.* Centralia, WA: Life's Footprints, Inc., 1991. www.RobertEWood.com.

Worden, J. William. *Grief Counseling and Grief Therapy.* New York, NY: Springer Publishing Company, Inc., 2009.

World Service Office, Inc., *Alcoholics Anonymous.* New York, NY: Alcoholics Anonymous World Service, Inc., 2002.

World Service Office, Inc. *Narcotics Anonymous.* (Fifth Edition Ed.). Van Nuys: AA World Service, Inc., 1988.

Acknowledgments

I am thankful and deeply touched by all the prophets and advocates who so generously shared their stories in the creation of this book—many from depths of vulnerability that few of us will ever know. Their stories prove that we all have wisdom to share, no matter our station in life. Each and every one of us is a story waiting to be told, and if we don't pass these stories of wisdom on, they follow us to the grave.

I gratefully acknowledge one of my spiritual mentors and friends, Father Ron Raab, CSC. Without his wisdom and spiritual insight, this book would sorely lack. Father Ron shares a story about taking his early-morning jog and coming across a man ready to jump off the Burnside Bridge! When he approached, the man yelled out, "I'm going to jump!" Father Ron rushed over to him, grabbed his arm, and yanked him off the railing. The man's eyes were fierce with anger and rage. He glared at Father Ron and said, "I just want to be loved!" Father responded, "Well, I love you, and today, you're not going to jump off this bridge!" Father Ron is a healer of brokenness. He rescues all of us in the parish and on the Old Town streets from jumping off bridges. He reaches out his hands to pull us off or to catch us should we fall. This job is one of tremendous responsibility, but for Father Ron, it's second nature.

Monica Beemer, the director of Sisters of the Road, is a remarkable friend and teacher of nonviolence. She is also a phenomenal expert on stereotype-encouraging adjectives. She graciously read the manuscript and saved me from using such descriptions—descriptions I had no idea I was using and which were supporting such a mindset. I cannot thank her enough for her thorough cleanup. She has blessed every page.

I wish to thank Dr. Cecilia Ranger, SNJM, Dr. Jeroid O'Neil Roussell, Jr., and Dr. Sheila O'Connel-Roussell, my professors in the Masters of Arts in Applied Theology Program at Marylhurst University, where I studied interfaith religions. It was there I came across the Jewish mitzvah of the ethical will. These professors were also mentors. They encouraged me to publish my homework. I thought it was ridiculous. Who would actually want to print my school papers? They knew more than I did. Four papers were published in the pastoral care journal, *Healing Ministry*. They also enthusiastically urged me forward in the writing of this book.

I appreciate the keen eye and the swift sword of my editor, Joan Maiers, SNJM, who crisply tightened the interviews honoring all of the presenters.

I want to thank my husband, David, for his contribution, insight, generosity, and cheerleading in the formation of this manuscript.

And, above all, I want to thank my Creator for the opportunity to honor and give voice to the people within these pages.

About the Author

Photo by Tracy Stewart

Linda Ross Swanson holds a variety of degrees and certificates, including a master's in applied theology and a diploma in pastoral care from Marylhurst University. She is certified in grief and loss counseling and education through the Association of Death Education and Counseling (ADEC). She is an associate Sister of the Holy Names of Jesus and Mary (SNJMA), which strongly advocates for social justice. Swanson has her own private grief counseling practice. She helps clients memorialize their experience in a way that honors both them and their loved one. Swanson is a recovering alcoholic of 25 years. Alcoholism also affected two of her brothers, who lived on and off the streets for years. She resides in Portland, Oregon, with her husband, David, and her little dachshund, Punkey Doodle. She has three grown children and two grandchildren.

Swanson is available for readings and book signings, interactive talks, and Wisdom Will workshops where she teaches people how to record their wisdom for posterity. She can be contacted through her websites: www.wisdomunderthebridge.com or www.wisdomwill.net You may email her at: LindaRossSwanson@yahoo.com/ Purchase the book directly at: www.CreateSpace.com/3611937/ or through Amazon.com and other retailers.